I0136095

A Reader in Philosophy of Education

Philip Higgs
Yusef Waghid

JUTA

A Reader in Philosophy of Education

First published 2017

Juta and Company (Pty) Ltd
PO Box 14373, Lansdowne 7779, Cape Town, South Africa
© 2017 Juta and Company (Pty) Ltd

ISBN 978 1 48511 707 0

All rights reserved. No part of this publication may be reproduced or transmitted in any form or by any means, electronic or mechanical, including photocopying, recording, or any information storage or retrieval system, without prior permission in writing from the publisher. Subject to any applicable licensing terms and conditions in the case of electronically supplied publications, a person may engage in fair dealing with a copy of this publication for his or her personal or private use, or his or her research or private study. See section 12(1)(a) of the Copyright Act 98 of 1978.

Project manager: Carlyn Bartlett-Cronje
Copy editor: Danya Ristić-Schacherl
Proofreader: Simone van der Merwe
Cover designer: Drag and Drop
Typesetter: LT Design Worx
Indexer: Michel Cozien

Typeset in Rotis Serif Std 55 Regular 10.5 on 14pt

The author and the publisher believe on the strength of due diligence exercised that this work does not contain any material that is the subject of copyright held by another person. In the alternative, they believe that any protected pre-existing material that may be comprised in it has been used with appropriate authority or has been used in circumstances that make such use permissible under the law.

Acknowledgement
Figure 6.1 The logos, pathos and ethos in the construction of arguments on page 78. Springer Nature. A Theory of Philosophical Fallacies. *Argumentation Library*, Volume 26 (Lecture viii): 73-81. 08 August 2015, Leonard Nelson. © Springer International Publishing Switzerland. With permission of Springer Nature.

Table of Contents

About the authors

Ronald Barnett is Emeritus Professor of Higher Education at University College London Institute of Education, where he was Dean of Professional Development, and also Pro-Director, responsible for the Institute's longer-term strategy. He is a past chair of the Society for Research into Higher Education (SRHE), was awarded the inaugural prize by the European Association for Educational Research for his 'outstanding contribution to Higher Education Research, Policy and Practice', and is a fellow of the Academy of Social Sciences, the SRHE and the Higher Education Academy (HEA). He is also a visiting professor at several universities in the UK and across the world, and has been a guest speaker in 40 countries. Throughout his career, he has been working to establish and develop a social philosophy of higher education. His (26) books include – most recently – a trilogy on understanding the university: *Being a University* (Routledge, 2011), *Imagining the University* (Routledge, 2013) and *Understanding the University* (Routledge, 2016).

Søren Bengtsen is Associate Professor, PhD, at the Centre for Teaching Development and Digital Media, Aarhus University, Denmark. His main areas of research include educational philosophy, doctoral education and higher education. Dr Bengtsen works especially under the influence of Martin Heidegger's and Emmanuel Levinas's philosophies, and recently he has focused on the concept of darkness derived from such philosophies and its implication for the philosophy of higher education. His most recent publications include his journal paper (co-written with Ronald Barnett) 'Confronting the dark side of higher education' in the *Journal of Philosophy of Education*, his book chapter 'An exploration of darkness within doctoral education: Creative learning approaches of doctoral students' in *Handbook of Research on Creative Problem-Solving Skill Development in Higher Education* (edited by (Zhou, IGI Global, 2017) and his book *Doctoral Supervision: Organization and Dialogue* (Aarhus University Press, 2016).

Tina Besley is Professor and Director of the Centre for Global Studies in Education at Waikato University, New Zealand. Tina has wide research interests, including philosophy of education, school counseling, educational politics and policy, research assessment in higher education, subjectivity, youth studies, interculturalism and global knowledge economy and cultures. Her recent work now extends to e-learning, social networking and global studies in education. She is President and a fellow of the Philosophy of Education Society of Australasia (PESA) President of the Association of Visual Pedagogies, a member of the New Zealand Association of Counsellors (NZAC) and a fellow of the Royal Society of Arts, UK (RSA).

Galit Caduri earned her PhD at the Faculty of Education, University of Haifa, in Israel, in the field of philosophy of education. She had her post-doctoral training at Stellenbosch University in the field of citizenship. Her main interests are educational research and teachers' narratives. Currently, she is involved in several research projects relating to the use of social networking sites such as Facebook and WhatsApp in educater–learner communication.

Nuraan Davids is a senior lecturer in the Department of Education Policy Studies at Stellenbosch University. Her research interests include philosophy of education, democratic citizenship education and Islamic education. She has previously published *Women, Cosmopolitanism, and Islamic Education: On the Virtues of Education and Belonging* (Peter Lang, 2013), *Citizenship Education and Violence in Schools: On Disrupted Potentialities and Becoming* (co-written with Yusef Waghid, Sense, 2013), *Ethical Dimensions of Muslim Education* (with Yusef Waghid, Palgave Macmillan, 2016), *Educational Leadership-in-Becoming: On the Potential of Leadership in Action* (with Yusef Waghid, Routledge, 2017) and *Education, Assessment and the Desire for Dissonance* (with Yusef Waghid, Peter Lang, 2017).

Pradeep Dhillon is Associate Professor in the Department of Educational Policy, Organization and Leadership, University of Illinois at Urbana–Champaign (Urbana, IL). She holds courtesy appointments in the Linguistics and Comparative Literature departments and the Unit for Criticism and Interpretive Theory. Her research straddles philosophy of language (both analytic and continental) and mind, aesthetics and international education, and she has a strong interest in Kantian value theory as it relates to aesthetics, cognition and human rights education. She is the editor of *The Journal of Aesthetic Education*, and has served as Chair of Education for the American Society for Aesthetics. She has presented papers on philosophy and aesthetics at several international philosophy conferences and has organised a two-part interdisciplinary symposium titled 'Art and the Brain' (2006-2007). She has published widely within her areas of research interest. Her publications include the co-edited volume (with P Standish) *Lyotard: Just Education* (Routledge 2000, 2013), the edited volume *Somaesthetics and Education* (University of Illinois Press, 2017) and *Kant: The Art of Judgment* (Continuum Press, in preparation).

Joseph Divala is a senior lecturer in philosophy of education and Head of the Department of Education and Curriculum Studies at the University of Johannesburg. He obtained his qualifications from Stellenbosch University, the University of the Witwatersrand and the University of Malawi. Dr Divala is active in initial teacher education for SEN/FET phase in philosophy of education and post-graduate education and research (MEd and PhD) in curriculum and transformation and philosophy of education. He has taught, researched and published in the areas of aims and conceptions of education, democracy and citizenship education in Africa, social justice in education, ethics and governance in African higher education systems. Dr Divala considers himself as neo-communitarian in approach to his intellectual projects. He is also a member of a number of both national and international journal review boards, such as the *South African Journal of Higher Education* and *Educational Philosophy and Theory*.

Philip Higgs is Emeritus Professor and Research Fellow in the College of Education at the University of South Africa. He is a National Research Foundation-rated researcher and his academic interests focus on philosophy of education and the transformation of higher education. His most recent book publications, co-authored with Jane Smith, include *Rethinking Truth* (Juta, 2006, second edition), *Rethinking our World* (Juta, 2015, fourth edition) and *Philosophy of Education Today: An Introduction* (Juta, 2015).

Joseph Hungwe is currently a PhD candidate in the Department of Education and Curriculum Studies at the University of Johannesburg. He holds an MPhil degree from the University of Zimbabwe and an MEd degree from the University of the Witwatersrand. He has extensive experience in lecturing in philosophy and education at tertiary level in Zimbabwe and South Africa. His research interests are in the internationalisation of public higher education, student social diversity, political philosophy and critical thinking in the African context.

Tracey Isaacs is a senior researcher completing her PhD in the Department of Education Policy Studies at Stellenbosch University. She received her MSc in reading and literacy and continues to work in schools to advance literacy development in young children. Her recent publications include 'The blame game' (*SAJHE* 2015), 'Legitimising critical pedagogy in the face of timorous, mechanistic pedagogy' (*SAJHE* 2015) and 'Critical agency in educational practice: A modern South African perspective' (*Future Human Image* 2014). Her current research interests include the issue of critical student agency in relation to the current upsurge in university and high school student activism in South Africa.

Khosrow Bagheri Noaparast is currently a professor of philosophy of education at the University of Tehran. He has made contributions to a wide range of topics in philosophy of education, religion and personal construct psychology, including topics from different viewpoints such as constructive realism, neo-pragmatism, action theory, deconstruction, hermeneutics and Islamic philosophy of education. In 2011 he was awarded a First Order Medal of Research (The Distinguished Researcher) by the University of Tehran. Among his important works are 'Toward a more realistic constructivism' in *Advances in Personal Construct Psychology* (edited by GJ Neimeyer, Jai Press, 1995), 'Celebrating moderate dualism in the philosophy of education: A reflection on the Hirst-Carr Debate' (*Journal of Philosophy of Education* 2013) and 'Richard Rorty's conception of philosophy of education revisited' (*Educational Theory* 2014).

Michael A. Peters is Professor in the Wilf Malcolm Institute for Educational Research at Waikato University, Emeritus Professor at the University of Illinois at Urbana–Champaign and Professorial Fellow at James Cook University. He is the executive editor of *Educational Philosophy and Theory* and the founding editor of several other journals, including *Open Review of Educational Research* and *Video Journal of Education and Pedagogy*. His interests are in education, philosophy and social policy and he has written over 60 books, including most recently *The Global Financial Crisis and Educational Restructuring* (co-edited with JM Paraskeva and T Besley, Peter Lang, 2015), *Paulo Freire: The Global Legacy* (co-edited with T Besley, Peter Lang, 2015), *Educational Philosophy and Politics: The Selected Works of Michael A Peters* (Routledge, 2012), *Cognitive Capitalism, Education and Digital Labor* (co-edited with E Bulut, Peter Lang, 2011) and *Neoliberalism and After? Education, Social Policy, and the Crisis of Western Capitalism* (Peter Lang, 2011). He was made an honorary fellow of the Royal Society of New Zealand in 2010 and awarded honorary doctorates by the State University of New York (SUNY) in 2012 and the University of Aalborg in 2015.

Rachel Shanyanana holds a PhD in philosophy of education (2014) from Stellenbosch University. Dr Shanyanana was a post-doctoral research fellow at the University of Johannesburg, Department of Education and Curriculum Studies, in 2014. She has also worked as an educator, education officer, lecturer and co-ordinator in the educational sector. She is currently Assistant Pro-Vice Chancellor at the University of Namibia, Khomasdal Campus. Her research interests include higher education, African ubuntu, deliberative democracy, citizenship education, education for social justice, ethics of care, girls' and women's access to education in Africa and transformative education in African universities. She is also a reviewer of the *South African Journal of Higher Education* (*SAJHE*) and *Namibia Journal of Managerial Sciences (NJMS)*.

Alison Taysum is an international researcher at the University of Leicester, UK, and leads an international research team who focus on the philosophical enquiry into education systems' leadership and the empowerment of young societal innovators for equity and renewal. She is programme leader for the MSc Educational Leadership, and supervises doctoral students. Alison is a committed Christian who, first, loves God and, secondly, believes in an ethos of equity for all regardless of a person's race, ethnicity, faith or lack thereof, or whether they have any of the protected characteristics of the Equality Act, 2010 (Equalities and Human Rights Commission 2010). For Christians, all other rules hang upon these two.

Kam-por Yu is currently Director of the General Education Centre of the Hong Kong Polytechnic University. He has been an associate professor in the Department of Public and Social Administration at the City University of Hong Kong, and a research officer in the Department of Philosophy at the University of Hong Kong.

His main area of interest is ethics, especially Confucian ethics and applied ethics. His recent publications include *Ethical Dilemmas in Public Policy* (Springer, 2016), *Taking Confucian Ethics Seriously* (State University of New York Press, 2010) and a series of papers on the Confucian views on war, peace, harmony, civility, rights, toleration and pluralistic values.

Yusef Waghid is Distinguished Professor of Philosophy of Education in the Department of Education Policy Studies at Stellenbosch University. He is the author of *African Philosophy of Education Reconsidered: On Being Human* (Routledge, 2014), *Pedagogy out of Bounds: Untamed Variations of Democratic Education* (Sense, 2014), and co-author (with Nuraan Davids) of *Educational Leadership in Becoming: On the Potential of Leadership in Action* (Routledge, 2017) and (with Faiq Waghid and Zayd Waghid) of *Educational Technology and Pedagogic Encounters: Democratic Education in Potentiality* (Sense, 2016).

Foreword

The editors and authors of *A Reader in Philosophy of Education* have produced a fascinating, well-written and highly significant book.

Readers of this work will gain enormously from the insights offered into vitally important areas. The 13 areas covered allow for clarification of key ideas alongside encouragement for readers to develop their own insights. Work on critical realism focuses on universities highlighting ways in which we can go beyond narrow perspectives into activity that may be unknown and impure but which, through imaginative approaches, allows for speculative energy to be released. The emphasis that is placed on hermeneutics in terms of the vital role of interpretation is welcome. A consideration of pragmatism, systems theory, post-structuralism and rationality raises a wide variety of issues, including interpretive and sceptical insights. Discussions about phenomenology take us beyond a scientific outlook in highlighting ethical and critical perspectives. There are issues raised about beliefs, including fascinating insights into Islam and Buddhism. Traditions and philosophies are explored in relation to specific contexts, with important work on critical theory in the African context, feminism in the African context, African philosophy of education through a (post)critical lens and Chinese philosophy and education, with emphasis on philosophy of education in classical Confucianism.

These challenging ideas are presented in a well-structured manner. There are sensible and appropriate variations between chapters, but there is also a clear, reasonably common structure that may be seen in each chapter. An introduction is followed by the description and discussion of philosophical underpinnings and of key ideas and issues. There are reflections upon and arguments about key issues, enlightening consideration of educational implications that have been raised by these discussions and, finally, conclusions and recommendations for future research. There is a genuine sense of engagement not only with fundamental ideas but with what those ideas mean in relation to education, schooling (at various levels), teaching and research.

The book is refreshingly and determinedly international and global. The editors have done well to establish a team that is individually strong, with high-profile and highly experienced academics contributing insightful work. It is particularly impressive that voices from many locations are heard in this book: The chapter authors are based in countries that include Israel, Iran, the USA, China and parts of Africa. This issue of location is important not only for demonstrating a commitment to inclusivity, but also for allowing issues regarding the contextualisation of ideas to be made clear.

This welcome diversity of ideas and issues means that the book may be read in various ways. There is a great deal of value to be had from reading individual chapters. The common structure across chapters referred to above allows for some comparative insight. The variation in emphasis on context and fundamental ideas encourages readers to think about the interplay between theory and practice.

There is a clear commitment to the value of deliberation throughout the book. Moreover, a sense of philosophy provides a means not just of thinking more clearly, but also of reflecting on – and through – action. The close connection between key ideas and education is very welcome, as it generates insights into what, in rather crude terms, may be thought of as competing purposes of schooling. For some there is a virtuous circle between education and engagement. In other words, those who are well educated will achieve the fundamental purpose of schooling, which is to take part in society, and then that involvement will in itself be educational. For others, there is a vicious circle in which those teachers who deliberately promote engagement may come uncomfortably close to closing down avenues of enquiry in favour of promoting a particular form of involvement that is in itself designed to achieve specific outcomes rather than broaden understanding.

The authors of this book show very helpfully that thought and action may be usefully – educationally – intertwined. And they do so, as the editors declare in their preface, not by requiring some sort of falsely rigorous approach to reading the chapters, as if they were part of a simple scientific truth, or by approaching the publication as a textbook, but rather by promoting dynamic, critical reading. Such readers will gain in several ways through the focus on cosmopolitanism, deliberation, rationality and the emotions by developing their powers of critique and their capacity to engage. For this to be achieved in less than 200 pages is a significant achievement indeed.

The principal audience of this book is given by the publisher as 'postgraduate students and subject specialists in education'. There is no doubt that the book will be of enormous value to those people – and I confidently predict that it will also be welcomed by many more in many parts of the world.

Ian Davies
University of York
March 2017

Preface

In search of meanings

The anthology of chapters in this reader depicts multiple understandings and applications of philosophy of education vis-à-vis 13 distinctive themes: pragmatism, phenomenology, systems theory, post-structuralism, realism, Buddhism, Chinese philosophy, African philosophy of education, Islamic philosophy, hermeneutics, rationality, critical theory and feminism – all in relation to education. We have deliberately not enumerated these thematic contributions in the order in which they appear in the reader, because we do not want our readers to consider these chapters as chronologically or systematically intertwined. Instead, we envisage that these chapters be read, on the one hand, as interconnected with education, and on the other hand in relation to concomitant discourses constitutive of teaching, learning, management and ethics. In this regard, we have identified 13 genres of thinking that contribute to the advancement of philosophy of education as a practice.

By implication, our exposition of various themes in relation to education has a distinct connection with what it means to embark on a practice. Here, practice refers first to the notion of philosophic activity in the sense that a person thinks, reflects, analyses, contemplates and critiques particular understandings with the aim of influencing how he or she enacts (that is, puts into action) what he or she philosophises about. Simply put, analysing concepts is connected to how concepts are enacted, or put into action. Secondly, practice also has a bearing on how a concept is realised in various pedagogic activities, for instance in teaching, learning, management, governance and other ethical forms of human engagement. The point about practising philosophy of education is to examine what concepts mean, and concurrently to consider their implications for human action. In this sense meaning is connected to action, and action is implicit in meaning. Stated differently, it is through action that meaning is enacted, and it is through meaning that human action is realised.

At the core of all 13 chapters is the idea of getting to know what concepts *mean*. The reader offers particular insights and debates on how these concepts manifest within human action. Following an Aristotelian account of ascertaining meanings of concepts primarily involves uncovering the thinking, or understanding, or ways in which concepts are presented. Consequently, when searching for meanings, we look for those ideas that make concepts what they are. More specifically, uncovering meanings involves finding out what understandings or thinking patterns constitute such meanings. Meanings, therefore, do not simply exist; meanings take shape and become meaningful as they unfold in relation to human action. It is for this reason that we might be inclined to ask about the context of a particular word or concept before considering what that concept might mean. The latter practice is what we refer to as looking for *reasons* that make concepts what they are. In short, acquiring meanings is about ascertaining reasons that constitute concepts.

In recognising that the discourse of looking for meanings, or searching for reasons, is tantamount to the practice of philosophy of education, the contributions in this reader are actively concerned with meaning-making. Now that we have explained what the practice of looking for meanings, and by implication searching for reasons, is about, we need to say something more about the quest for reasons. When we asked the authors to give account of concepts they have been working with over extended periods of time, we had in mind the practice of justification. To offer a justification for why concepts are what they are is to give an account of such concepts – that is, explicating the reasons that constitute such concepts. In a way, we invited the authors to critically engage with concepts, as well as to give reasons for the concepts revealing themselves in particular ways. The authors, therefore, did not merely state their understandings of concepts and that such concepts manifest in human actions, but rather that their understandings were premised on justifications, referred to as reasons that underscore concepts.

In a different way, the accounts of concepts and their manifestations in actions presented in this reader have some connection to what it means to theorise. Thus, when we act in a way whereby we explicate meanings of concepts on the basis of outlining reasons as to why concepts are what they are, we engage in some kind of philosophic activity that can be named 'theorisation'. By implication, it would not be implausible to suggest that the authors in this reader have endeavoured to offer reasons in defence of particular concepts. That is, the authors offer theoretical accounts of concepts. And considering that giving theoretical accounts of what we do involves some kind of philosophic activity in the form of stating our reasons for concepts being what they are, it can be said that the very act of theorising involves participating in a practice itself.

Thus, this reader is underscored by a non-dichotomous claim that theory and practice are intertwined. The contributions are therefore not limited to an account of reasons for actions; they also show how reasons manifest in particular kinds of actions. In other words, the authors perform the philosophic activity of thinking about concepts and showing how concepts give rise to particular ways of doing in multiple ways. That is, they theorise about concepts, and by implication perform a practice. Theory and practice – more specifically, giving an account of reasons and showing how reasons manifest in human actions – are not two independent philosophic processes. Instead the two activities are interdependent, because the very act of giving reasons, or theorising for that matter, involves participating in some kind of practice.

Equally, when authors practise philosophy of education they not only give justifications as to the reasons that constitute concepts, but also point out how reasons live themselves out in actions – that is, how reasons are practised. As the theory becomes more pronounced, so the practice of theorising yields more clarity of meaning or understanding in and about the concepts under examination. In short, what the authors of the reader envisage is that concepts should be *read* simultaneously as theoretical pieces on account of the justifications offered in their (concepts') defence, as well as practical notions that have some kind of legitimate practical concern or orientation in mind.

This reader has been designed to summon those who engage with concepts to reason in and about concepts. In this way, when thinking about a concept, we are simultaneously invited to make claims about the use or application of concepts – a matter of doing a practice with the idea of clarifying the affinity of concepts to particular actions as well. In other words, the authors of this book invite readers to come to reason. More specifically, this reader explicitly appeals to its audience to become practical reasoners. Thus, first, readers are invited to engage with reasons; secondly, they are summoned to give an account of how they make sense of the concepts; and thirdly they are asked to point out how the reasons unfold and guide human action. By implication, readers are asked to engage with reasons and to relate reasons to various educational actions – a matter of showing how reasons manifest in actions.

When doing the latter, we are referred to as practical reasoners. Yet practical reasoning (*phronesis*) in the Aristotelian sense is not just about giving an account of reasons and a justification of how reasons engender particular actions, such as in education. Rather, giving and enacting reasons have a connection with situating the reasons appropriately. This seems to be the task of practical reasoners: They engage with reasons and simultaneously show how reasons manifest in various actions. And often the rationale behind their offering of reasons for this or that matter is connected with the act of doing things correctly or fittingly for this or that purpose. It is the latter aspect that will now be explored in more detail.

We have accentuated the point that the chapters should not be read sequentially but rather as essays intertwined with understandings of education. Our understanding of education connects with practical reasoning – that is, reasons underscore and guide human actions. It is not that humans merely engage in action. Rather, they do so thoughtfully – with reasons, and by implication justifications, for their actions. Put differently, humans' practices are supported by reasons for acting or doing things in particular ways. What follows from the latter is that humans' education is constituted by the notion of practical reason(ing). This brings us to the question: What does practical reasoning entail? Throughout this book, the reader is invited to come to reason. Therefore, in a way, this reader emphasises an appeal to the practice of caring. Caring for humans in the Aristotelian sense implies evoking our potentialities to come to reason.

In his seminal work, *Dependent Rational Animals: Why Human Beings Need the Virtues*, MacIntyre (1999:82) suggests that to develop the capacities of humans as independent practical reasoners involves fostering in them 'the ability to evaluate, modify, or reject [...] [their] own practical judgements [...] *and* the ability to imagine realistically alternative possible futures'. Thus, when we care for humans we instil in them not only 'the ability to reach their own conclusions, but also [...] [to] be held accountable by and to others for those conclusions' (MacIntyre 1999:84). This seems to be the spirit of argumentation in this reader: The authors open themselves up to the critical judgements of others and make themselves accountable to the judgements of others for reaching their conclusions.

Likewise, this book encourages readers to act independently, that is, with an 'ability and [...] willingness to evaluate the reasons for action advanced by others [authors]' (MacIntyre 1999:105). In this way, we account for our endorsements of the practical conclusions made by the authors as well as 'for one's [a reader's] own conclusions' (MacIntyre 1999:105). By implication, to become practical reasoners involves giving an intelligible account of our reasons in relation to the reasons of others (authors). In this way, as readers and authors we engage in 'reasoning together with others' (MacIntyre 1999:107). In MacIntyrean terms, such a form of reasoning together – that is, readers engaging with the text of authors – can be referred to as a textual *deliberation*. That is, learners (readers) engage with the texts of educators (authors). Both give an account of their reasons on the basis of reading and reflecting on the text with insight. This means that authors and readers engage with the text and offer practical judgements on what they have produced through writing and reading. They make sense of the reasons that they offer in defence of particular concepts and practices – that is, the ways in which concepts manifest in actions. Thus authors do not merely give an account of their reasons, and their reasons are not unquestioningly endorsed by the readers. Instead, textual deliberation demands that readers take into systematic controversy that which constitutes texts.

As a result of textual deliberation, there is always space for new understandings to emerge. New understandings or meanings of texts, and by implication the concepts that are espoused through the texts, emanate as a consequence of readers' (learners') engagement with texts – that is, they reflect on, contemplate and offer other possibilities for how texts ought to be analysed or interpreted. Such a form of enquiry happens only because readers or learners are prepared to take a stand in relation to concepts and practices that confront them. Readers situate themselves within texts and begin to think about, and even think differently about, the texts that confront them.

In a way readers disrupt texts, as they do not merely accept everything they encounter in exactly the same way. They disrupt texts on account of seeing texts differently even to what authors might have intended. Simply put, readers take the risk of disrupting texts that can give rise to their specific understandings of the texts and are even provoked to construct alternative meanings to those of the authors. Hence, there cannot be a single or monolithic understanding of texts, as disruption means that texts can be seen in a different light as well. If the latter does not happen, and readers merely accept the text uncritically and unquestioningly, they would be considered as passive recipients of knowledge and not deliberative practical reasoners.

Of course, deliberative practical reasoners do not just find fault with everything in texts. Rather, they analyse and at times look beyond what the texts intend to offer. Deliberative practical reasoners deconstruct texts (in addition to analysing them), because they have developed the capacity to offer alternative meanings for future possibilities. And this is one way in which we encourage readers or learners to read the texts and to make sense of the concepts therein.

But there is also another way in which texts can be read. At times, readers construct meanings of texts and suspend any further examination of them. Yet simultaneously they open up opportunities for themselves to look at texts differently – that is, to present texts in alternative ways. Thus, when we both suspend and present meanings of texts, we offer a *rhythmic analysis* of text. In this regard, Agamben (1994:100) proposes that 'rhythm holds, that is, gives and holds back'. In a similar manner we expect our readers or learners to hold back and consolidate understandings of concepts. We also encourage them to search for deeper meanings and present alternative understandings of concepts rather than merely regurgitating what they think the authors might have intended.

Finally, every chapter in this reader is considered as a text, and should be critically approached and analysed as such. The authors have not just given their specific interpretation of the texts. They have also referred readers or learners to particular concepts that require some analytical enquiry – that is, what the reasons are that constitute concepts and their implications for human actions. Human actions are the repositories of concepts, and hence they can be considered as practices. So what we are interested to know is our readers' and learners' particular understanding of every main concept in this reader and how these concepts guide practices of education. In the examination of concepts, we encourage our readers or learners to search for reasons that make concepts what they are. Thereafter we summon them to find out the practical implications of reasons for educational practices. And for the latter to occur, readers or learners have to imagine themselves as practical reasoners intent on engaging deliberatively and rhythmically with texts. More specifically we challenge them to theorise and practise their own understandings of concepts, and to offer alternative possibilities for future educational endeavours. Simply put, we urge all readers and learners to become deliberative enquirers who can make a contribution to shaping the practices with which they engage.

Yusef Waghid
University of Stellenbosch
March 2017

References

Agamben G. 1994. *The Man without Content.* Translated by G Albert. Stanford: Stanford University Press.

MacIntyre A. 1999. *Dependent Rational Animals: Why Human Beings Need the Virtues.* London: Duckworth.

African philosophy of education through a (post)critical lens

Chapter

1

Yusef Waghid and Philip Higgs

Introduction

As the authors of this chapter, our current understandings of the notion of an African philosophy of education have arisen from our pedagogical encounters with learners and insights of philosophy of education obtained over the past two decades. We have been greatly influenced by the (post)analytical tradition of philosophy of education that, first, takes a critical view of education and, secondly, has a post-structuralist understanding of education. In other words, while we are attracted to an African philosophy of education that aligns with critical discourse and post-structuralist thought, we are concerned with concepts and practices that seek the achievement of socially just human relations, specifically on the African continent. Rather than taking an exclusively analytical view of such philosophy and focusing intently on ideas that make the concept what it is, we concentrate on how practices of this philosophy attune to the achievement of social justice within human forms of engagement – that is, we consider an African philosophy of education *in action*. Drawing on established understandings of this philosophy, we first show why and how the concept can be linked to critical understanding, and secondly we make a case for an African philosophy of education from the post-structuralist perspective.

Philosophical/conceptual underpinnings of an African philosophy of education

An African philosophy of education and what it means to be 'an African'

What is unique about an African philosophy of education? Does the construction of such a philosophy exclude it from other forms of philosophy? To prefix the notion of 'African' to philosophy of education suggests that this philosophy is framed by what it means to be African. In this chapter, we use the term 'African' not to mean that every African adheres to such a philosophy, but rather in the sense that an African philosophical system arises from, and thus is somewhat related to, African thought, practices and traditions. And just as European, Western and Oriental philosophy are labels accorded to the different experiences, traditions, cultures, values and attitudes of the people living in the various areas, we use 'African' in a non-essentialist way. In other words, we see an African philosophy of education as a means of bringing to light and making sense of the experiences and enactments that speak to this philosophy's African-ness yet remain accessible to other thoughts and traditions. Since the ideas fund in African philosophy are also present also in other traditions, these similarities are echoed, seen, interpreted and analysed in the theories of African thinkers. Drawing on our foundational understanding of this philosophy, we contend that being 'African' is an identity which accentuates human beings' concern to act in the interests of Africa even if we do not reside on the continent. Having an African identity does not restrict us to a particular geographical realm; it orientates us to act in the interests of Africa's demands and expectations wherever we may find ourselves.

As South Africans, we authors find that our African identity has been shaped significantly by traumatic histories of segregation and othering. Thus our political and societal concerns with democratic justice for all human beings are embedded in our personal life stories, our particular histories. Our concern for Africa, and for what it means to be African, is not limited to a political construction of identity. Because of our own encounters with oppression and dis-location, we are engrossed in what it means to act with humanity, dignity and justice. The idea of democratic justice is linked with engaging with human beings on the basis of equality and freedom to speak our minds in an atmosphere of deliberation, where there is also the opportunity for us to agree and disagree on particular matters without having to alienate and exclude one another from any form of human engagement. Such exclusion would undermine the possibility of justice being achieved, considering that the practice of justice involves listening to the voices of others and being willing to speak our mind in a responsible manner.

Thus our African identity is guided by our willingness to engage with all other human beings on the continent, and to work towards justice for all Africa's people on the basis of deliberation and freedom of expression. This account of African identity resonates with Masolo's (1994) depiction of the concept. For Masolo (1994:1–2), African identity invokes two terms: 'negritude' and 'return'. *Negritude* refers to 'the dignity, the personhood or humanity, of black people' (Masolo 1994:1–2). The notion of *return* refers to a conscious state of the mind in which Africa's people become aware of and rebel against the manipulative power relations that control them (Masolo 1994:1–2). In the same way in which democratic justice is committed to African people's emancipation from subjugation and control, so Masolo's (1994:2) depiction of an African identity aims to recognise Africans – and we would add across racial categories – as dignified human beings who reject alienation and domination.

An African philosophy of education and democratic justice

Unlike Masolo (1994), our (the authors') African identity is not racialised in terms of 'blackness' and 'whiteness', as if exclusion and marginalisation involve only 'black' people on the African continent. Instead, our African identity transcends the notion of 'race', because exclusion and alienation are human sufferings that are not dictated by the colour of our skin. As 'white' and 'black' South Africans, we have both suffered the inhumanity of apartheid in that, because of our social differences, we have not been permitted to engage with one another in the same social contexts. Not being granted the spaces for social engagement has meant, and continues to mean, that in many instances people do not 'see' one another. By denying us the possibility of intersubjectively sharing our cultural spaces, segregation and domination have harmed our human psyche and distorted our identities as Africans. Our quest for justice for all South Africans was a real concern, but our prejudicial views – imposed upon us by the apartheid government – kept us physically apart.

Yet even with prejudiced African identities we both yearned for democratic justice for all citizens in our country. So we identified apartheid as a major problem in our society, and this stance shaped our philosophy of education towards one of recognising all humans as equal and having the same rights to enact their autonomy and freedom. Our subsequent views on justice and equality for all South Africans have been shaped by our commitment to enhancing democratic justice through our educational advances. Our African philosophy of education has been informed by an understanding that problems – albeit political and societal problems – ought to be changed in conjunction with the cultivation of democratic justice for all. The understanding of the African philosophy of education that we have contended can be achieved only if the human encounters among all South Africans can be enacted along the lines of democratic and just actions. Such an understanding of this philosophy therefore invokes the following meanings and actions: Humans recognise major problems in their societies and respond to such problems before examining the educational implications thereof. In our view, apartheid segregation was a major wrong. Our response was not just to wish apartheid away – we also had to examine how education as a form of human engagement would be negatively affected.

In our view, the negative consequences of apartheid are that our universities remain segregated institutions, and knowledge production is still dominated by a privileged view. Our knowledge interests continue to be subjected to control by the more 'powerful' other. Our educational spaces have been unjustly guided by manipulation, control and exclusion of the other. In response we consider our African philosophy of education as being committed to the cultivation of critical action, and as pursuing unimagined and unexpected human encounters that could enhance democratic justice for all. In the next section we highlight how our allegiances to critical and post-structuralist thought assisted us to engender a more defensible understanding of an African philosophy of education.

Key issues and debates within critical and post-structuralist views of African philosophy of education

An African philosophy of education, culture and the struggle for scientific meaning

Hountondji (2002:xix) suggests that ethnophilosophy, in focusing on the cultural practices of Africans, is defective – it is not real science in the strictest sense of the term. We authors contend that such a philosophy does not undermine an African philosophy of education. Hountondji (2002) is correct to critique an over-reliance on ethnophilosophy, such as in the forms of Africans' traditional ethnic views, artefacts, languages and prose, and cultural forms of living. And we agree with him that any philosophy of education cannot ignore the 'struggle for [scientific] meaning' (Hountondji 2002:xvii). Meanings of a 'scientific' kind are developed through argumentation and the putting forward of different points of view that are considered equally on the basis of refutation and agreement. For the latter to take place we must look at reasons. Reasons give arguments their distinctive features in terms of which views are modified, refuted and accepted. We thus concur with Hountondji (2002:30) that 'science' can be valorised only on the basis of its significance for human beings and 'its meaning for life'.

However, even Hountondji would not argue against the importance of culture, as he acknowledges its significance in producing new human understandings (Hountondji 2002:243). Culture, and its ability to produce new understandings, also plays a role in argumentation that relies on reasons. Even if our reasons are culturally grounded, argumentation remains valid. Rather, argumentation relies on a different source of justification: human cultural understanding. Therefore our understanding of an African philosophy of education is not remiss of culture. We instead maintain that culture and human reason are used in an integrated manner to develop particular or perhaps alternative points of view. Such an understanding of culturally informed reasons has the potential to guide an African philosophy of education differently. We now consider two views – critical and post-structuralist – of a culturally reasonable understanding of this philosophy.

A critical notion of an African philosophy of education

Gyekye (1992:27) offers an integrated account of African philosophy that can have an alternative impact on education. On the one hand, the *particularist* thesis 'perceives philosophical ideas or doctrines as particular – that is, relative and relevant only to the times and cultures out of which they emerge' (Gyekye 1992:28). By implication, meanings associated with Africans' experiences on the continent are constituted in the culturally informed reasons that shape such meanings. For instance, when reasons are given in defence of African women cultivating their farmland, these reasons are not only grounded in the women's cultural understandings of farming but also influence the ways in which meaning is given to their cultivation of crops. On the other hand, the trans-particular or universalist understanding of African philosophy suggests that African thought transcends 'the times and cultures that begat them' (Gyekye 1992:28). That is, African philosophy has a universal impetus and affects education in relation to critical reasoning that goes beyond magic and superstition.

Thus, in agreement with Gyekye (1992), our understanding of a critical African philosophy of education is constituted by the way culturally dependent reasons can be used to respond to problems on the African continent before examining the educational implications of such a discourse. The point about a culturally dependent and reasoned understanding of an African philosophy of education is that reasons related to the concerns on the continent are grounded in the lived experiences of Africans, who can offer justifications based on their critical and deeply rooted cultural understandings of predicaments on the continent with the aim of liberating themselves from control and domination. For example, when some Africans reflect critically about why they are subjected to the authority of a military dictatorship, they may ascertain that an over-reliance on the traditional wisdom of unquestionable sages in some ethnic communities leads to an uncritical compliance with the will of tribal leaders. In this way, their reasons are culturally grounded and inform their critical understandings of how tribal authority can evolve into some people assuming control over the lives of others without the latter having a say in how they are ruled. Often a military dictatorship, for example, has the effect of people being governed and controlled perhaps against their will. These people are subjected to a form of governance that does not involve their freedom to live in harmony with others and the government.

If Africans extend such culturally dependent reasons in thinking about how education will be adversely affected, they would begin thinking along the lines of an African philosophy of education. Educational relationships among Africans, say in institutions of civil society such as universities and schools, could be framed according to the dictates of obedience and the lack of freedom to question and disagree. Human relations at educational institutions would thus be subjected to exclusion and would result in learners and educators being unwilling to speak their minds for fear of political reprisals being perpetrated against them by the government. Practising an African philosophy of education involves ascertaining not only the culturally dependent reasons that inform and guide human practices – in this case, a military dictatorship – but also which educational opportunities Africans need in order to alter their undesirable human experience. In short, a critical African philosophy of education is associated with uncovering culturally dependent reasons that inform human practices and at the same time suggests ways in which such practices can be liberated educationally.

A post-structuralist notion of an African philosophy of education

The claims of Wiredu (1980) about African philosophy give education a different, 'post-structuralist' character. For Wiredu (1980:172), '[African] philosophy seeks to be comprehensive and endeavours to *transcend* the ordinary levels of insight in both accuracy and depth. As a result it is complex [...] because it deals in uncommon ways with ideas which are the common stock of our ordinary thought and experience'. Moreover, African philosophy 'should be approached in a spirit of *openness* and *freedom* or not at all' (Wiredu 1980:173). Wiredu thus reminds us that African philosophy is not some constrained doctrine of knowledge that inhibits human thought and practice. Rather, African philosophy goes beyond assumed insights in an atmosphere of 'openness' and 'freedom', thus paving the way for previously unimagined and unexpected 'truths' to emerge. It follows that African philosophy is not just enveloped in a paradigm of critical understandings, but lends itself to a discourse of thought and practice that goes beyond the ordinary and assumed, on the basis of being open and free to what is still to come. Following Wiredu (1980), in this way African philosophy connects with a (post)critical or post-structuralist notion of education in the sense that not everything can be known in advance and subsequently resolved critically – that is, on the basis of justification and renewal towards something better. African philosophy can also become open to the unexpected and as yet unconsidered ideas that can be used to freely and uninhibitedly engage with any predetermined expectations.

The post-structuralist notion of an African philosophy of education proposes that human thought and practice cannot be constrained, and that new ideas and understandings are always in the act of becoming on the basis of our opening ourselves up to the unimagined and unpredictable. For instance, with regard to the abovementioned military dictatorship dilemma, the post-structuralist notion of an African philosophy of education brings about a critical view of the discourse, with the idea that there is always more to know and to encounter. If we do not become open and free to the possibility that a military dictatorship can be counteracted, and even suppressed, and that ways can be reimagined to transcend its inhibiting imperatives to human freedom and thought, then we will remain trapped conceptually and pragmatically in an atmosphere of hegemonic domination, where the unexpected is not even considered as a possibility for meaningful change. Certainly the post-structuralist view of an African philosophy of education engenders opportunities for the unimagined possibilities to address undesirable and repressive practices on the African continent. This brings us to some of the implications of such a philosophy for educational theory and practice.

Implications of a (post)critical view of an African philosophy of education for educational theory and practice

Thus far we have addressed an African philosophy of education in relation to critical and post-structuralist thought. Whereas a critical African philosophy of education relates to the emancipation of human beings from practices of domination and control, a post-structuralist view of the discourse is concerned with looking at things anew, with the possibility that the unexpected and unimagined can be forthcoming. The question is how such understandings of an African philosophy of education affect educational theory and practice.

We authors' assimilation into the Anglo-Saxon tradition of analytic philosophy of education has brought us into contact with the uncovering of meanings on the basis of looking for reasons that constitute concepts and practices. Wiredu (1980:15), schooled in the analytic tradition of philosophy, makes a case for African philosophy in relation to the analytical as he tackles authoritarian practices related to traditional African communities, such as the principle of unquestioning obedience to elders, witchcraft and an 'unscientific attitude of mind'. By contrast, we are concerned with how a reasoned and culturally dependent understanding of African philosophy can influence education in pedagogical encounters among learners and educators. In this way we seek to address how critical and post-structuralist notions of an African philosophy of education affect educational experience.

The view of educational theory and practice that we adopt in this chapter is one of mutual attunement – that is, theory and practice serve one another equally. A theory or set of ideas is not simply conjured up independent of human experiences. Rather, humans' propositions and contentions are presented as justifiable ideas that give educational theory its distinctive form. An educational theory informs the practices in a certain way, and in turn the practices reinforce the theory. The notion of educational theory and practice as being intertwined underscores the African philosophy of education, and in the same way, when a theory of African education informs its practices, its practices reinforce the theory. Equally, when Africans' practices – their lived experiences and/or pedagogical encounters – alter the respective theory that underscores them, the theory is either modified or altered according to the demands of the practices. When a theory of human engagement that involves people listening attentively without questioning to what others in authority have to say is altered to a theory whereby people engage with the views of those in authority in a critical way without fearing intimidation or exclusion, then such a theory has resulted in the practices having been modified. The rationale for human action has been adapted from uncritical obedience to elders' views to a questioning of and engagement with the assumptions and perspectives of others.

Our point is that a theory of human engagement alters the way people act, just as people's practices modify or reinforce the underlying guiding principle (reason) that makes the actions what they are. Theory and practice are thus intertwined.

We now consider how a critical-cum-post-structuralist or (post)critical view of an African philosophy of education affects educational encounters among learners and educators.

A (post)critical view of an African philosophy of education and autonomous human action

According to the (post)critical understanding of an African philosophy of education, dilemmas on the continent have to be looked at in relation to what it means to become liberated. For several decades Africans have been subjected to political hegemony to the extent that their autonomy as persons has been undermined. The now (in)famous 'Arab Spring', for example, highlights why and how several Arab-speaking African countries experienced mass protests against inflexible governments. The demands of the various peoples for recognition of their 'voice' had initially been attended to. But a lack of individual autonomy resulted in these countries quickly reverting to their pre-revolutionary contexts of repression and control.

How does an African philosophy of education as a (post)critical discourse respond to such a dilemma? We suggest that educational encounters in schools and universities should encourage autonomous human action. Learners and educators ought to be regarded as people who have the right to think for themselves, to be imaginative and to question others' points of view and assumptions without having to suffer persecution and exclusion. Our argument resonates with the seminal thoughts of Zeleza (2004:66), who posits that autonomy of persons (educators and learners) is significant in the production of 'critical social knowledge' which can advance ethical and responsible change in universities on the continent. Zeleza (2004:66) further contends that if African universities do not remain committed to the cultivation of autonomy of learners and educators, they will fail to respond adequately to the challenges of democracy, development and self-determination. We maintain that a (post)critical understanding of an African philosophy of education ought to be responsive to the unexpected and previously unpredicted challenges of democratic engagement and development. Failing to do this would be not only an injustice to Africa but, more poignantly, detrimental to the imperatives of what it means to enact a (post)critical African philosophy of education.

A (post)critical view of an African philosophy of education and deliberative encounters

The (post)critical notion of this philosophy is also committed to the cultivation of more open and reflexive human encounters. To be critical is to recognise the potential in deliberative encounters whereby educators and learners can engage unconstrainedly in the pursuit of becoming more open and reflexive towards human understandings and events. The practice of ubuntu (considered in traditional African parlance as a communal form of human engagement) would be extended from mere participation to engagement. In other words, when learners and educators participate in pedagogical encounters, they would do so on the basis of wanting to act in community, contributing to one another's shared understandings. Participation alone does not always engender change, as participants can become passive and disconnected from their pedagogical concerns to changing undesirable forms of human action. For instance, learners and educators can participate in an atmosphere of ubuntu in a pedagogical encounter, but their participation does not automatically lead to some desirable form of change for humanity. Moreover, certain tribal communities on the continent participate in community to reflect on the dilemma of child labour, but if their actions do not contribute to addressing this wrong, they cannot have engaged in ubuntu.

Ubuntu upholds the willingness of people to engage with one another with the intention of altering an undesirable situation. When people engage deliberately they state why a more favourable situation should be sought. When learners and educators become persuaded by the capacity of deliberation to change their understandings of a particular situation to one whereby change is worked towards, then they will have become more open to and considerate of the possibility of change. This happens only when they engage with one another as equals, legitimately speaking their minds in the pursuit of desirable action.

An African philosophy of education that recognises the importance of ubuntu in the pursuit of desirable human action towards change is considered a critical discourse. Thus we concur with Gyekye's (1995:160) suggestion that the discourse is associated with human practices geared towards the cultivation of humanness, caring and distributive justice – that is, towards people becoming more inclined to resolve societal deficiencies not only through a genuine concern for one another but also by contributing towards changing their undesirable situations. Thus, enacting ubuntu is a way of realising a critical understanding of an African philosophy of education. Africans not only reflect on the desires for societal change, they are stimulated to *bring about* change.

Moreover, the practice of a (post)critical African philosophy of education implies that people's deliberative encounters should extend beyond a *desire* for tangible societal change. An education seeking social justice involves educating people about the reasons for combating and alleviating poverty and hunger, but such an education cannot be confined to altering these debilitating conditions. Thinking (post)critically about an education for social justice implies that we imagine situations beyond the alleviation of injustices. We need to expand our thinking towards what it means to experience conditions of equality, freedom and societal advancement. A (post)critical notion of an African philosophy of education plays an important role here. If we can imagine an African continent where communities live in conditions of profound equality and freedom, the possibility for flourishing would be enhanced as well. A (post)critical notion of education can contribute towards uninhibited thinking, where every challenge to societal advancement could be overcome. Such a discourse would urge educators and learners to imagine new, alternative possibilities and to offer ways of building more just human relations.

A (post)critical view of an African philosophy of education and cosmopolitanism

The assertion that a (post)critical African philosophy of education can engender open, reflexive and previously unimagined educational encounters is an implicit acknowledgement of the existence of such a philosophy of education. Like Gyekye (1995:190), we believe that there cannot be a single and uniform African philosophical perspective on education, because in terms of human experiences, traditions, cultures, values and attitudes, African thinking and life are different and multifold. Difference as well as similarities are to be found among various African cultures, Gyekye (1995:192) points out:

> A painstaking comparative study of African cultures leaves one in no doubt that despite the undoubted cultural diversity arising from Africa's ethnic pluralism, threads of underlying affinity do run through the beliefs, customs, value systems, and sociopolitical institutions and practices of various African societies.

The (post)critical notion of an African philosophy of education is aimed at giving what Gyekye (1995:211) describes as 'analytical attention to the intellectual foundations of [diverse] African culture[s] and experience[s]'. And when we recognise the prominence of Africa's 'cultural variability [...] as a way of establishing deeper recognition and respect for fundamental differences' (Hansen 2011:74), such a philosophy of education takes a cosmopolitan view. Considering that cosmopolitanism recognises 'humanity in both its generality and particularity' (Hansen 2011:74) in much the same way as a (post)critical African philosophy of education considers the particular in relation to the global (general), it can be argued that such a philosophy is drawn to a 'hospitality to intellectual, moral, aesthetic, and cultural diversity' (Hansen 2011:76). When the latter occurs, African persons 'are brought into the world, and the world into the person[s]' (Hansen

2011:86). Thus, the cosmopolitan experience is more concerned with what African communities and individuals can become 'through the experience of reflective openness to the new fused with reflective loyalty to the known' (Hansen 2011:86).

So when learners and educators enact a (post)critical African philosophy of education, they show a conscious concern not just to conduct themselves in deliberative encounters, but also to being reflectively open to what is strange as well as familiar to them – 'the surprising and the expected' (Hansen 2011:86). We contend that a (post)critical African philosophy of education orientates people to 'the core value of reflective openness to the new and reflective loyalty to the known' (Hansen 2011:113). For instance, when Africans reflect on their ways of seeing and living in the world, they do not abandon their traditional understandings of life in the communities. Rather, they bring their understandings and practices into conversation with what is unfamiliar and other. Their loyalty to what they know becomes subjected to their reflectiveness towards the unfamiliar. In this way, people's ways of living may be influenced by what is still to come. When pedagogical encounters among learners and educators are provoked by a reflective loyalty to the known and a concurrent openness to the new and unexpected, their willingness to engage deliberatively will not only be enhanced but will also be geared towards what is not yet there – that is, people's imaginations will be enlarged.

Conclusion and recommendations for future research

We have begun this chapter by implicitly juxtaposing two strands of an African philosophy of education – traditional ethnophilosophy and culturally reasoned philosophy – that can affect education differently. Our argument defends an African philosophy of education that transcends the dichotomy between ethnophilosophy and culturally reasoned philosophy, and we make a cogent case for a (post)critical African philosophy of education. Such a form of philosophy is geared towards the cultivation of just human relations in deliberative ways, with the possibility of being reflectively open to the new while remaining reflectively loyal to the known. A reflective loyalty to the known does not imply that such a philosophy of education cannot be questioned. On the contrary, the mere fact that such a philosophy is brought into conversation with the unfamiliar subjects our loyalty to the possibility that we might see things differently.

In our defence of a (post)critical African philosophy of education along the lines of deliberation and cosmopolitanism we have not overlooked the traditional essentialist depictions of the discourse. We have pointed out some of the limitations associated with an exclusive emphasis on ethnophilosophy and a culturally reasoned philosophy. Instead, our argument recognises that a unitary and uniform philosophy of education is not possible. We are also interested to know some of the limitations of such a philosophy of education and how pedagogical encounters might be enacted in institutions of learning. We recommend that our readers construct their own understandings of an African philosophy of education, and especially of how such a philosophy would address some of Africa's major societal, political and economic issues. In this way, we would honour the discourse of enacting philosophy of education.

Finally, in other texts we have cogently argued for a reasoned and culturally dependent notion of such a philosophy of education (Higgs et al 2000; Waghid 2014). This chapter should be read as an extension of these understandings. We are interested in how our readers may subvert and/or extend our views.

References

Gyekye K. 1992. *Tradition and Modernity: Philosophical Reflections on the African Experience.* Oxford and New York: Oxford University Press.

Gyekye K. 1995. *An Essay on African Philosophical Thought: The Akan Conceptual Scheme.* Revised ed. Philadelphia: Temple University Press.

Hansen DT. 2011. *The Teacher and the World: A Study of Cosmopolitanism as Education.* London and New York: Routledge.

Higgs P, Vakalisa NCG, Mda TV & Assié-Lumumba NT. (eds). 2000. *African Voices in Education.* Cape Town: Juta.

Hountondji PJ. 2002. *The Struggle for Meaning: Reflections on Philosophy, Culture and Democracy in Africa.* Translated by J Conteh-Morgan. Athens, Ohio: Ohio University Center for International Studies.

Masolo DA. 1994. *African Philosophy in Search of Identity.* Bloomington and Indianapolis: Indiana University Press.

Waghid Y. 2014. *African Philosophy of Education Reconsidered: On Being Human.* New York and London: Routledge.

Wiredu K. 1980. *Philosophy and an African Culture.* Cambridge: Cambridge University Press.

Zeleza PT. 2004. Neo-liberalism and academic freedom. In PT Zeleza & A Olukoshi. (eds). *African Universities in the Twenty-first Century. Volume 1 – Liberalisation and Internationalisation.* Dakar: Codesria. 42–68.

Pragmatism and education:

From experience to linguistic turn to pragmatic turn

Khosrow Bagheri Noaparast

Introduction

This chapter first introduces the philosophical insights of pragmatism. Then the challenges that these insights have raised are addressed. Finally, based on the preceding discussions, the relation of pragmatism to education is explored, with special emphasis on Dewey.

Pragmatism as an American philosophy started around 1870. The founders of pragmatism are Charles Sanders Peirce (1839–1914), William James (1842–1910) and John Dewey (1859–1952). Each of these founders developed pragmatism in terms of his own interests. Peirce was interested mainly in semantics and logic, James dealt with experience particularly in the realms of psychology and religion, and Dewey focused on education.

Pragmatism is genuinely an American philosophy, because its development is based on social necessities to solve problems and provide social cohesion in the United States of America (USA). Social cohesion is vital in the USA, as the country was composed of immigrants from different parts of the world. In a country with no past, the present is highly important and dealing with current pressing problems can be a criterion for having an identity of belonging to the land.

Pragmatism has had different readings since the time of its founders. For the founders themselves, the focal point of pragmatism was experience. However, in the middle of the 20th century, during a linguistic turn, a neo-pragmatism appeared in which direct experience was replaced with a linguistic version of experience. Wilfrid Sellars was a brilliant figure in this direction change. Relying on Sellars's legacy, Richard Rorty (see, for example, 1980) pushed post-Deweyan pragmatism forward. In a further step, the linguistic turn culminated in the works of Robert Brandom (1994, 2011), who attempts to combine pragmatism with its rival, analytic philosophy, and suggests an analytic pragmatism. In another development, as Richard Bernstein (2010) suggests, pragmatism showed a pragmatic turn, a sort of return to the founders' emphasis on experience in seeking to overcome some dead ends of the linguistic turn without ignoring the insights provided by neo-pragmatism.

When it comes to the relation of pragmatism to education, Dewey carries the burden of developing a pragmatist philosophy of education and, we might say, philosophy of education in general. As Kaminsky (1986) believes, philosophy of education began in the mid-1930s with the founding of the John Dewey Society. Nevertheless, neo-pragmatists such as Rorty have put forward insights about education that need to be taken into account in dealing with the relationship between pragmatism and education.

The philosophical/conceptual underpinnings of pragmatism

Pragmatism started simply as a method rather than a philosophical tradition that deals with philosophical problems and provides a philosophical point of view. James (1975:28), who coined the term 'pragmatism', regarded it as a method for solving metaphysical disputes – 'that might otherwise be interminable' – including clashes between science, on the one hand, and ethics and religion on the other. The pragmatic method was intended to clarify concepts involved in the disputes and thereby resolve the misunderstandings. However, soon pragmatism went beyond a mere technique and became a philosophical viewpoint with relevant conceptual underpinnings.

We now examine the basic philosophical and conceptual insights of pragmatism. The various strands of pragmatism referred to above are at issue.

Experience as the touchstone of pragmatism

In contrast to James, Peirce (1992:132) initially formulates the maxim of pragmatism as follows: 'Consider what effects, which might conceivably have practical bearings, we conceive the object of our conception to have. Then, our conception of these effects is the whole of our conception of the object'. The strong relation between thinking and doing is evident in Peirce's (1998:142) later suggestion that 'pragmatism teaches us, what we think is to be interpreted in terms of what we are prepared to do'.

This reliance of thinking on doing is the touchstone of pragmatism, and shows the role played by experience therein. According to the maxim, a concept is made clear by assessing its employment in practice. This indicates an operational definition, in which a concept is defined in terms of the measurable consequences of its employment in practice. For instance, intelligence might be operationally defined as the score we may achieve when taking an intelligence test.

James (1983:217) elaborated Peirce's maxim by distinguishing between two sorts of knowledge: 'knowledge by acquaintance' and 'knowledge about something'. *Knowledge by acquaintance* refers to a direct knowledge in which experience is important, whereas *knowledge about something* relates to an appeal to concepts. We may know something by acquaintance without being able to describe it. For instance, how can we 'make a blind man guess what blue is like' by means of a mere description? (James 1983:217). James (1983:217) believes

14

that the direct knowledge acquired by experience is basic, suggesting that 'all the elementary natures of the world, its highest genera, the simple qualities of matter and mind, together with the kinds of relation that subsist between them, must either not be known at all, or known in this dumb way of acquaintance without knowledge-about'.

Dewey (1938) introduces the situation as the context of thinking. According to Dewey (1938), thinking starts with a problem in an indeterminate situation in the course of life, and ends with solving the problem and turning the indeterminate situation into a determinate one. When our acquired habits work and we can rely on our predictions, the situation is determinate, but as soon as our habits are broken, we are confronted with an indeterminate situation. This centrality of situation indicates that all conceptual and logical endeavours have an instrumental nature focused on solving a problem that has turned a determinate situation into an indeterminate one. Taking situation as the starting and ending point of thinking, and thereby considering thoughts as plans of action, shows the place of experience in Dewey's (1938) view.

Pragmatism and reality: Situation

Dewey's (1938) view of situation can show what account pragmatism makes of reality. In fact, reality is replaced with situation in pragmatism. While the world can exist without any human beings living in it, situation is not separable from humans. Heidegger (1996) proposed a state of 'being-in-the-world' – we may use similar hyphens with regard to pragmatism and talk about a human as a being-in-the-situation. That is to say, humans and situations are connected so deeply that they cannot be separated from each other.

Among the founders of pragmatism, Peirce (1992) has the most affinity with reality, in that he takes a semi-realistic position. However, even Peirce (1992) takes humans to be intertwined with situation. As Bernstein (2010:136) puts it: 'We do not need to reify a realm of facts that exist independently of any language, thought, or inquiry. Peirce does justice to the fallibility and openness of all justificatory practices and inquiry without losing touch with a reality "that is independent of the vagaries of me and you" (Peirce 1992, p.52)'. That is to say, while Peirce (1992) takes the independence of reality for granted, he considers meeting the reality beyond our language, thought or enquiry impossible. We may say that we always deal with 'our reality' rather than with 'reality' as such.

James (2003) takes the interrelation of humans and the world as the building blocks of reality. Thus he does not see human consciousness as distinct from material things (James 2003). Such distinction is replaced with relation: 'Consciousness connotes a kind of external relation, and does not denote a special stuff or way of being' (James 2003:13). According to James (2003:12), this relation is immediate and direct, thus he refers to it as 'pure experience'. Consciousness is an arrow that starts from humans and ends in things. This relational character of consciousness with reality is so profound that James (2003) talks about plural truths, coming from various relations that people may have with their environment. Take, for example, an experience described by James (1975:27f):

> *This human witness tries to get sight of the squirrel by moving rapidly round the tree, but no matter how fast he goes, the squirrel moves as fast in the opposite direction, and always keeps the tree between himself and the man, so that never a glimpse of him is caught. The resultant metaphysical problem now is this: Does the man go round the squirrel or not?*

James (1975) suggests that 'yes' and 'no' are both possible answers to the question. It depends on what 'going around' means. If it means moving from the man's north to east, then to south and at last to west, then 'yes' is true. If it means being in front of him, then going to his right, then behind him and to his left without getting in front of him again, then 'no' is correct. It follows that reality is not absolute, and instead there are different perspectival relations to the situation, each constituting a reality. Therefore, we can talk of plural realities.

Reality seen as being separate from humans, as realists propose, is not acceptable for pragmatists. For pragmatists, relations between humans and the world – that is, situations – are at issue.

Pragmatism, facts and values

Facts and values have been two sides of a profound controversy in philosophy. While some philosophers, such as logical positivists, talk about the fact/value distinction, pragmatists usually see facts and values as merged.

James's (1975) main concern is to overcome the gulf between science, which deals with facts, and religion and ethics, which focus on values. James (1975) refers to supporters of science as tough-minded and to supporters of religion and ethics as tender-minded. James uses Peirce's pragmatic maxim to try to bring these supporters together, arguing that whether we are dealing with a scientific hypothesis or a value statement, we should look at its operational consequences as the criterion for its significance. Thus, according to James (1975), if belief in God makes a person capable of coping with a serious illness, then this is sufficient for taking the belief as true. The operational and behavioural effects of a belief are the best criteria for deciding about the belief. In terms of this maxim, science and religion are on the same level. Furthermore, according to James (1975), we do not need to appeal to scepticism or the Cartesian method of doubt in order to provide a profound certainty about our beliefs. We should check our beliefs only when they are faced with difficulties. If our beliefs work, then we do not need to doubt them in order to achieve certainty. Thus we can hold our values until they are shaken, and by appealing to the pragmatic maxim we can decide about them.

Peirce (1877) proposes how to settle a doubtful belief using the criterion of the methods of science. By introducing experiments, we can look for their consequences and thereby decide about a belief (Peirce 1877). Again, this scientific method can be used equally for factual statements as for value statements.

Dewey (in Reisch 2005) disagrees with logical positivists such as Carnap and Neurath. Logical positivists suggest a distinction between scientific sentences and value sentences, taking value sentences as meaningless and scientific sentences as meaningful. Dewey (in Reisch 2005), by contrast, rejects this fact/value distinction and believes that value statements are the subject of scientific study. Operationally defined, values can be studied in terms of their sensible consequences. Thus, in his letter of 1938 to Neurath, Dewey comments: 'In a strict sense of thing language there can be no genuine evaluation propositions or sentences. In terms of a behavior or operational language I think the case can be clearly made out in behalf of the genuinely logical character of some – though not all – value-expressions' (in Reisch 2005:89).

We do not forget the case in which Dewey (in Reisch 2005) shows agreement with logical positivists on the meaninglessness of metaphysical statements, but takes their rejection of these statements as being in error. In his letter of 1939 to Morris, Dewey wrote: 'Of course I agree that "metaphysical" statements in the sense of non- or anti-empirical are unverifiable. But I think the attempt to dismiss them entirely at one swoop by calling them "meaningless" is a serious tactical mistake' (in Reisch 2005:95). Dewey's agreement can be taken as a tactic for dismissing Thomists who, according to Dewey (1939), attempted to regard science as value-neutral in order to introduce religion as the sole source of values. This was a motive for him to see science as being intertwined with values.

However, the main urge for rejecting the fact/value distinction comes from Dewey's (1939) pragmatist view that a value statement's meaning is related to its behavioural effects. Thus, contrary to logical positivists who take ends in the relationship between means and ends as subjective, and means and their impacts as objective, Dewey (1939:423) puts means and ends in a continual relation in which means can become ends as achieved ends can be taken as means for some other ends: 'Every condition that has to be brought into existence in order to serve as a means is, in that connection, an object of desire and an end-in-view, while the end actually reached is a means to future ends as well as a test of valuations previously made'. Dewey's (1939) pragmatic stance is evident as he takes the achievement of an end as a test of its significance.

The pragmatists' emphasis on situation, instead of on reality, along with the involvement of facts and values that this orientation requires, is too human-centred to be able to confront the hard face of reality. James (1983:335) suggests that 'the only meaning of essence is teleological, and that classification and conception are purely teleological weapons of the mind. The essence of a thing is that one of its properties which is so important for my interests that in comparison with it I may neglect the rest'. Likewise, Dewey (1971:29) insists: 'Necessary means needed; contingency means no longer required – because already enjoyed'. James (1983) takes the only meaningful teleology to be a mental teleology, while Dewey (1971) reduces all necessities to psychological or logical ones. This is too uncompromising a conclusion. Talking about ontological necessities might face the problem of induction, an inference that rests solely on the past. However, the power of negating the duration of the past to the future is no stronger than the power of induction – both supporting and rejecting the induction rely on the past. A more reasonable pragmatist should take, at best, an agnostic position to the effect that we do not know what the future holds and that we do not know whether there are ontological necessities.

Pragmatism in recent times

As described, the pragmatism of the founders Peirce, James and Dewey declined mid-century. This was due to the rush of logical positivists to the USA, caused by the Second World War and the new sphere of thought that they brought with them. Because of his longevity, Dewey alone was in touch with the logical positivists. The new wave of thought dominated for some time, until pragmatism experienced a revival. Thinkers who are generally regarded as forming part of the revival of pragmatism include, among others, CI Lewis, WVO Quine, Murray Murphey, George Herbert Mead, Hilary Putnam and Philip Kitcher, though some of them reject this categorisation. For example, Putnam (1994) denies being a pragmatist on the grounds that the pragmatic maxim is a poor way to deal with truth.

As mentioned, there have been two main trends in the revival of pragmatism: the linguistic turn and the pragmatic turn. While the linguistic turn is more critical of classical pragmatism, the pragmatic turn calls for a return to classical pragmatism without neglecting the insights provided by the linguistic turn. We now explore these two trends briefly.

The linguistic turn

The linguistic turn, or neo-pragmatism, is championed by Rorty and Brandom. Rorty greatly admires the work of Dewey, but also pays attention to Peirce's pragmatic maxim and its consequential requirements. Rorty (1980) tries to demolish the realistic interest in truth as the representation of reality. He sees the negation of representation as the core element of pragmatism (Rorty 1980). Rorty critiques the tough-minded Dewey and supports the tender-minded Dewey, in James's (1975) terms. That is to say, he is uneasy about Dewey's strong inclination towards scientific method and instead aligns himself with Dewey's preoccupation with cultural values, in particular democracy in Western culture. Pragmatism without method is a desired pragmatism for Rorty. For him, the core element of pragmatism is that true beliefs are not those which represent the 'nature of things' but the beliefs which give us the rules of successful action (Rorty 1991:65).

By accepting this, according to Rorty (1991:65–66), we would admire an experimental and fallible attitude without making a commitment to a certain 'method'.

Brandom (1994, 2011) attempts to combine the insights of analytic philosophy and of pragmatism, referring to his view as analytic pragmatism. In taking the side of analytic philosophy, influenced by his teacher, Sellars, Brandom (1994) accuses the classical pragmatists of being trapped in the 'myth of the given'. This term refers to the supposedly false view that humans can have in their perceptions a direct non-conceptual knowledge through an immediate relation to any object in the world. While neither Sellars nor Brandom denies that humans take something from objects during their perceptions, either consciously or unconsciously, Sellars and Brandom both reject the view that this 'something' could be, by itself, knowledge. In order to turn into knowledge, the naïve sense data need to enter the 'space of reasons' (Sellars 2007), in which concepts and their relations make it possible for a person to participate in the play of giving and taking reasons. What Brandom has in mind in accusing the early pragmatists is, for instance, James's (2003:12, 1983:217) 'pure experience', and 'knowledge by acquaintance' and all that he includes in it, such as the elementary natures of the world and the simple qualities of matter and mind. Thus Brandom (1994) maintains that 'experience' is not one of his words.

For Brandom (1994), the core element of pragmatism is the primacy of know-how over know-that. That is to say, pragmatism's basic insight is that human normative activities are regulated implicitly by certain norms of which humans are not explicitly aware. Human activity is not the applied form of some antecedent theoretical knowledge. What comes first is the activity itself being implicitly under the guidance of certain norms. Brandom's (1994) programme for combining analytic philosophy and pragmatism is to make explicit that which is implicit in human cognitive activities and behaviour, using the insights put forward by analytic philosophers in terms of logical rules of inference. Thus, Brandom (1994) calls his approach inferential. Gaining these insights includes taking practices as both the starting point and the end point in testing the suggested explicit formulations.

The pragmatic turn

Used by Bernstein (2010) as the title of his book, the pragmatic turn is another recent trend in pragmatism. On the one hand, harking back to the classical pragmatists, he gives experience the central position (Bernstein 2010). Such emphasis provides the objective basis of our knowledge: 'Acknowledgement of this bruteness – the way experience "says NO!" – is required to make sense of the self-corrective character of inquiry and experimentation' (Bernstein 2010:134). On the other hand, Bernstein (2010) does not want to ignore the role of language and logic in the linguistic turn in dealing with the structure of human beliefs and knowledge.

Bernstein's student Steven Levine (2012) also suggests that we need to heed the classical pragmatists' legacy of experience. Against the charge of the myth of the given, he argues that the notion of experience for early pragmatists does not require adopting the myth (Levine 2012). This is because, according to Levine (2012), Peirce views experience as having a mediated character due to the involvement of concepts in it. Moreover, Levine (2012:138) believes that Dewey avoids the myth by introducing habits which involve human experience: 'But for Dewey, and all the pragmatists, there is a stratum of pre-reflective yet rationally intelligible habits and bodily skills that are neither conceptual nor merely causal. It is only once this stratum is identified that the pragmatists' true account can come into focus'. Levine (2012) accedes, however, that Brandom's attempt to explore the complex semantic system of our thought is appreciated.

Key issues and debates concerned with pragmatism

The philosophical underpinnings of pragmatism have raised various challenges. The challenges and issues we now address include instrumentalism with regard to meaning and truth, and consequentialism in morality.

Instrumentalism, as related to meaning and truth

Pragmatism gives a focal position to instrumentalism. Taking human thought as an instrument for handling the environment is also related to the issue of truth. The challenge is whether the workability of our thoughts can be taken as sufficient for their truths.

With regard to the relation of instrumentalism with meaning, Brandom (1994:71) critiques classical pragmatists for their reliance on instrumentalism:

> *They understand truth in terms of usefulness and take the contents possessed by intentional states and expressed by linguistic utterances to consist in their potential contribution to success of an agent's practical enterprises. Peirce, James, and Dewey are at base (though not always, and in every respect) instrumental normative pragmatists.*

Brandom (1994) rejects instrumentalism by claiming that the meanings of our utterances cannot just be explored functionally, in terms of their potentiality in providing an activity. Instead, the interpersonal relations and interplay of giving and taking reasons are also vital in providing meaning for our utterances and the norms that guide our behaviour (Brandom 1994). Inferential relations between our statements cannot be ignored in dealing with meaning. That is to say, the relation of a statement we utter with prior statements of ours or of our interlocutor matters in meaning. The content of a belief depends on these prior statements and on how the belief is derived from them. The source for determining the content of a belief is not only its potentiality for success in action.

Levine (2012), a defender of the early pragmatists, admits that this critique has some purchase with regard to James and Dewey, though not with Peirce. Levine (2012) suggests that early pragmatists can be defended in this regard because of the feedback structure they propose for enquiry. This structure requires that when in the enquiry an abduction or prediction is inferred from our belief system and is shown to be successful in action, it enters the belief system through being fed back by a new statement. When the new statement enters the belief system, there must be a coherence between the two. Fulfilling this requirement might in turn need a change in the belief system. Then, in future enquiries, the new belief system would be the source of inference along with its new meanings. In this way, Levine (2012) proposes that pragmatists can have a semantic view which accounts for meaning in terms of prior beliefs, and not merely consequences.

A related debate is the tension between experience and meaning in pragmatism. Some claim that early pragmatists' emphasis on experience and neo-pragmatists' inclination towards language and logical relations show a tension in pragmatism (see, for example, O'Shea 2014). Others attempt to synthesise these two seemingly contradictory inclinations (see, for example, Bernstein 2010). O'Shea maintains that Bernstein cannot easily resolve this tension because reliance on experience as the objective constraint on our beliefs, or 'secondness' as Peirce (1976:823) puts it, does not put an end to our concerns. Rather, when we ask what it is in experience that constrains us from holding some of our beliefs, we are obliged to hold a 'thirdness' (Bernstein 2010:135) – conceptual content inferentially constructed. In other words, the 'NO!' (Bernstein 2010:134) of the experience cannot be explored without appealing to the conceptual relations involved in the structure of our thoughts.

Instrumentalism in relation to truth has also raised some challenges. A workable idea or hypothesis is not necessarily true. Workability can be due to different reasons. As Rescher (1987) points out, a wrong hypothesis might work because it is at the scope of nature's error-tolerance. The wrong hypothesis of the flat Earth worked in the past and still works because buildings are of such small scale that they do not breach the tolerance of nature. Thus, pragmatism is confusing in equating workability with truth.

Consequentialism, as related to morality

The main contrast comes from the ethics of principles supported by Kant (1997). While ethics of principles requires that people do the right thing no matter in which situation they are or what consequences they confront, consequentialism evaluates moral actions in terms of their successful effects. This is a contrast between duty and success, between principles and prudence. There was a return to Kantian morality in the USA in the wake of the Vietnam War (1955–1975), in which a million Vietnamese people were killed. Rorty (1998), however, supports prudence over principles and holds that what we should do depends on situations rather than fixed principles. Hence, if a pragmatist seeks to condemn the Vietnam War, he or she will do so not in terms of fixed moral principles but in terms of its consequences (Rorty 1998:33). This indicates that, given successful consequences, such a war might be taken as acceptable. But what are successful consequences? And what is the scope of the consequences? A war might have successful consequences for a nation but disastrous consequences for the world. These ambiguities lead to relativism in morality. The resultant relativity in which ends justify means is at the core of the challenge against consequentialism.

The educational implications of pragmatism

In line with the pragmatist urge, Dewey attempts to overcome the theory–practice gap in philosophy of education. He rejects the thinking that such philosophy is 'an eternal application of ready made ideas to a system of practice having a radically different origin and purpose' (Dewey 1916:331). Instead, he takes philosophy as 'the general theory of education', and educational settings as 'the laboratory' for testing the philosophical distinctions being made concrete in these settings (Dewey 1916:328–329).

In order to illustrate the basic pragmatist concept of education, Dewey (1938) appeals to the concept of experience. Experience in Dewey's version, as we have seen, deals with fixation of situation through enquiry. Dewey (1938:105f) defines enquiry as 'the controlled or directed transformation of an indeterminate situation into one which is determinate in its constituent distinctions and relations as to convert the elements of the original situation into a complete whole'. The work of Darwin and Hegel are the source of Dewey's thinking here: The emphasis on transformation of the situation is due to the Darwinian urge, and looking for a 'complete whole' refers to the Hegelian urge.

Relying on his conceptions of experience and enquiry, Dewey (1916:49–62) regards education as reconstruction of experience, which he calls 'growth'. In this view, education has no criteria other than experiment and problem-solving. Growth is achieved when we can solve problems through enquiry and the result of enquiry can feed future enquiries. The process and methods of enquiry are thus more important for Dewey (1916) than the product or contents to be learned. Knowledge for its own sake is at odds with this view; the school curriculum and contents should address the problems learners face rather than being learned for their own sake.

New pragmatists such as Rorty have challenged Dewey's (1916) view, claiming that process and enquiry are not enough and content should be equally emphasised in education (Bagheri Noaparast 2014). Referring to ED Hirsch's critique of Dewey concerning the necessity of enculturation, Rorty (1999:122) comments: 'As Hirsch quite rightly says, that narrative will not be intelligible unless a lot of information gets piled up in the children's heads'. This is not to say that Rorty (1999) takes education as the transmitting of culture. When it comes to critiquing culture, Rorty (1999) is quite open, suggesting that there is no final vocabulary – that is, one concept of culture can be replaced with alternatives. However, in the early years of education he considers enculturation necessary as a background that makes critique possible (Rorty 1999).

A further characteristic of education in Dewey's (1916) view associated with the emphasis on process and method is to prioritise the interests of learners. This characteristic weakens the authority of the educator, who used to be regarded as the 'sage on the stage'. In pragmatist education the learner is active and the educator is a facilitator who helps the learner to learn mostly *how to learn*. Thus, the alternative saying, the 'guide on the side', is more fitting to the pragmatist view.

The pivotal elements of pragmatist education – enquiry and learners' interests – remind us of the issue, addressed above, of emphasising method/experience/interest at the price of undermining content/traditional values/discipline. White (2015) attempts to reject the charge that Dewey undermines content knowledge, moral values or social discipline in educational circles. According to White (2015), Dewey instead replaces the direct method of imposing these things with an indirect method in which learners start with their interests but, through facing the problems to be solved, acquire content knowledge, moral values and discipline in terms of their collaborative actions.

Dewey himself faced this issue. Along with his wife, Dewey administered a school that was set up by the University of Chicago, called University Elementary School and more popularly known as the 'Laboratory School'. Dewey (1972:437) had two aims for the school: 'To exhibit, test, verify, and criticize theoretical statements and principles, and to add to the sum of facts and principles in its special line'. He administered this school from 1896 to 1904, but his administrative style elicited some complaints about discipline and morality. Dewey (1976:65–66) responded as follows:

Upon the moral side, that of so-called discipline and order, where the work of the University Elementary School has perhaps suffered most from misunderstanding and misrepresentation, I shall say only that our ideal has been, and continues to be, that of the best form of family life, rather than that of a rigid graded school. [...] If we have permitted to our children more than the usual amount of freedom, it has not been in order to relax or decrease real discipline, but because under our particular conditions larger and less artificial responsibilities could thus be required of the children, and their entire development of body and spirit be more harmonious and complete [...]

Dewey (1976) attempts to reconcile his reliance on freedom and interest with the equally important concepts of discipline and morality. However, the tension between the two poles is intense, particularly in societies in which tradition is strong. This tension makes it very difficult to apply pragmatism in these societies' education systems. In Iran, for instance, a strong religious culture has led to an education system characterised by the indirect education that Dewey suggests is not recommendable because moral and traditional values are not sufficiently observable. Ironically, Dewey's pragmatism has not been practised in the USA either. As Kliebard (2002:94) points out, 'One can find almost nothing in American school practice of the educational ideas that Dewey propounded over the course of his long life.' This is no doubt partly due to the strength of tradition in the USA, as the conservatives have strongly rejected Dewey's ideas.

Conclusion and recommendations for future research

The components of 'pragmatism' and 'education' need further attention, contrary to the wide discussions that have been held on the history of pragmatism.

While almost all pragmatists have accepted the pragmatic maxim, different versions of pragmatism do not agree as to what exactly constitutes pragmatism. Early pragmatists upheld pure or immediate experience; neo-pragmatists emphasised the linguistic character of behaviours, with Rorty focusing on description and re-description of things while Brandom concentrates on logical relations involved in our behaviours. Quine, who does not name himself a pragmatist, is regarded as being influential in new directions of pragmatism by giving more attention to theoretical flexibility and less attention to action (Godfrey-Smith 2014). McDowell (2011) critiques Brandom for losing the pragmatist intuition when he talks about intention in action as a disposition to say 'yes' to an action. According to McDowell (2011), Brandom takes intention out of action, while pragmatists take intention in action to be a practical skill within actions. This emphasising of action rather than theory or language, as post-Deweyan thinkers did, is strongest in Bernstein's view in which a new pragmatic turn is addressed. Such vacillation between behaviour and belief, or action and theory, shows that the demarcation question is still an open question.

With regard to education, Dewey's invaluable attempts are challenged not only by other critics but also by neo-pragmatists such as Rorty. For instance, Dewey's most basic pragmatic attempt to overcome the theory–practice gap has arguably had little success. Wain (2001:176–177) suggests that Dewey failed to resolve this and other dualisms, while Rorty (1990) also sees Dewey's endeavour as wrong from the start because the realms of philosophy and education are distinct.

Therefore, the following questions need to be addressed: What constitutes pragmatism? Are characteristics of instrumentalism and consequentialism necessary components of pragmatism? Should pragmatism be understood in a limited sense in terms of the pragmatic maxim, or in a broad sense, and what is this broad sense? What is the relation between theory and practice in education? Is there an optimal point for educators between the two extreme points of being a 'sage' and being a 'guide'?

References

Bagheri Noaparast K. 2014. Richard Rorty's conception of philosophy of education reconsidered. *Educational Theory*, 64(1):75–98.

Bernstein RJ. 2010. *The Pragmatic Turn*. Cambridge: Polity.

Brandom RB. 1994. *Making it Explicit: Reasoning, Representing, and Discursive Commitment*. Cambridge: Harvard University Press.

Brandom RB. 2011. *Perspectives on Pragmatism: Classical, Recent, and Contemporary*. Cambridge: Harvard University Press.

Dewey J. 1916. Democracy and education. In JA Boydston. (ed). *John Dewey: The Middle Works. Volume 9*. Carbondale: Southern Illinois University Press. 1–370.

Dewey J. 1938. *Logic: The Theory of Inquiry*. New York: Henry Holt.

Dewey J. 1939. Theory of valuation. *International Encyclopedia of Unified Science*, 2(4). Chicago: University of Chicago Press.

Dewey J. 1971. The superstition of necessity. In JA Boydston. (ed). *John Dewey: The Early Works. Volume 4*. Carbondale: Southern Illinois University Press. 19–36.

Dewey J. 1972. The university school. In JA Boydston. (ed). *John Dewey: The Early Works. Volume 5*. Carbondale: Southern Illinois University Press. 43–76.

Dewey J. 1976. *The School and Society*. Edited by JA Boydston. Carbondale: Southern Illinois University Press.

Godfrey-Smith P. 2014. Quine and pragmatism. In G Harman & E LePore. (eds). *A Companion to WVO Quine*. Oxford: Wiley-Blackwell. 54–68.

Heidegger M. 1996. *Being and Time*. Translated by J Stambaugh. New York: State University of New York Press.

James W. 1975. *Pragmatism: A New Name for Some Old Ways of Thinking* [1907]. Cambridge: Harvard University Press.

James W. 1983. *The Principles of Psychology*. Vol 1. Cambridge: Harvard University Press.

James W. 2003. *Essays in Radical Empiricism* [1912]. New York: Dover.

Kaminsky JS. 1986. The first 600 months of philosophy of education 1935–1985: A deconstructionist account. *Educational Philosophy and Theory*, 18(2):42–48.

Kant I. 1997. *Critique of Practical Reason*. Cambridge: Cambridge University Press.

Kliebard H. 2002. *Changing Course: American Curriculum Reform in the 20th Century*. New York: Teachers College Press.

Levine S. 2012. Brandom's pragmatism. *Transactions of the Charles S. Peirce Society*, 48(2):125–140.

McDowell J. 2011. Some remarks on intention in action. *The Amherst Lecture in Philosophy*, 6:1–18. Available: http://www.amherstlecture.org/mcdowell2011/. (Accessed 7 February 2017.)

O'Shea JR. 2014. A tension in pragmatist and neo-pragmatist conceptions of meaning and experience. *European Journal of Pragmatism and American Philosophy*, VI(2):40–63.

Peirce CS. 1877. The fixation of belief. *Popular Science Monthly*, 12 November:1–15.

Peirce CS. 1976. *The New Elements of Mathematics*. Vols 1 to 4. Edited by C Eisele. Paris: Mouton.

Peirce CS. 1992. How to make our ideas clear [1878]. In N Houser & C Kloesel. (eds). *The Essential Peirce: Selected Philosophical Writings. Volume 1 (1867–1893)*. Bloomington: Indiana University Press. 124–141.

Peirce CS. 1998. *The Essential Peirce: Selected Philosophical Writings. Volume 2*. Bloomington: Indiana University Press.

Putnam H. 1994. *Words and Life*. Cambridge: Harvard University Press.

Reisch GA. 2005. *How the Cold War Transformed Philosophy of Science: To the Icy Slopes of Logic*. New York: Cambridge University Press.

Rescher N. 1987. *Scientific Realism*. Dordrecht: D Reldel.

Rorty R. 1980. *Philosophy and the Mirror of Nature*. Oxford: Blackwell.

Rorty R. 1990. The dangers of over-philosophication: Reply to Arcilla and Nicholson. *Educational Theory*, 90(1):41–44.

Rorty R. 1991. *Objectivity, Relativism and Truth: Philosophical Papers I*. Cambridge: Cambridge University Press.

Rorty R. 1998. *Achieving our Country: Leftist Thought in Twentieth-century America*. Cambridge and London: Harvard University Press.

Rorty R. 1999. Education as socialization and as individualization. In R Rorty. *Philosophy and Social Hope*. New York: Penguin. 114–126.

Sellars W. 2007. *In the Space of Reasons: Selected essays of Wilfrid Sellars*. Edited by K Sharp & R Brandom. Cambridge: Harvard University Press.

Wain K. 2001. Richard Rorty and the end of philosophy of education. In MA Peters & P Ghiraldelli Jr. (eds). *Richard Rorty: Education, Philosophy, and Politics*. Oxford: Rowman & Littlefied. 163–178.

White B. 2015. Scapegoat: John Dewey and the character education crisis. *Journal of Moral Education*, 44(2):127–144.

Rationality and education:
On releasing imaginative human action

Chapter

3

Yusef Waghid and Nuraan Davids

Introduction

In this chapter we suggest three interrelated forms of rationality: interpretive rationality, practical rationality and sceptical rationality. We argue for such integration on the basis that a consistent articulation of reasons towards a desirable or morally worthwhile end, coupled with openness towards what is as yet unimagined and unexpected, ought to be commensurable with humans' application of rationality. We defend sceptical rationality, which can engender pedagogical openings whereby educators and learners engage with one another beyond merely offering clear and consistent reasons for some practically worthwhile purpose. In this regard we examine how sceptical rationality reveals the possibility of seeing things anew, prompting in educators and learners awareness that reasons can lead to the release of the imagination. Such a form of rationality launches educators and learners towards the unexpected, unimagined pedagogical breakthroughs that are always in becoming. Drawing on the seminal thoughts of Charles Taylor (1931–), Alasdair MacIntyre (1929–) and Stanley Cavell (1926–), we argue for a form of human rationality that is commensurable with imaginative human action.

We begin our exposition in reference to the work of Karl Popper (1963), who argues for a humanist conception of rationality. Popper's (1963:515) idea of rationality is connected to what he calls an 'imaginative intervention' of the human mind. He seems to assert that being imaginative and intervening are both related to what it means for humans to act responsibly, morally and intellectually – that is, to act *rationally* (Popper 1963:516). When people act rationally, they 'contemplate and adjudicate, and [...] discriminate between, competing theories' (Popper 1963:516). In other words, following Popper, we have the capacity to think for ourselves, and in this way we can be reflective about what we think and, in turn, present reasonable justifications for our thoughts. In addition, our judicious act of reasoning enables us to distinguish between alternative understandings of human action.

Conceptual underpinnings and key debates

Popper (1963) extends his notion of a rational human being to a person who not only acts contemplatively and judiciously, but also rethinks and challenges his or her conclusions. Rationality implies that a person 'use[s] his imagination in trying to find whether and where his own conclusions are at fault' (Popper 1963:516). This is an admission that people are fallible and that rationality is a form of criticism which we use to consider various truth claims on the basis of contemplation and justification. Thus, reasons are not just offered but thought about over and over again, and justified on the grounds of being exposed to more persuasive reasons in turn.

Consequently, a particular reason once accepted does not have to be taken as carved in stone – that is, 'objective' – but can be subjected to continuous scrutiny and intervention until more convincing reasons arise. Popper (1963:516) insists that people use their rationality on the basis of 'trial and error in every field'. Thus, once a reason has been accepted, it does not have to be valid for all time, as through experimentation new reasons and eventually more plausible reasons might ensue to address relevant concerns. For instance, once a reason has been considered as to why learners' learning can be improved, such a reason does not have to remain valid for all time. Similarly, a justification for teaching a particular subject in a particular way might not necessarily hold true at a different time or in a different context – a more convincing reason in support of improved learning may be found.

Indeed, good teaching ought to be shaped by bringing what is taught into question, by holding accountable that which is usually taken for granted. Good teaching happens when educators are prepared to take the risk of considering new ways of teaching, and to disrupt the way things have always been done. Through 'trial and error', reasons can be modified and even repudiated on the grounds that more plausible but up-to-now unconsidered reasons can justify a practice, such as engaging in particular pedagogical activities. An educator might not only apply reason to renewed ways of teaching and learning, he or she may also reflect on his or her reasons for doing things in a certain way. And when we improve on our reasons, we show our willingness to listen to others' criticism of these reasons, acceding that there is much more to know than what we already know – that is, we rethink our reasons in the light of new insights. Rationality is thus a human experience on the basis of which we articulate defensible reasons for our perspectives. In this way, human rationality can ensure growth and transcendence of reasons.

Next we examine some of the philosophical underpinnings of rationality in relation to three accounts of the concept.

Rationality as human practice

Having established rationality as a human practice guided by criticism, imagination and rethinking, we now analyse certain strands of rationality. We focus on how Taylor, MacIntyre and Cavell promote notions of interpretive rationality, practical rationality and sceptical rationality respectively.

Interpretive rationality

Taylor (1985:151) depicts rationality as a human activity in which articulation plays a significant role. According to Taylor (1985:137), 'we have a rational grasp of something when we can articulate it, that means, distinguish and lay out the different features of the matter in perspicuous order' – in other words, 'say[ing] clearly what the matter in question is'. For instance, when an educator understands teaching, he or she is capable of putting into words the meanings associated with the practice of teaching and then making a systematic argument for what teaching is or ought to be. An educator with a rational grasp of what he or she is doing can form judgements – that is, find reasons for clarifying or defending particular decisions or actions. Teaching is explained as a human practice on the grounds that an educator gives an account of meanings linked to the practice of teaching. And when he or she offers meanings to explain and justify the teaching practice, he or she does so clearly and simply, using an order of justification whereby one reason is built on another. These reasons do not contradict each other; they combine to present a systematic argument because, following Taylor (1985:137), 'consistency is plainly a necessary condition of rationality'. When we articulate reasons clearly, we have not only rational understanding but also 'theoretical understanding' (Taylor 1985:137). It comes as no surprise then that rationality is associated with contemplation (which used to be known as 'theoria').

Having a rational grasp of a concept or practice is not confined to articulating it clearly and consistently. It also entails being genuinely attuned to the concept or practice. To rationally grasp a concept or a practice is to embed ourselves in the way in which that concept or practice unfolds, and to acclimatise it in relation to the world. Understandings of what it means to teach are closely linked with how those understandings are articulated and thus made meaningful. Articulating meanings of teaching consistently is not a sufficient condition for teaching being what it is. Teaching is not made visible by being described as this or that practice; teaching is lived, shared and contested through the practices that constitute it. Following Taylor (1985:142), to be attuned to the practice of teaching an educator must 'love it'. For an educator to articulate his or her understanding of teaching clearly, consistently and in an attuned way, he or she also has to have the 'wisdom of self-knowledge and self-reconciliation' (Taylor 1985:142). When educators recognise what it means to love teaching, they understand and express that love through their teaching. In turn, they make what they teach lovable to their learners. It is not unusual, therefore, to hear learners say that they enjoy this or that educator's classes because of the love that the educator reveals through his or her teaching. Moreover, when educators love their teaching, they show love to those whom they teach, making the learners feel recognised, included and respected.

In sum, *interpretive rationality* entails articulating our understanding of a concept or practice by offering our reasons for why it is what it is in a clear and consistent manner, and by being attuned to it.

Practical rationality

MacIntyre (1999) offers an Aristotelian account of practical rationality or reasoning, otherwise known as '*phronesis*'. Aristotle (2004:151) describes *phronesis* as an intellectual virtue, a state that allows the individual who attains it to be able to ascertain what is good for humankind, and then to deliberate how best to reach that good:

> *Thus prudence must be a true state, reasoned and capable of action in the sphere of human goods. Moreover, whereas there is an excellence in art, there is no such thing in prudence; and in art the man [or woman] who makes a mistake is rated higher if he makes it voluntarily, but in the case of prudence he is rated lower, just as in the case of the [moral] virtues. Clearly, then, prudence is a virtue, not an art.*

To MacIntyre (1999), practical reasoning is the capacity of human beings to make independent rational choices. He emphasises individual autonomy whereby we exercise our rational agency to make judgements based on 'powers of perception, perceptual attention, recognition, identification and reidentification [together with] [...] having and exhibiting desire and emotion [...] of directing [our] actions towards ends that constitute specific goods' (MacIntyre 1999:27). Making independent rational choices on the grounds of articulating autonomous 'speech acts' involves making assertions, and expressing doubts through asking questions (MacIntyre 1999:30).

Practical rationality, for MacIntyre (1999:14), also requires us to engage with others 'by making their actions intelligible to us, [and] enable[s] us to respond to them in ways that they too find intelligible' – a matter of engaging in interpreting the speech of others (MacIntyre 1999:34). Acting with practical rationality thus implies that we embark on activities 'in concert and communication with others' (MacIntyre 1999:51). As MacIntyre (1999:74) points out,

> *to learn how to become an independent practical reasoner is to learn how to cooperate with others in forming and sustaining those same relationships that make possible the achievement of common goods [...] Such cooperative activities presuppose some degree of shared understanding of present and future possibilities.*

The idea of engaging with others on the basis of practical rationality is linked to an understanding that we can reach our own conclusions, but simultaneously 'can be held accountable by and to others for those conclusions' (MacIntyre 1999:84). In other words, practical rationality can be described as people simply using their common sense – not unlike an educator, who needs to assess his or her learners, or the context of the classroom, so as to determine the most appropriate methods of teaching. In this way, an acknowledgement of autonomous (independent) action is inextricably linked to a dependence on others for their intelligible contributions. MacIntyre (1999:97) asserts:

> *There is no point then in our development towards and in our exercise of independent practical reasoning [rationality] at which we cease altogether to be dependent on particular others [...] [because] our co-workers [...] make us aware both of our particular mistakes in this or that practical activity and of the sources of those mistakes in our failures in respect of virtues and skills.*

MacIntyre (1999:54) further explains practical rationality as 'the ability to stand back from one's initial judgements about how one should act and to evaluate them by a variety of standards'. Once we have offered reasons in defence of a particular argument, we should also demonstrate an ability to distance ourselves from our initial reasons because we can devise more imaginative reasons for various possible futures (MacIntyre 1999:74). Practical reasoners can evaluate, modify or reject their own practical judgements, questioning whether reasons that they take to be good are in fact good enough, and exercising their 'ability to imagine realistically alternative possible futures, so as to be able [to make] rational choices' (MacIntyre 1999:83). As practical reasoners we show that we are not attached to particular points of view or ways of doing. Practical reasoners have the capacity not only to offer reasons but also to evaluate these reasons and become detached from these reasons if more justifiable evidence emerges. We act more intelligently, being in a position to be cautious because our decisions are influenced by reasons, but also being able to take risks because we can distance ourselves from reasons that are perhaps not as plausible as they at first seemed. Put differently, our risk-taking capabilities are demonstrated when we offer reasons, and, after we have taken other evidence into consideration, we either modify or reject these reasons in response to the more justifiable reasons that are available.

In sum, *practical rationality* involves offering reasons for our particular points of view, engaging with other people and their reasons, and detaching ourselves from our reasons so that we can evaluate, modify or even perhaps reject these previously held reasons in order to construct more defensible ones.

Sceptical rationality

Cavell (1979:130) extends the understandings suggested by Taylor (1985) and MacIntyre (1999) by introducing doubt into the process of offering reasons. Cavell (1979:131, 132) suggests the possibility that in our clear and consistent articulation of reasons for some practical purpose, there can be 'grounds for doubt', that what we claim or argue for 'can reasonably be doubted'. Not every reason can conclusively be articulated as reasonable and therefore beyond criticism or challenge. Teaching, for instance, has been articulated above as being a practice.

But if the very idea of a 'practice' were to be reconsidered, reasonable doubt would be raised and teaching could no longer be referred to conclusively as a practice.

MacIntyre (2002:8–9) proposes that while educators are involved in a variety of practices, and while teaching is an ingredient in every practice, teaching is never more than a means, an endeavour towards making something. Teaching has no function, MacIntyre (2002:8–9) maintains, beyond that of introducing learners to the purpose of activities. All teaching is for the sake of something else, and so teaching does not have its own goods.

Scholars such as Dunne (in MacIntyre 2002) and Noddings (2003) challenge MacIntyre's view. Noddings (2003:241) believes that teaching is about accepting responsibility for the development of learners as whole persons, which in turn demands that education becomes a virtuous endeavour and encounter.

> An education worthy of its name will help its students to develop as persons, to be thoughtful citizens, competent parents, faithful friends, capable workers, generous neighbors and lifelong learners. It will try, too, to develop aesthetic, ethical and spiritual sensitivity. It offers programs and activities designed to enhance these ends and it tries to choose means compatible with them. Where possible, it avoids coercion. It prefers the language of invitation, offering, encouragement, guidance, sharing, advice and trying-out to that of requirement, compulsion, prescription, testing and assignment. (Noddings 2006:339)

As a relational practice, argues Noddings (2003:241), teaching benefits learners and educators. So even if teaching is considered to be just a means, as MacIntyre (2002) maintains, it is underscored by something that affects human actions in particular ways, though we may never know with certainty what those actions are. An educator cannot be certain that because he or she demonstrated a particular virtue while teaching – be it respect, compassion, patience – the learners will have understood it and learnt to have it as well. Cavell (1979:431) proposes that 'to live without doubt, without so to speak the threat of skepticism [...] would be to fall [...] [out of] love with the world'. For Cavell, as Macarthur (2014:2, 3) explains, scepticism is not the name of

> a negative epistemological thesis – say that we cannot know, or know for certain, that the external world or other minds exist – but a pervasive threat to something he calls (after Wittgenstein) "the ordinary". What is at issue is nothing less than our capacity to apply words to the world at all. [...] [Moreover,] while scepticism about the external world is not straightforwardly true there is a 'truth' in scepticism.

'The human creature's basis in the world as a whole, its relation to the world as such, is not that of knowing, anyway not what we think of as knowing', suggests

Cavell (1979:45). Scepticism is thus not a matter of our failing to satisfy some demanding standard of justification or certainty. Instead, scepticism 'arises from a reflection on how the application of criteria comes to seem disappointing within a certain kind of philosophical reflection in so far as it fails to conclusively establish the reality of whatever the criteria are criteria of' (Macarthur 2014:15–16).

Following Cavell (1979:448), the 'claim of reason' is that there is always more to know, and that looking at reasons sceptically opens up the possibility of pursuing alternative meanings. Educators would seek to instil scepticism in their teaching in order to encourage learners to come to their learning with openness and doubt – so that they never accept what they are taught without questioning it and pondering and reasoning about it. This ought to be the habit of teaching, whereby educators and learners encounter one another in mutually attached detachments that always subject the other to conscious reasoning.

Implications: On releasing imaginative human action

Our understanding of education in the Aristotelian sense is connected to the idea of a human encounter whereby people do things in association with one another, whether in conversation or within particular communities. For Aristotle (2004), the goals of education cannot be separate from the goal of life, which is the self-realisation of being human. In this sense, education is an implicitly relational practice – it can unfold only in relation to another human. Education is also embedded in what it means to be human and happy, as to be happy is to be educated:

> Since all knowledge and every pursuit aim at some good, what do we take to be the end of political science – what is the highest of all practical goods? Well, so far as the name goes there is pretty general agreement. "It is happiness" say both ordinary and cultured people; and they identify happiness with living well or doing well. (Aristotle 2004:7)

Education, therefore, is constituted through educators offering reasons that are justifiable from their various perspectives. And in the quest to find more plausible ways of understanding, educators bring into doubt their offered reasons. In turn, they create the possibility of thinking differently about their reasons in pursuit of enhancing their human encounters. We are drawn to Hogan's (2011:31) description of a learning environment as being focused on the educational practices of teaching and learning, rather than being distracted by this or that allegiance or value system. Such focus, suggests Hogan (2011:31), is marked by a commitment to building and sustaining a community of enquiry – that is, educators and learners embarking on teaching and learning in association. Such a community calls attention to inherent benefits as distinct from extrinsic goals, but not to what these benefits might be (Hogan 2011). Moreover, a commitment to building and sustaining a community of enquiry is necessarily constituted, on the one hand, by the acknowledgement and recognition of learners, and on the other hand, by an educator who exercises attentive restraint so that he or she might listen to and think about the standpoints of learners (Hogan 2011:31).

Like any human encounter, a pedagogical encounter is also guided by the reasons people offer consistently for this or that purpose, and about which they simultaneously raise doubts. In seeking to show the power of sceptical rationality in guiding the ways in which educators teach and learners learn, we turn to the work of Maxine Greene (1995).

Greene (1995:25) suggests that '[p]eople trying to be more fully human must not only engage in critical thinking but must be able to imagine something coming of their hopes; their silence must be overcome by their search'. So when educators and learners participate in pedagogical encounters they not only engage in critical thinking, by accounting for their reasons, but also 'release [their] imagination', by orientating their search for reasons 'to awaken, to disclose the ordinarily unseen, unheard, and unexpected' (Greene 1995:28). Such educators and learners are open to a reflectiveness about their reasons that will move them towards 'what is not yet' (Greene 1995:48). Following Greene (1995), Thayer-Bacon (2010:3) maintains that releasing the imagination of learners further develops 'their attending skills and their ability to respond to ordinary and unusual experiences, as well as recognize patterns and commonality that exist in our diverse world'. To Greene (1995:3), it is imagination that makes empathy possible, and that allows people to accept the possibility of alternative realities. A lack of imagination, explains Greene (1995:37), results in 'an incapacity to create or even participate in what might be called a community'.

> All we can do is to speak with others as passionately and eloquently as we can; all we can do is to look into each other's eyes and urge each other on to new beginnings. Our classrooms ought to be nurturing and thoughtful and just all at once; they ought to pulsate with multiple conceptions of what it is to be human and alive. They ought to resound with the voices of articulate young people in dialogues always incomplete because there is always more to be discovered and more to be said. We must want our learners to achieve friendship as each one stirs to wide-awakeness, to imaginative action, and to renewed consciousness of possibility. (Greene 1995:43)

In releasing their imaginations in pedagogical encounters, learners and educators are not constrained by imposition and control. Rather, they are provoked to reach out for meanings, to go beyond conventional limits in their seeking of consistency and explanations (Greene 1995:57). This also means that educators cannot constrain themselves by thinking that their voice is the only pedagogical voice worth hearing. Going beyond conventional limits entails educators thinking and re-thinking not only about how meaning is cultivated and expressed, but also about how to construct and position themselves in relation to those they teach. Such pedagogical encounters, unrestricted by the dominance and control of conclusive reasons, are open to learners' and educators' narratives. For these narratives to find expression – so that human flourishing might be cultivated – educators need to be prepared to listen to their learners. When learners recognise that they are being listened to, and that their voices are being respected, Noddings (2012:774) suggests, they willingly enter into the educator–learner encounter and share their narratives. Such encounters invite conversation, debate and disagreement, and recognise that the pursuit of explanations or clarity often resides in the unexpected and the unforeseen. Thus, according to Greene (1995:121), in pedagogical encounters educators would have to be 'attentive and vigilant' if they were to open texts and spaces in their provocation of learners. In other words, pedagogical encounters should be about sceptical rationality that prompts in learners an awareness of seeing things anew.

In sum, pedagogical encounters inspired by *sceptical rationality* involve not only an articulation of reasons in a clear and consistent manner, and an orientation of reasons towards some transformative activity, but also educators instilling in themselves and in learners a willingness to move towards relations that encourage them to 'imaginative action, and to renewed consciousness of possibility' (Greene 1995:43). Unless learners are provoked into thinking about situations anew, or into doubting strongly held views, they will not be encouraged to consider other perspectives. And unless learners can imagine themselves in circumstances they might otherwise never encounter – described by Greene (1995:43) as acknowledging 'the harshness of situations' – they will not learn to have empathy for others. It is not enough to acknowledge or express knowledge of a particular harshness. Greene argues for not only visualising the 'harshness', but visualising it to the extent of *feeling* it, so that empathy might be evoked. How may learners acknowledge hunger, poverty, displacement or oppression if they are not motivated to visualising themselves into the harshness of these situations?

Thus, exercising sceptical rationality is especially pertinent in societies where there is less likelihood of particular groups encountering one another. In the South African landscape, for example, it is possible for people to live unscathed by the harshness of poverty even while driving past it on a daily basis. How may learners conceive of the plight of migrants, as they wash from shore to shore in pursuit of security and human dignity, if not through releasing themselves from their own experiences? In other words, learners have to be provoked out of the conventions of their thinking, their ways of doing and acting, so that they might imagine the fear and hopelessness felt by others. And to provoke their learners in this way, educators need to disrupt the conventional limitations of their classroom, and of what and how they teach; educators need to be prepared to undo their own constraints. This becomes evident in the way that educators understand and relate to their learners.

The educator recognises the diverse individuality of each learner, and teaches in such a way that those facets of diversity are acknowledged and respected.

Conclusion and recommendations for future research

In this chapter we have explored the interrelated forms of interpretive, practical and sceptical rationality. We have implicitly argued for an integrated notion of rationality, meaning that when people apply their rationality, they open themselves to that which is unknown and unexplored. This is especially pertinent in a classroom setting, where educators should invite their learners to think, and apply reasons, and to consider perspectives and arguments anew. Such an understanding and application of rationality depends on articulating reasons clearly and consistently. The argument in favour of sceptical rationality has been offered with the intention of showing that educational encounters are not always predictable, and that a comprehensive and conclusive account of reasons do not always bring about pedagogical 'breakthroughs' (Greene 1995:vii).

Educating for 'openings' (Greene 1995:vii) is closely linked with the cultivation of democratic educational relations. We are interested to know how democratic pedagogical encounters would unfold in the wake of the sceptical, practical and interpretive forms of rationality. First, in *Citizenship, Education and Violence: On Disrupted Potentialities and Becoming* (Waghid & Davids 2013), we argue for democratic citizenship education as a response to violence in communities. This is an example of how reasons are offered in defence of a particular understanding of democratic community, and how citizens ought to articulate their reasons. As readers you are encouraged to refer to this book, as it is hoped that through your engagement with our thoughts on reasons, you would be prompted to think differently about democratic citizenship education in relation to addressing a wrong such as violence in communities.

Secondly, Roland Martin's (2013) *Education Reconfigured: Culture, Encounter, and Change* explores what it means to produce democratic citizens. She proposes, significantly, that the making of a democratic citizen depends on the cultivation of a 'rational decision-maker' (Roland Martin 2013:150). Such a person is capable of being open to questioning and committed to cultivating democracy along a theory of education whereby learners are 'in control of their own learning' (Roland Martin 2013:154). We are interested to know whether education for a democratic citizenry should be amenable to the cultivation of sceptical rationality. Thus, in cultivating democratic citizens through education, the possibility exists of seeing rationality as a means as to why and how the former can be engendered. We recommend that you consider examining the possibility of cultivating democratic citizenship education on the basis of the forms of rationality put forward in this chapter.

One of the fundamental aspects of education, Bailin and Siegel (2003:188) point out, is the use of rationality, which they equate with the practice of critical thinking. Fostering critical thinking in learners is a matter of treating them respectfully as persons (Bailin & Siegel 2003:189). This involves enabling learners to judge educational matters for themselves, preparing them for self-sufficiency and self-direction, and allowing them to do careful analysis, good thinking and reasoned deliberation in democratic life (Bailin & Siegel 2003:189). Consequently, critical thinking (and so rationality) aims at 'the promotion of independent thinking, personal autonomy, and reasoned judgement in thought and action' (Bailin & Siegel 2003:189). Rationality (and so critical thinking) involves the ability to assess the probable strength of reasons and the disposition to do so (Bailin & Siegel 2003:192). Thus we recommend that you examine the viability of critical thinking for education and for democratic citizenship education.

References

Aristotle. 2004. *The Nicomachean Ethics* [350 BCE]. Translated by JAK Thompson. London: Penguin.

Bailin S & Siegel H. 2003. Critical thinking. In N Blake, P Smeyers, R Smith & P Standish. (eds). *The Blackwell Guide to the Philosophy of Education.* Oxford: Blackwell. 181–193.

Cavell S. 1979. *The Claim of Reason: Wittgenstein, Skepticism, Morality and Tragedy.* Oxford: Oxford University Press.

Greene M. 1995. *Releasing the Imagination: Essays on Education, the Arts and Social Change.* San Francisco: Jossey-Bass.

Hogan P. 2011. The ethical orientations of education as a practice in its own right. *Ethics and Education*, 61:27–40.

Macarthur D. 2014. Cavell on skepticism and the importance of not-knowing. *Conversations: Journal of Cavellian Studies*, 2:2–23. Available: http://www.academia.edu/6795921/Cavell_on_Skepticism_and_the_Importance_of_Not-Knowing. (Accessed 8 February 2017.)

MacIntyre A. 1999. *Dependent Rational Animals: Why Human Beings Need the Virtues.* London: Duckworth.

MacIntyre A. 2002. Alasdair MacIntyre in dialogue with Joseph Dunne. *Journal of Philosophy of Education*, 361:1–19.

Noddings N. 2003. Is teaching a practice? *Journal of Philosophy of Education*, 372:241–251.

Noddings N. 2006. Educational leaders as caring teachers. *School Leadership and Management*, 264:339–345.

Noddings N. 2012. The caring relation in teaching. *Oxford Review of Education*, 386:771–781.

Popper K. 1963. *Conjectures and Refutations.* London and New York: Routledge.

Roland Martin J. 2013. *Education Reconfigured: Culture, Encounter, and Change.* New York and London: Routledge.

Taylor C. 1985. *Philosophy and the Human Sciences. Philosophical Papers 2.* Cambridge: Cambridge University Press.

Thayer-Bacon B. 2010. *Releasing the Imagination: Essays on Education, the Arts, and Social Change* by Maxine Greene. Review. *Journal of Educational Controversy*, 5(1):1–6.

Waghid Y & Davids N. 2013. *Citizenship, Education and Violence: On Disrupted Potentialities and Becoming.* Rotterdam/Boston/Taipei: Sense.

Phenomenology and education:
Have we opted for epistemology before ontology?

Tracey Isaacs

Introduction

Educational research is viewed, rather narrowly, by some as an essentially scientific enterprise. But educational research should be research *for* education and not research *about* education. Research *for* education is based on the ethical and critical dimensions of our social practice, as educators, that communicates meaning, value and identity to ontological beings. In bypassing the positivist view centred on facts and truth, a more subjective and personal language might help to give expression to new arguments that frame the debate on educational ontology.

Thus, in this chapter, we emphasise a theory of education grounded more in ontology and less in epistemology. Even when epistemology is studied for philosophical meaning, it begins with the imagination rather than with positivism. In this way more clarity may emerge around aspects of phenomenology and the curriculum, and around how a particular curriculum may be reconceptualised phenomenologically. The chapter seeks to develop a philosophical account of educational theory that supports ontological positions embedded in social justice, equality and active agency. We explore the work of existentialist scholars (James Magrini and others), criticalists (Joe L Kincheloe and Patti Lather), constructivists (Maxine Greene, Patrick Slattery and David M Dees) and curriculum theorists (Fazal Rizvi and Nel Noddings) to further justify the need for a community of pedagogues committed to ontological educational theory.

The philosophical/conceptual underpinnings of philosophy of education

The debate on phenomenology in education

Magrini (2012) demystifies the link between existentialism and phenomenology by clarifying that *existentialism* is concerned with the subjective and personal aspects of existence. *Phenomenology* in its turn is the way of observing, recording and interpreting how we enquire into our existence through lived experience (Magrini 2012:2). Thus, given the subjectivity of experience and the many ways of interpreting it, phenomenology can be characterised as philosophical hermeneutics. The aim of the hermeneutic approach is not to arrive at solutions, but to clarify and deepen our understanding of phenomena (Magrini 2012:2). Consequently, what emerges from this theorising, as seen from an educational perspective, is a sense that our ontological position (a way of existing wherein we enquire into our existence) should be deeply foregrounded in pedagogical encounters. This position suggests that interpretation involves personal growth and self-formation through co-creative pedagogical arrangements (Magrini 2012:2). Therefore this thinking breaks with epistemological models based on grand narratives.

Magrini (2012) exposes the deficit thinking attached to educational policy and research that ignores ontological diversity and multiple educational logics, or 'multilogicality' in Kincheloe's (nd:1) terms. As it relates specifically to the curriculum, following Greene (1995), Magrini (2012) proposes curriculum content from the humanities (literature and art) to draw out a multi-perspectival view of being-in-the-world. This position opposes a curriculum conceived from dominant natural scientific schemes that, according to Kincheloe (nd:3), follow a '"culture of positivism" [and] emphasize certainty and prediction as [they] organize verified facts into certified theories'. Positivist rationality is dangerous in that it subscribes to epistemological rigidness and closes off opportunities for diversity (cultural, gendered, racial, ability and so on), thereby circumscribing the 'quality of knowledge we produce' about elements of being-in the-world, such as 'selfhood' (Kincheloe nd:1).

Similarly, Kincheloe (nd:3) addresses the short-sightedness of positivism by proposing a critical theoretical system of meaning seeking the emancipation of the subject. Kincheloe (nd:3) frames the problem of positivism in education in terms of 'monologicality', through which we assume that 'formal cognitive operations represent the highest level of human cognition'. He advocates for a more 'ethically informed theory of cognition' that expands ontological and epistemological boundaries (Kincheloe nd:4). Here, 'value' is given to the 'voice' and experiences of all human beings-in-the-world, including the 'subjugated and marginalized' (Kincheloe nd:5). Consequently, an embrace of rationalities and knowledges provides rich insight and understanding of what occurs when we 'encounter the world', and it deepens our 'ontological awareness' (Kincheloe nd:8). What this means phenomenologically is that our subjectivities demand a deviation from the 'safe', 'decontextualized' and 'obvious answers' that fragment us from our world (Kincheloe nd:17). Our selfhood and our lifeworld are instead characterised by 'uncertainty and ambiguity', and our perspectives are 'limited by time and space, by history and culture' (Kincheloe nd:21, 22).

We have sought to understand how phenomenology and education are integrated. Next, we will develop clearer insight into how a theory of education grounded in ontology fits into a framework of contemporary schooling.

A theory of education grounded in ontology

Ontologically, learning can be seen as a way of being (Magrini 2013:1). Thus, Magrini (2013:1) argues that the aim of education is perceived in human beings' primordial search for meaning. Gathering life experiences as text, he proposes, and analysing this text provides conceptual lenses for inspiring improved educational practice (Magrini 2013:2). He also warns, however, that it will disappoint positivists who may believe that the phenomenological approach can solve problems; that theory is far removed from praxis; and that theory can be applied to praxis to predict, control and direct it (Magrini 2013:2). Magrini (2013:2) therefore makes it clear that phenomenology is informed by practical theory (the content and experiences of daily life), and cannot be equated with scientific theory (abstraction, objectivity, the 'right method'). The most ardent critics of phenomenology argue that, as a philosophical method of enquiry, the results it can deliver may at best be described as 'speculative and tentative insight into the things we might find useful in praxis' (Magrini 2013:2). Critical theorists respond that far from seeking verifiable facts (through the scientific method) to make meaning of our lives and of living, we should be engaged in moral action aimed at reducing human suffering (Steinberg & Kincheloe 2010:140).

The criticalist perspective

Regarding our ontological (and even epistemological) awareness, Steinberg & Kincheloe (2010:140) consider the ways that society is structured along power differentials that 'make us feel comfortable in relations of domination and subordination, rather than equality'. Therefore Steinberg & Kincheloe (2010:141) find support in the critical paradigm for self-direction aimed at moral reasoning and moral practice, which takes criticality and lenses of complexity as its guideposts. Epistemologically this means that social analysis sees experience as socially constructed. This view deeply conflicts with the positivist notion that is grounded in instrumental rationality, which has method, efficiency and fact as its central concerns (Steinberg & Kincheloe 2010:144).

In sum, these theorists help to clarify that we take certain epistemologies as natural because we have come to believe and rely on their claims of providing evidence through 'prediction, explanation and verification' (Lather 2004:762). Not disclosed in this narrow-minded view of reality is that there are so many categories organising our existence, and that this stable and unified idea of science forestalls description, interpretation and discovery, which is closer to the way we play, talk, learn and tell stories to better understand our world, ourselves and others (Lather 2004:762). Furthermore, as Magrini (2013:3) points out, 'in an era of social efficiency and scientific management, we are trapped in a way of seeing, understanding, interpreting and discoursing about our existence that distorts and restricts our vision'. To him, education has been reduced to a series of problems that need to be solved (Magrini 2013:3). Moreover, parents are seen as clients, learners are recast as products and educators work as technicians to remediate learners' 'faults' cognitively and behaviourally (Magrini 2013:3). Consequently, the technological management of education brings us to a vacuous ontological point and a dangerous educational cul-de-sac that Magrini (2013:3) characterises as the 'forgetfulness of being'.

Scientific versus critical methodologies

Yet Lather (2004:760) is quick to remind us that the grandiose quantification (through the scientific method and technological management) has thus far not been able to settle any important issues of public policy. She remains unconvinced that so-called evidence-based practice actually works in schooling (policy, research, practice) (Lather 2004:763). Furthermore, Lather (2004:763) highlights the unavoidable reality of everyday classroom encounters with the profound question: How many problems that educators face have been resolved by policy and research?

Nevertheless Lather (2004:765) helps us to understand how we are ontologically conditioned by social structuring. To this end, she draws on Foucault's (1998) technologies of governmentality. First, our rulers use the technology of policy to regulate our behaviour (Lather 2004:765). Secondly, we are controlled by diplomatic and military technologies instituted by our governments to minimise dissent and resistance (Lather 2004:765). And finally, the government seduces us through the instrument of the economy with the promise of wealth stimulation (Lather 2004:765). Lather (2004:762) proposes that in the face of the sophisticated scientific management of society, which unknowingly disciplines us through normalising practices and behaviours, we need to respond with a 'counter-science'.

Following Foucault (1998:320), Lather (2004:765) perceives this counter-science as a field where strategic possibilities might become apparent, and where we are ontologically self-directed as beings of understanding, reflection and action. Ultimately, Lather (2004:765) illuminates how complexity theory is embedded in ontology. She skilfully builds a notion of 'otherness' within a postcolonial framework that acts as a striking metaphor for being (particularly for beings-in-becoming-educated) (Lather 2004:765). She proposes that we (beings) are likened to the postcolonial situation, which can be characterised by a 'politics of unevenness; contradictory outcomes; disjunctures; delays; contingencies; and uncompleted projects' (Lather 2004:767). Phenomenologically, lived experience resonates with the postcolonial situation in that it is 'rich in ambiguity; and it stays close to the complexities and contradictions of existence' (Lather 2004:767). Critical theorists, on the whole, have contributed to an alternative view of the sciences that epistemologically contests the ('infallible') natural sciences in the sense that they advocate for 'an applied social science that can cope with the multiplicity of the social world' by admitting its and their limitations and possibilities (Lather 2004:768).

We have attempted to understand the limits and potentials of an educational model that deviates from the overwhelming reliance on the scientific method, and that instead would choose to entertain diverse epistemological and ontological positions. Let us now look more closely at the learning environment from the curricular and pedagogical point of view, particularly at how these sites promote certain notions of being-in-the-world.

Key issues and debates in philosophy of education

A change in epistemology: Start with the imagination?

Magrini (2013:4) identifies the impoverished nature of being educationally in pointing out that learning occurs only when there is an 'observable and demonstrable change in student behaviour' and cognition. This understanding of being-in-education suggests that there is an absolutely 'correct method' (Magrini 2013:4), and that the process of education has stable, definite and predictable outcomes, or products. To develop his argument, Magrini (2013:5) draws a parallel between the natural world and our learning environment, suggesting that in the context of biology, for example, organisms and stimuli interact (Magrini 2013:5). Yet to treat learners as objects who react in response to a powerful external stimulus assumes a reality far removed from human meaning, and thus brings into question such concepts as free will, autonomy and agency.

This level of learner objectification also presupposes that education is something (we have) to do or give to learners, when in fact it may be more correct to believe that learners bring their own education (through their lifeworlds) into schooling. Magrini (2013:6) sees the learning sciences as limiting when learning is defined only in terms of the 'retention, retrieval and transmission of pre-determined skills, dispositions and knowledge'. This deficit view of education is inconsistent with educational models and approaches premised on an authentic curriculum and subject matter. Furthermore, in a problem-based approach to learning as advanced through the scientific method, education is centred on the abstraction of concepts and mastery over an external world (Magrini 2013:6). It could also be understood differently: Concepts are part of our lived experiences, and we are not 'over' the world but embedded within it. Therefore we learn and make meaning (daily) perhaps more at the subconscious level, because our everyday experiences are not governed routinely by the scientific method (where knowledge is retained, retrieved and transmitted, and where we experience the external world only as an exercise of the mind in books).

We interpret Lather's (2004:762) 'counter-science' as being in line with Magrini's (2013:7) concept of practical knowledge, where the emphasis is far removed from describing, predicting, explaining and determining appropriate action. Instead, as phenomenological subjects in education, we are fully present ontologically – we learn and come-into-presence with our whole body (sensory-motor and affectively) and not exclusively through cognition (Magrini 2013:14). Furthermore, in this model of learning, the fragmentation of the world is replaced by an attempt to see as much as possible of the total picture concerning a particular reality, and even to look beyond it. Thus, to institute a phenomenological turn in contemporary education means that an epistemology fixated on conceptual knowledge (procedural, factual and metacognitive knowledge) gives way to other epistemologies – those turned towards emotional intelligence and affective forms of knowledge, such as intuition and aesthetics (Magrini 2013:14).

This phenomenological focus takes seriously the notion that as autonomous beings, we are able to freely construct meaning by interpreting, repudiating or reaffirming experience, and this focus rejects the notion that we can know the world only in a systematic way (Magrini 2013:14). To reinforce his argument, Magrini (2013:9) proposes that we are always learning in response to the demands the world makes of us. For example, a practical activity such as grasping a doorknob or crossing a room is a response to our world, yet we do not approach it through thematic, well-laid plans and strategies (Magrini 2013:19). Instead, our practical knowledge and experience creates the openings for us to respond to the world in new and unique ways (Magrini 2013:19).

Thus the original ways of being in the world and understanding the whole person in authentic learning situations are far more educationally instructive than mislabelling and misrecognising (children, learners, adults and educators) through deficit models of schooling and education. Magrini (2013) suggests that embracing phenomenology indicates that as educators we look beyond what is (materially) in front of us and strive to discover what lies there (context, history, perspective) in order to respond hermeneutically. This kind of educational vision coincides with Greene's (1995) theorising on the re-emphasising of the humanities in the curriculum.

A curriculum that embraces aesthetic literacy

Greene (Slattery & Dees 1998:46) believes that the ontologically focused curriculum should encourage learners' imaginations through literary, artistic and phenomenological experiences. Therefore she challenges educational approaches that 'reduce learning and living to fragmented and quantifiable components devoid of the aesthetic and narrative' form (Slattery & Dees 1998:46). Furthermore, Greene perceives the curriculum as a continuous interpretation and a conscious search for meaning (Slattery & Dees 1998:46). Here the phenomenological perspective gains dominance because it supports social and educational transformation by way of engaging learners and educators in the literary, performative and creative arts (Slattery & Dees 1998:46). Practically this could be through a reliance on the autobiographical narrative, where storytelling is a veritable way of knowing, and where our own stories establish authentic projects and stronger identities (Slattery & Dees 1998:46).

Pedagogically, Greene's (1995:49) propositions are meant to provoke a heightened sense of agency on the part of learners and educators, because she feels that the humanities curriculum draws from and moves beyond our lived world. Thus this kind of education rationalising bypasses mere functional and technical approaches to learning based on prescriptions, measurements and solutions (Greene 1995:49). Greene (1995:55) therefore suggests a counterbalance: a pedagogical space that fosters the growth of the human person and spirit in a caring, hopeful and sustainable community. The significance of this educational view informs a pedagogical practice that cannot be scientifically planned, because educators and learners cannot chart in advance the spaces where they have not been.

Magrini (2012, 2013), Lather (2004) and Greene (1995) propose a more ethical pedagogy that goes beyond conformist conceptions of education. Magrini (2012, 2013) provides a practical and transparent understanding that challenges the stable and definite theories of education. Seen in the light of social justice for marginal learners who might not excel at retention, retrieval and transmission of information, phenomenologically innovative pedagogical approaches might be more profitable to confirm their ontological presence. In this way learner disengagement (boredom and absenteeism, for example) could be circumvented through a truer connection between the educational being (not only the cognitive being) and an authentic curriculum, to foster authentic projects, provide meaning and create stronger learner identities.

Lather (2004) provides an educational vision where counter-science creates adequate space for practical knowledge. The ethical dimensions of such thinking might have practical implementation when learner autonomy and free will are exercised in self-selected learning, rather than learners having to follow regimented, testing-focused learning. Learning particularly relevant to decisive community issues (such as pollution and safety) stands out as an example where counter-science learning supersedes positivist learning. In this instance learner agency may mean action or activism (rather than abstract, theoretical testing) to understand and solve complex social problems.

Greene (1995) inspires a humanities-focused curriculum that particularises interpretation and meaning-making. The overturn from a rigid, quantitative educational model to an aesthetic and intuitive phenomenological account of the educational subject is a welcome shift towards amplifying human value and identity over static subject matter. In the humanities-distinct curriculum, room is created for broader agency by authentic projects that grasp ontology through the lens of literary, performative and creative arts, which help to accentuate human complexity and diversity.

In sum, this discussion has been predominated by the theorising of academics and scholars who advocate for a greater phenomenological emphasis in curriculum and pedagogy. However, these theorists have not participated in the realm of policymaking, which is entangled within a wider network of meanings. In the next section we seek a better understanding of the complexity involved in curriculum design by looking at some of the discourses that shape policy and curriculum engineering, albeit to the exclusion of learners', educators' and parents' phenomenological ontology.

Implications of philosophy of education for educational theory and practice

Phenomenology and the curriculum

Since there is no single, commonly held view of how curriculum plans are conceived, we may assume that policymakers adopt particular worldviews and develop local policy within global contexts (Rizvi 2006). Rizvi (2006:20) interprets Noddings's (2005) view that progressive education policymakers emphasise 'global citizenship [centred on] social justice, [...] social and cultural diversity, treating the earth as a single unified place [...] and educating for peace'. In contrast, policymakers with a neoliberal and managerialist educational perspective (Lather 2004:759) emphasise Gardiner's (2006) skills-based paradigm, focusing on learners' 'cognitive flexibility; cultural sophistication; and ability to work collaboratively in diverse groups', all framed by an economic imperative for global interconnectivity (Rizvi 2006). Thus, curriculum theorists Lingard and Rizvi (1998:62) interpret Greene's (1996) notion of curriculum formation in this way – policy designers display 'dominance of a particular organisational paradigm that brings together the hegemonic convergence of a particular way of thinking about educational policy-making and governance'.

How do these understandings inform an account of the subjective and personal aspects of learners as beings? First, global and national policy formulations have already created too great a distance between 'themselves' and the ontological subject they serve to influence. The phenomenological ontology of learners would perhaps be better served by an emphasis on the local as a referent for the learners' lived experiences. Secondly, epistemological hegemony (reliance on the natural sciences for accountability and reliability) and a dependence on managerialism (the management of education for efficiency) run counter to any defensible notion of admitting the closeness and intimacy of concrete, everyday learner experience in curriculum planning.

Thirdly, the managerialist approach to curriculum development relies too heavily on the economic dimensions of lived experience, which suggests that as beings learners are primarily economic beings who employ cognitive skills to engage the world and make meaning of reality. And ultimately, while progressive curriculum policymakers might conceptualise curricular matters more phenomenologically, it remains to be seen how their theoretical propositions are implemented in classrooms in the contemporary context of 'quantification' (standardised testing), 'behaviourism' and 'cognitivism' (Lather 2004:760).

So, while on a large scale, non-progressive educational policy frameworks support a global vision of the learner (as citizen) as a globally interconnected being, they have lost sight of the particularities (autobiography: context, history, culture, gender) of the learner where he or she really is, and of who he or she is (or wants to be, or wants to become). This specific view of curriculum and educational policy formulation has also prescribed in advance (almost to the point that the learner is seen more as an automaton than an authentic being) the kind of beings learners are allowed to be: cognitively flexible, culturally sophisticated and able to work collaboratively in diverse groups (for economic efficiency).

The construction of new subjectivities in education

Following on the work of critical and progressive theorists, Rafferty (2011:385) calls for the curriculum to be reconceptualised with clearer phenomenological thrusts in order to subvert hegemonic barriers and to give greater validity to authentic learner experience in classroom encounters. Rafferty (2011) submits that understanding the curriculum phenomenologically is better seen from the perspective of the learners and educators than from the bureaucratic position of policymakers. In this way learners' and educators' individual perceptions and experiences, and that which they live, gain higher priority than what is theorised, researched or written about in policy documents (Rafferty 2011:386). Similar to Greene's (1997) phenomenological propositions on education, Rafferty (2011) believes that to reify classroom engagement is to create an authentic curriculum through learner and educator autobiographies that have unique developments, shape individual identities, create avenues for agency and provide a canvas for our praxis. This thinking overcomes the abstraction and emptiness of curriculum implementation that is uncritical, unreflective and aligned to strategies and practices that are divorced from learner and educator experience.

Furthermore, Rafferty (2011:386) argues that critical and reflective curriculum praxis creates vistas for educators to attach new meanings to understanding learner experience, and to develop greater clarity on what it might mean for learners to have a particular educational experience. With regard to the critical paradigm for the development of understanding, Rafferty (2011:387) suggests that, as educators, we need to consider how to maintain power relationships both through the curriculum and our pedagogical practice. In an effort to counteract some of the more damaging effects of the curriculum, we need to put greater effort into elevating learner point of view and learner experience, and valuing learner perception by seeing the totality of learner experience (learners as political, racial, social and gendered beings with issues and lives that are wider and richer than the curriculum and classroom arrangements) (Rafferty 2011:387).

Curriculum interpretation as a phenomenological enquiry is thus more concerned with those aspects of learner and educator experience that remain hidden in regular pedagogical engagement. Phenomenological educational enquiry also shows that to cause learner and educator lifeworlds to remain obscured forecloses on opportunities for curricular and educational change. Consequently, the inability to disclose what remains hidden phenomenologically (because of an allegiance to rote implementation of a static curriculum and bureaucratic management from policy engineers), unreflective pedagogy from educators and disinterested learning from learners will be allowed to continue, with no provocation to transform the way we think and act, and no further demand for an ethical pedagogy.

We have sought to understand how educators and learners might recover a phenomenological ontology in response to global and local curriculum policy imperatives in their everyday educational encounters. We now turn to the South African National Curriculum Statement (NCS) and the Curriculum and Assessment Policy Statements (CAPS) to learn how aspects of phenomenology feature therein.

Reconceptualising the curriculum

The South African national curriculum is the culmination of 17 years of experimentation, revision and implementation of bureaucratic policy formulation (DoE 2011:4). While some argue that curriculum revolutions should not occur as regularly as they have in South Africa, others defend frequent curriculum transformation in the effort to create as much distance as possible from the race-based, unequal and undemocratic apartheid curriculum. Underwritten by the Constitution (Act 108 of 1996), the NCS Grades R–12 (DoE 2011) strives to establish a democratic society, improve the quality of life of all citizens and free the potential of each person, and institute a government based on the will of the people with equal protection under the law. Thus the Minister of Basic Education declares that the curriculum and education play a vital role in the restructuring of society (DBE 2011a:4).

The policy documents that complement the NCS Grades R–12 are:
- the CAPS
- national policy pertaining to the programme and promotion requirements of the NCS Grades R–12
- National Protocol for Assessment Grades R–12.

These documents seem to suggest what Magrini (2013:3) calls 'social efficiency and scientific management' (or managerialism), and what Lather (2004:763) calls the 'auditable management' and control of educational systems. A cursory analysis of the language of these policy documents conveys the message of a curriculum preoccupied with quantification and accountability through performance measurement – that is, testing and other forms of evaluation. In order to avoid prejudging the aims and intentions of the NCS, we now perform a first-level critical discourse analysis, followed by a more detailed analysis.

Educational policy analysis

Generally, the NCS:

> *gives expression to the knowledge, skills and values worth learning in South African schools. This curriculum aims to ensure that children acquire and apply knowledge and skills in ways that are meaningful to their own lives. In this regard, the curriculum promotes knowledge in local contexts, while being sensitive to global imperatives.*

> *The [NCS] serves the purposes of:*
> * *equipping learners, irrespective of their socio-economic background, race, gender, physical ability or intellectual ability, with the knowledge, skills and values necessary for self-fulfillment, and meaningful participation in society as citizens of a free country;*
> * *providing access to higher education;*
> * *facilitating the transition of learners from education institutions to the workplace; and*
> * *providing employers with a sufficient profile of a learner's competences.*
> (DBE 2016)

The language of the policy initially appears to be neutral and phenomenologically grounded in its references to 'knowledge' and 'values' (DBE 2016), and in its mentions of 'meaningful to their own lives' and 'local contexts' (DBE 2016). But these phenomenological nuances are soon betrayed by the language of technological management indicated by terms such as 'skills' and 'global imperatives' (DBE 2016).

The function of the NCS is seen to accommodate various ontological possibilities, even while it attaches itself to a notion of democratic pluralism (Greene 1995:68). But the policy soon disappoints in detaching from the phenomenological and reducing learners to epistemological objects. The emphasis on vocationalism, skills and competencies, and the aspiration for (usually technical) advanced education, creates an assumption that our ontological significance is brought to bear primarily when we are technically skilled and able to work in industry. Even more worrying is the statement 'providing employers [...]' (DBE 2016), which seems to suggest that learners are perceived as beings-for-another (an employer), rather than authentic, autonomous beings.

The NCS

> *is based on the following principles:*
> - *Social transformation: ensuring that the educational imbalances of the past are redressed, and that equal educational opportunities are provided for all sections of the population;*
> - *Active and critical learning: encouraging an active and critical approach to learning, rather than rote and uncritical learning of given truths;*
> - *High knowledge and high skills: the minimum standards of knowledge and skills to be achieved at each grade are specified and set high, achievable standards in all subjects;*
> - *Progression: content and context of each grade shows progression from simple to complex; ENGLISH HOME LANGUAGE GRADES R-3 CAPS 5*
> - *Human rights, inclusivity, environmental and social justice: infusing the principles and practices of social and environmental justice and human rights as defined in the Constitution of the Republic of South Africa. The National Curriculum Statement Grades R-12 is sensitive to issues of diversity such as poverty, inequality, race, gender, language, age, disability and other factors;*
> - *Valuing indigenous knowledge systems: acknowledging the rich history and heritage of this country as important contributors to nurturing the values contained in the Constitution; and*
> - *Credibility, quality and efficiency: providing an education that is comparable in quality, breadth and depth to those of other countries.*
> (DBE 2016)

These principles seem to be predominated by phenomenologically attuned sensibilities. First, social transformation and educational equality through opportunity receives high esteem. Secondly, critical pedagogy and the questioning of grand narratives are encouraged. Thirdly, human rights, inclusivity, and environmental and social justice issues are highlighted. Fourthly, epistemological diversity is valued through admitting indigenous knowledge systems. However, the NCS also harbours some dangerous analytical–logical sentiments (such as social efficiency, managerialism, competition and objectivity) that are attendant with the scientific method.

Among the phenomenologically conducive undertones of the NCS is an allegiance to progression that is inherent in the scientific method (for example civilisation and technological advancement). Moreover, concepts such as 'high knowledge' and 'high skills' (DBE 2016) seem to invalidate a respect for indigenous knowledge systems, which may be inferred to hold 'low/lower knowledge' and 'low/lower skills'. Curriculum terminology such as 'credibility', 'quality' and 'efficiency' (DBE 2016) is closely aligned with technical rationality and accountability movements that are characterised by an obsession with bureaucratic efficiency.

Thus far we have addressed the general aims, purposes and principles of the NCS, which could be considered to be on a level of abstraction, because its broad discourse has up to now not really dealt sufficiently with the subjective and personal as they relate to learners. It would thus appear that learners are overshadowed by the bureaucratic system of education and policy formulation. We now study the more specific aims that relate directly to how the NCS perceives learners generally, and particularly in education.

The NCS

> *aims to produce learners that are able to:*
> - *identify and solve problems and make decisions using critical and creative thinking;*
> - *work effectively as individuals and with others as members of a team;*
> - *organise and manage themselves and their activities responsibly and effectively;*
> - *collect, analyse, organise and critically evaluate information;*
> - *communicate effectively using visual, symbolic and/or language skills in various modes;*
> - *use science and technology effectively and critically showing responsibility towards the environment and the health of others; and*
> - *demonstrate an understanding of the world as a set of related systems by recognising that problem solving contexts do not exist in isolation.*
> (DBE 2016)

Here, first, the NCS's aim to produce learners with certain skills and attributes is problematic, because education framed in this manner is too closely aligned with the productive cycle. This introductory framing creates scepticism that phenomenological, constructivist and progressive models of education may survive. Secondly, the technical language throughout is synonymous with Gardiner's (2006) skills-based framework of policy formulation, which heavily emphasises efficiency and managerialism (economic, educational, political and social management). Thirdly, an overemphasis on efficiency creates an ontologically reductionist and mechanical picture of learners. Fourthly, this curricular framing puts education at the centre of problem-solving and learners function as objects for finding solutions to problems. Productive concepts such as collaborative work groups, effective organisation and management, scientific data processing, effective and flexible communication, effective use of science and technology and the ability to integrate knowledge also reinforce a curricular commitment to one-dimensional educational theories based on social efficiency, transmission (of specific skills, knowledge and values) and vocationalism (Magrini 2012:3).

We have sought to understand how aspects of phenomenology are featured within the NCS with a view to considering what spaces exist for ethical, existential and phenomenological expressions. We now discuss the theoretical positions in this chapter to help us form a more coherent picture of what this might mean for contemporary education, and how these views might shape future research.

Discussion

A key component supporting the NCS is made up of the CAPS. While the CAPS focus on content (concepts and skills), time allocation, and informal and formal assessment requirements, the Foundation Phase of schooling (Grades R–3) provides the potential for phenomenological development. The time allotted to subject areas is as follows: 10 hours for Home Language, seven hours for Mathematics and six hours for Life Skills (Beginning Knowledge, Creative Arts, Physical Education, and Personal and Social Well-being) (DBE 2011a:6). Thus it appears that adequate room is made for interpretation of the curriculum as phenomenological, moral and ethical. However, the implementation of the curriculum by classroom educators would still require the overcoming of an essentialist, natural science epistemology (concepts and skills, assessment).

In contrast to the Foundation Phase, the CAPS for the Senior Phase of schooling (Grades 7–9) allocates time as follows: five hours for Home Language, four and a half hours for Mathematics, three hours for Natural Sciences and Social Sciences, and two hours each for Technology, Economic Management Sciences, Life Orientation and Creative Arts (DBE 2011b:7). Thus it seems that the curriculum favours a natural science epistemology (abstraction, fact-driven and cognitive). The scientific subjects have replaced the humanities that dominated the Foundation Phase. Yet theoretical propositions hardly coincide absolutely with pedagogical practice or as curriculum planners envision. In other words, even though the CAPS makes adequate provision for a humanities curriculum, it would still have to be interpreted as superficial since implementing a humanities-dominant curriculum within a larger natural science (positivist, instrumental) worldview would continue to submerge the phenomenological presence that we seek to uncover in education, as suggested by Greene (1995, 1996, 1997; and Slattery & Dees 1998:46–50).

In studying what might appear to be the phenomenological expression in the NCS and the CAPS, admittedly there are opportunities for elevating the ontological position of learners and educators. But the threats inherent in educational theories premised on social efficiency, knowledge and skills transmission, and vocationalism are unavoidable. Thus, progressive and constructivist undertones in the NCS become circumspect given that the CAPS present a double discourse: How do we conceive of the phenomenological in the light of an added emphasis on assessment, mathematics, the natural sciences, technology and the economic management sciences? The problem that a purely scientific epistemology presents in education is one in which our knowledge of ourselves, the world and others is one-dimensional and perhaps grossly distorted. On the other hand, a theory grounded in ontology strives to recoup exactly those elements of our being that become obscured within the scientific tradition and its attendant rationalities. In this instance the educational focus shifts from solving problems and is challenged phenomenologically as a search for meaning.

In more concrete terms, Magrini (2012) proposes that a curricular focus on intuitive–perceptual models may be seen to be more phenomenologically responsive for this reason – given that we cannot provide a curriculum in advance of learner learning, we should be influenced towards curriculum development that evolves autonomously. The curriculum, Magrini (2012:4) suggests, should be seen as 'transitory' and 'malleable', with 'temporary benchmarks for learning'. The phenomenological approach in education thus makes various demands on pedagogy: the development of learner-unique possibilities, the rejection of standardised curricula, varied pedagogical methods and the abandonment of authoritarian teaching (Magrini 2012:4).

Conclusion and recommendations for future research

According to Lather (2004:765), technologies of power are used to condition us ontologically and regulate our behaviour to prevent dissent. But if we consider ourselves as ontologically self-directed beings, we are capable of understanding, reflecting and activating our agency. Thus the fragmentation and generalisation of the curriculum runs counter to ontological diversity, and limits opportunities to develop educational approaches that take seriously the personal and subjective. And while the NCS and the CAPS did attempt to adjust an undemocratic apartheid curriculum, they remain too bureaucratic (functioning at the level of systems) and do not adequately deal with the human person and spirit (Greene 1998). Simply stated, curriculum transformation resulting in the NCS and the CAPS and their educational propositions is not convincing enough to inspire a belief in changed ontological and epistemological positions. But it is precisely on account of such limitations that we are induced towards phenomenological enquiry wherein more interesting questions can emerge, where possibilities for social justice and equality are considered, and where a heightened sense of agency is provoked in educational beings.

Left unattended, curricular and pedagogical practices will continue to drift, embedded in notions of behaviourism, transmission, social efficiency and vocationalism. This dangerous stream of thought creates little space for true educational reform and social transformation. Moreover, these grievous educational approaches especially bode poorly for non-elite learners (through the education process), whose already fragile ontology (social value and identity) is overshadowed in dominant educational discourses by elitist ideology. Thus, researchers must begin the serious work of looking at the ethical and critical categories that magnify the ontological positions of non-elite learners. So as not to create a caricature of non-elite reality and experience, educationalists (comprising both academics and professionals in the field of education) must also commit through theory and practice to adjust education in ways that are more inclusive, just and equitable, by creating room for all forms of critical and positive social agency. And lastly, research efforts should ideally mobilise and be visibly evident in classroom practice, where a broad-based humanities curriculum is understood to be just as robust, viable and demanding as a positivist curriculum.

References

DBE (Department of Basic Education). 2011a. National Curriculum Statement (NCS). Curriculum Assessment Policy Statement. Foundation Phase Grades R–3. Available: http://www.education.gov.za/Portals/0/CD/National%20Curriculum%20Statements%20 and%20Vocational/CAPS%20English%20HL%20GRADES%20R-3%20FS. pdf?ver=2015-01-27-154201-167. (Accessed 9 February 2017.)

DBE (Department of Basic Education). 2011b. National Curriculum Statement (NCS). Curriculum Assessment Policy Statement. Senior Phase Grades 7–9. Available: http://www.education.gov.za/Portals/0/CD/National%20Curriculum%20Statements%20 and%20Vocational/CAPS%20SP%20%20HL%20%20ENGLISH%20GR%207-9%20%20 web.pdf?ver=2015-01-27-155553-090. (Accessed 9 February 2017.)

DBE (Department of Basic Education). 2016. Curriculum: National Curriculum Statements (NCS) Grades R–12. Available: http://www.education.gov.za/Curriculum/ NationalCurriculumStatementsGradesR-12.aspx. (Accessed 9 February 2017.)

Foucault M. 1998. *Aesthetics, Method, and Epistemology. Volume 2*. Edited by JD Faubion & P Rabinow. Translated by R Hurley. New York: New Press.

Gardiner H. 2006. How education changes: Considerations of history, science and values. In M Suarez-Orozco & DB Qin-Hilliard. (eds). *Globalization: Culture and Education in the New Millennium*. Berkeley: University of California Press. 1–25.

Greene M. 1995. *Releasing the Imagination: Essays on Education, the Arts and Social Change*. San Francisco: Jossey-Bass.

Greene M. 1996. A constructivist perspective on teaching and learning in the arts. In CT Fosnot. (ed). *Constructivism: Theory, Perspectives and Practice*. New York: Teachers College Press. 120–141.

Greene M. 1997. Metaphors and multiples: Representation, the arts and history. *Phi Delta Kappan*, 78(5):387–394.

Greene M. 1998. I am not yet. 256-257. In WF Pinar (ed). *The Passionate Mind of Maxine Greene*. Bristol: Falmer Press, Taylor & Francis Inc.

Kincheloe JL. nd. The power of difference in knowledge production: Multilogicality in the bricolage and postformalism. Available: http://freireproject.org/wp-content/critical_ pedagogy_reading_room/CP_research/ThePowerofDifferenceinKnowledgeProduction. doc. (Accessed 9 February 2017.)

Lather P. 2004. Scientific research in education: A critical perspective. *British Educational Research Journal*, 30(6):759–772.

Lingard B & Rizvi F. 1998. Globalisation and the fear of homogenisation in education. *Change: Transformations in Education*, 1(1):62–71.

Magrini JM. 2012. *Social Efficiency and Instrumentalism in Education: Critical Essays in Ontology, Phenomenology and Philosophical Hermeneutics*. New York and London: Routledge.

Magrini JM. 2013. A 'fundamental theory' of education grounded in ontology? A phenomenological rejoinder. *Philosophy Scholarship*, 38. Also available: http://dc.cod.edu/cgi/viewcontent.cgi?article=1039&context=philosophypub. (Accessed 9 February 2017.)

Noddings N. (ed). 2005. *Educating the Global Citizen*. New York: Teachers College Press.

Rafferty P. 2011. The confluence of curriculum theory and the phenomenological for the critical pedagogue. *The Scholar-Practitioner Quarterly*, 5(4):385–393.

Rizvi F. 2006. Epistemic virtues and cosmopolitan learning. Radford Lecture, 27 November, Adelaide, Australia. Available: http://illinois.edu/cms/3943/rizvi___proofepistemicvirtues.pdf. (Accessed 15 March 2017.)

Slattery P & Dees DM. 1998. Releasing the imagination and the 1990s. In WF Pinar. (ed). *The Passionate Mind of Maxine Greene: 'I am ... not yet'*. London and Bristol: Falmer. 46–60.

Steinberg SR & Kincheloe JL. 2010. Power, emancipation and complexity: Employing critical theory. *Power and Education*, 2(2):140–151.

The role of dialectical hermeneutics in education

Introduction

The relations between hermeneutics and educational theory, practice and research currently seem obvious. Since hermeneutics is the art of interpretation, and education involves practices such as understanding, explanation, the use of texts, reading and writing, the connection between hermeneutics and education appears self-evident. However, Hans-Georg Gadamer (1900–2002) (1975:399), known as the father of philosophical hermeneutics, maintains that:

> [i]nterpretation is not something pedagogical for us [...] it is the act of understanding itself, which is realized – not just for the one for whom one is interpreting but also for the interpreter himself – in the explicitness of verbal interpretation. Thanks to the verbal nature of all interpretation, every interpretation includes the possibility of a relationship with others. There can be no speaking that does not bind the speaker and the person spoken to. This is true of the hermeneutic process as well. But this relationship does not determine the interpretative process of understanding – as if interpreting were a conscious adaptation to a pedagogical situation; rather, this process is simply the concretion of the meaning itself.

Gallagher (1992) shows, by contrast, how different conceptions of hermeneutics are tied to educational experience and theory. Following this line of thinking, the main concern of this chapter is to outline the connections between hermeneutics and educational research, practice and theory. In particular, we seek to demonstrate how dialectical hermeneutics may be used as a method of reinforcing philosophical studies in education. In order to do so, the next section presents in a nutshell the development of hermeneutics, while in the section after that we assess the relevance of hermeneutics to educational experience, research and theory. Following the idea that interpretation involves a discursive dialectical process, in the next section we explore the concept of dialectical analysis in the Socratic tradition and its epistemic role in philosophical research in education. The concluding sections discuss the implication of the above analysis for educational theory and practice and provide recommendations for future research.

The nature of hermeneutics

Hermeneutics is a term derived from the Greek *hermeneutikos*, meaning to interpret (Palmer 1969). Thus, it is primarily concerned with understanding and interpretation, especially as related to language and text. While it was originally an approach used for the interpretation of ancient and biblical texts, Schleiermacher (1977) developed a general hermeneutics that deals not only with scripture but also with legal and classical texts. Dilthey (1988) took this approach a step further by suggesting the use of hermeneutic canons in social and human science. For these writers, as for many others, the basic problem of hermeneutics was methodological: how to found the science of interpretation in a way that would make it properly 'scientific'.

Heidegger (1962), who was inspired by the idea of framing hermeneutics in human experience, understood hermeneutics to be an existential characteristic of (human) being. According to his view, if we are to understand anything at all, we must already find ourselves 'in' the world 'along with' that which is to be understood. This shift has moved hermeneutics beyond its concern with the written text and spoken word to a more universal conception. The underlying idea is that social action and situations can also be understood and read as texts. When we try to understand a world, we use the same processes that are involved in understanding a written text, and so hermeneutic philosophy and theory may be employed in the social sciences to examine, describe and understand social phenomena (Ricoeur 1981).

Gadamer (1975), following Heidegger's (1962) ontological concerns, suggests that hermeneutics is not a method which seeks for and promises objectivity, because as readers we are conditioned by prejudices of our own historical existence and language. Interpretations are always biased in some way and meaning is to be found within the historical contexts of the interpreter and interpreted. In order to gain understanding we need to enter a dialogue or a conversation with the unfamiliar, strange or anomalous. This creative communication between us and our partner or text is an ongoing process that entails a 'fusion of horizons' (Gadamer 1975:305) – that is, the engagement of the familiar and of what is alien in which neither remains unaffected. As Gadamer (1975:306) puts it: 'The horizon of the present is continually in the process of being formed because we continually have to test all our prejudices. An important part of this testing occurs in encountering the past and in understanding the tradition from which we come. Hence the horizon of the present cannot be formed without the past'.

Here lies the most fundamental tenet of hermeneutics, which is that understanding has a circular structure, the 'circle of meaning' (Gadamer 1975:150). The hermeneutic circle traditionally signified a methodological process or a condition under which understanding is possible – that is, a dialectic between the understanding of the text as a whole and the interpretation of its parts.

Here, coming to understand the meaning of the whole of a text and coming to understand its parts are always interdependent activities. As Gadamer (1976:117) explains, 'It is a circular relationship [...]. The anticipation of meaning in which the whole is envisaged becomes explicit understanding in that the parts, that are determined by the whole, themselves also determine this whole.' It follows that understanding is a continual movement 'from the whole to the part and back to the whole' (Gadamer 1976:117).

We can sum up this concept of interpretation by identifying its three characteristics (Gallagher 1992:45):

1. Interpretation is existential – every human activity involves interpretation.
2. Interpretation is always constrained. There is never a presuppositionlessness of the world. Humans are always embedded in some kind of tradition, language, life story or set of values, and so we cannot escape the hermeneutic circle.
3. Interpretation is a process in which we already find ourselves.

Gadamer's (1976, 1992) claims for the universality of hermeneutics and the possibility of meaning and truth have been questioned by some philosophers, including Jurgen Habermas (1929–) and Jacques Derrida (1930–2004). They both offer a 'depth hermeneutics' that moves beyond constrained communication to critical reflection (Derrida 1976; Habermas 1971). They contend that interpretations are conditioned not only by individuals' 'being' in a certain culture, history and language (Derrida 1976; Habermas 1971). There are extra-hermeneutic factors such as economic facts of labour and class, and political factors of domination, that distort ordinary interpretation and communication (Derrida 1976; Habermas 1971). Gadamer's position, to them, is politically naïve (Derrida 1976; Habermas 1971). However, while Habermas's (1971) conception of hermeneutics is critical, Derrida (1976) proposes that all interpretations are false and there is no resolution to the hermeneutic situation.

Habermas (1971) draws on Ricoeur's (1970:27) notion of a 'hermeneutics of suspicion', which rejects Gadamer's (1975) idea that meaning, truth or consensus can be found in the process of interpretation. What usually passes for truth is ideologically distorted. Thus we need a hermeneutics of suspicion in order to reflect on structures of power and authority, and by so doing destroy false consciousness and emancipate individuals and society from political power and economic exploitation. Derrida (1976) offers a more radical approach (often called 'deconstructive hermeneutics'), as he views the critical interpretation as another text that presupposes some conception of truth – that is, an ideology-free situation and that thus promotes false consciousness. He rejects the idea of transcending language itself, as there is no ultimate escape from false consciousness; thus the task of hermeneutics is to unmask or deconstruct the meaning of a text in order to show its contingency and relativity (Derrida 1976).

Some links between the above approaches to hermeneutics and education are quite clear, for example critical pedagogy. However, in order for us to fully understand the contribution of hermeneutics to the field of education a deeper investigation is required. Our objective is to forge a possible link between hermeneutic concepts and educational practice, research and philosophy. In particular, we seek to demonstrate the epistemic role of dialectical analysis within the hermeneutic framework and how it may be applied in the pursuit of philosophical studies in education. Readers should note that the analysis presented here is not exhaustive, as it focuses on a certain conception of hermeneutics and education, mainly as developed by Gallagher (1992).

The philosophical/conceptual underpinnings of hermeneutics and education

Since every human activity involves interpretation (Gadamer 1975, 1976; Heidegger 1962), it seems reasonable to argue that practices such as teaching and learning, as well as studying empirically and philosophically educational phenomena, are by their nature hermeneutic. However, this statement is too general to allow us to understand the hermeneutic processes with which learners, educators, researchers and philosophers of education are engaged while being in the world. In order to do so, we need to unpack the hermeneutic principles and ideas that underlie educational practice and theory.

Educational experience as hermeneutic

We have seen that hermeneutics investigates the processes of interpretation, the communication of meaning through a text and within a dialogue, and so forth. Here, language has a central role to play in understanding the world. Communication and language are also central to education, yet what associates education with hermeneutics is the idea that learning in the classroom involves an interchange of interpretations. These interpretations may relate to subject matter, how the educator presents and communicates his or her understanding of the curriculum, how the learner presents and communicates his or her understanding to the educator and his or her classmates, how the educator understands what it means to be an educator and so on.

In his analysis of the relations between educational experience and hermeneutics, Gallagher (1992) presents principles that align pedagogy with Gadamer's conception of hermeneutics. These principles are discussed in the following sections.

Educational experience has a circular structure

Interpretation is the attempt to obtain the meaning of something. Communication occurring in the classroom is itself hermeneutics, since both learners and educator try to interpret and negotiate meaning via dialogue. The give and take of that discourse involves the hermeneutic circular process as the educator brings his or her own understanding on various pedagogical aspects to the hermeneutic circle, such as the subject matter, how it should be presented or what it means to be an educator. In the same way, the learner brings to this structure his or her preconceptions about the subject matter, conditioned by his or her past experience. Whenever the educational experience involves attending a lecture, reading a text, solving a problem or having a conversation, it involves a hermeneutic circle, as the fore-conceptions of learners and educators are continually being shaped within the dialectical interplay that takes place in the classroom.

Educational experience is always constrained by the process of tradition

Tradition effectively influences the individual's interpretation, as the past is operative in terms of helping to shape the interpreter's present. Our thinking and communicating with others is never unconditioned – tradition biases our view. Think about the concept of innovation: Although it builds on the past, it also extends beyond it. This is not to say that the past determines the present; it instead inspires it by revealing the possibilities of being. Educators and learners are situated within a certain tradition that informs their life and the way they negotiate the meaning of educational experiences.

Educational experience is always linguistic

To teach means to present something or to communicate with learners in some way. According to the hermeneutic principle of 'language as a way of being', every interpretation of the world is constrained by language. Here language is not independent of reality, but rather part of the dialogical process of encountering the world in a meaningful way. Put differently, every engagement with the world means engagement in a dialogue, which involves language. Thus, 'to deliberate, to argue, to judge, to apprise, and so on – these are all ways that we enter into dialogue with the world. Such dialogue is made possible by language and itself constitutes the learning process' (Gallagher 1992:116).

The hermeneutic structure of educational experience is the same as that of questioning

Educational experience, argues Gallagher (1992), depends on educator–learners involvement. This is not external, objective involvement in the sense of manipulating and controlling the experience. Rather, educational involvement means that the learner and educator are in a hermeneutic situation, as they both attempt to interpret and understand that which is to be learned or taught. Interpretation is structured as a question. This is due to the fact that by interpreting we try to make the unknown known – that is, reveal something about the world, which entails questioning (Gadamer 1975). There are no correct or incorrect questions, though some might be considered as 'proper' or 'improper' by a tradition. For example, the scientific tradition defines what would be considered as a scientific question.

In the educational context, learners and educators are engaged in the process of questioning as they challenge the unfamiliar and the familiar, the tradition, the possible and real. The logic of this dialectical process is of questioning, since it is by questioning that we come to understand the world.

Educational research and its relation to hermeneutics

By exploring the connection between hermeneutics and educational research, we can find the roots of hermeneutics in the ontology and epistemology of qualitative research in education. These philosophical underpinnings deal with reality, truth, the relationship between the knower and the known, and the ways in which the enquirer goes about finding out knowledge (Guba 1990; Howe 1988). The roots of qualitative (interpretive) research are found in Aristotle (1994) and his distinction between theory (*sophia*) and practical wisdom (*phronesis*). According to him, there are two ways of reasoning within which we can grasp reality: *techne*, designed to reveal the mechanical causes of events, and *episteme*, focusing on teleological (purposive) causes, which as we shall see are essentially interpretive (Aristotle 1994).

Mechanical causes 'push' events randomly into being. In terms of modern science (the positivist approach), this means that things, objects, facts, events and behaviours are related to one another in a mechanical way. Therefore there is a causal connection between them. According to this view the tasks of scientific enquiry are to discover universal laws or statistical generalisations by deductive and inductive reasoning, explain relations between dependent and independent variables, and predict some consequences from the initial conditions through randomised experimentation (Hempel 1966). In teleological causes, by contrast, the ultimate telos (purpose) 'pulls' an event toward a natural state inherent in the very rational design or meaning of things (Alexander 2006; Smith 2002).

Following this idea, qualitative researchers hold that when it comes to human affairs, scientific enquiry should strive to understand human behaviour and not predict or control it. People cannot be perceived as things, these researchers say, since they do not act mechanically because of the influence of independent variables, but rather they choose how to act in the light of some teloi that are established on the basis of culture, norms, language, tradition or past experiences. Taylor (1964) and Von Wright (1981) take this teleological thinking a step further by suggesting that humans are purposeful beings, and so to understand human behaviour we should enquire into the norms, customs and purposes that govern a person's deeds. For Taylor (1989:99) these teloi are always subordinate to higher ideals, which he calls 'strong values'. In other words, teleological explanations are essentially interpretive, having to do with the norms, experiences and interpretation of the world that motivate (in the sense of pulling forward, not pushing) us to behave in a particular way. Thus in order to be able to understand why people act the way they do, we need to explore the normative system that underlies their behaviour.

Qualitative research programmes in education – such as narrative research, feminism, post-structuralism, critical thinking, anthropology and ethnography, to name but a few – maintain that people engage in interpretive or hermeneutic activity when they encounter the world. This view entails investigating the meanings and interpretations of educators, policymakers, learners, managers and researchers in order to study the educational experience. This work is mostly descriptive, relating to interpreting what is going on in order to deepen and broaden the understanding of everyday experiences. Explanations are suggested for the sake of explanations (adding plausibility to what we see), and knowledge is by its nature constructive.

Another research programme in education that dovetails with hermeneutics is post-structuralism. We have seen that post-structuralists criticise the hermeneutic analysis for being naïve because it ignores the role of language as a differential system. The quest for a deeper understanding is thus converted by post-structuralists to the analysis of power relations in communication, so as to expose structures of domination and to interrupt relations of dominance and subordination. The aims of this type of analysis are emancipation and social change (Peters & Burbules 2004). Biesta, Allan and Edwards (2010:231) summarise the differences between the interpretive and critical–emancipatory research in education as follows:

> *While the ambition of both might be expressed in terms of "adding plausibility", there is a fundamental difference in how "plausibility" is understood [...] Whereas interpretative research would see theorising as contributing to reflection and learning, critical theory aims at a very particular set of learning processes, viz., those that lead to insight in how power and social position "structure" experience, articulation and interpretation.*

Researchers using post-structuralism engage in critical questions such as these: Whose knowledge is shaping the curriculum?, Whose interest does the knowledge serve?, Which images and activities are mentioned in the curriculum?, Who benefits and who loses if educators use this knowledge?, Which discourses are at work in the classroom? and so on. The studies of Davies (1989), Lubeck (1996), MacNaughton (2005) and Ryan and Grieshaber (2004) are some examples of post-structural research in education.

Philosophy of education and hermeneutics

We can find some principles of critical hermeneutics in critical theories of education (Apple 1982; Freire 1970; Gur-Ze'ev 2005, 2010) and radical pedagogy (Derrida 1976; Foucault 1980). As mentioned, critical hermeneutics has been developed in the writings of critical theorists such as Habermas (1971). According to his view, the aim of hermeneutics is to offer suspicious interpretation of those ideologies and institutions that repress people by maintaining ruling power structures (Habermas 1971). Since language, tradition, prejudice, ideology and other forces operate at the back of our minds, we ought to bring them forward and reflect on them. The purpose of such reflection is to assist in the achievement of emancipation, since it is by people's false consciousness being penetrated that unconstrained communication and autonomy are possible. The underlying idea here is that an ideology-free world is possible, even only as a regulative principle. This concept of hermeneutics is echoed in the work of Paulo Freire (1921–1997), who designed educational programmes to liberate urban and rural workers. Analysing the educator–learners relationship, he calls against the 'banking' concept of education in which the practice of depositing is at the centre: Educators are the depositors and learners are the depositories (Freire 1970:243). While educators are committed to 'fill' the learners with the proper knowledge, the learners are expected to patiently receive, memorise and repeat it. Freire explains (1970:243–244):

> In the banking concept of education, knowledge is a gift bestowed by those who consider themselves knowledgeable upon those whom they consider to know nothing. Projecting an absolute ignorance onto others, a characteristic of the ideology of oppression, negates education and knowledge as processes of inquiry. The teacher presents himself to his students as their necessary opposite; by considering their ignorance absolute, he justifies his own existence. The students, alienated like the slave in the Hegelian dialectic, accept their ignorance as justifying the teacher's existence – but unlike the slave, they never discover that they educate the teacher.

This approach, argues Freire (1970:244), aims at 'changing the consciousness of the oppressed, not the situation which oppresses them, for the more the oppressed can be led to adapt to that situation, the more easily they can be dominated'.

Apple (1982) offers a slightly different analysis of the asymmetrical relations of power dominating the school environment. Drawing on Gramsci's concept of 'hegemony', Apple (1982) argues that the relation between educator and learner is constrained by hegemonic factors such as power relations, economic interests, class, gender and race. According to this view, the educator's internalised race, gender and class prejudices are transmitted unconsciously to learners. This 'knowledge' is concealed in a false consciousness presented as 'objective truth'. These hidden processes are embodied in educational institutions, curricula, research practices, textbooks, educator training, educator performance, management, language of schooling and so on.

For both Apple (1982) and Freire (1970), libertarian education is possible by employing critical pedagogical practice ('depth hermeneutics', to use Habermas's [1971] language) that reveals the hegemonic character of educational institutions and experiences. According to Freire (1970), that means allowing educators and learners to critically reflect on the way they exist in the world by entering a genuine dialogue in which the educator–learners relationships are redefined by the new roles they play: Educators are now taught by the learners, who in turn teach. In this type of engagement, they become jointly responsible for a process in which all grow. Significantly, for Apple (1982) and Gur-Ze'ev (2005, 2010), one of the central tasks of critical pedagogy is to resist the homogeny as well as describe it. Gur-Ze'ev (2010) sees this as counter-education 'which is committed not only to criticize but also to overcome all versions of normalizing education'.

The radical approach to hermeneutics dovetails with the post-structuralist approach to education, especially with Derrida's (1976) notion of deconstruction. According to Derrida (1976), the idea that emancipation from false consciousness is possible falls into the trap of distorted ideology. Since the writer writes in a language that dominants his or her discourse, and a reader is also held within a language, which in principle he or she cannot dominate, there is no ultimate escape from false consciousness (Derrida 1976). Individual thought, it is argued, is being shaped by linguistic structures that are embedded in history, culture and time. Given this linguistic constraint, the task of the deconstructor is to look for the ways in which one term in the text, argument, historical tradition or social practice has been 'privileged' over another. The term may be privileged because it is considered the general, normal, central case, while the other is considered special, exceptional, peripheral or derivative. Something may also be privileged because it is considered more true, more valuable, more important or more universal than its opposite.

Derrida (1976) offers a deconstructive critique of educational institutions such as the university by questioning whether the principle of reason that underlies universities has a reason. Taking a deconstructive stance in the educational context also means asking questions about the academic staff's position within the institution and the language they use in their discourses (Gallagher 1992:295), and about the ways in which and the extent to which pedagogical mechanisms such as grading, reward and punishment, orders and so on are subject to 'normal' and homogeneous individuals (Foucault 1977).

Dialectical analysis as a method for philosophical research in education

We have looked at the way in which philosophical ideas in education dovetail with various strands of hermeneutics. In this section we demonstrate how hermeneutics could be used as a methodology to be applied in philosophical research in education. Nozick's (1981) notion of 'philosophical explanations' provides a useful conceptual framework to clarify the connection between dialectical hermeneutics and philosophical investigation. For Nozick (1981), most philosophical problems are aimed at understanding how something is or can be possible, given counter-claims, rather than at proving or rebutting its veracity: 'How [can] educational researchers [...] believe the subjective perceptions of qualitative participant-observers given the concern for objectivity and generalisability of experimental research in the behavioural and social sciences?' (Alexander 2006:205). What is needed to answer this question is not a theory that proves or refutes one of the claims, but rather a theory that finds harmony in apparent tension and incompatibility. The way to resolve this tension, by providing Nozick's (1981) 'philosophical explanations', is to examine these views within different and new conceptual frameworks – that is, to examine them dialectically. By confronting different arguments, comparing counter-perspectives and contrasting various ideas, we can show how it is possible for us to believe two ideas that are in tension with one another.

The concept of dialectics has various meanings. One of those meanings originates in the work of Socrates and the very origins of philosophy as a method of enquiry. This entails a living discussion between Socrates and his learner set in a particular time, place and context. Though Plato presented this sort of dialogue as spontaneous, Socrates constructed a rigorous and clear structure that led to the discovery of truth. At the outset he raised a fundamental question about moral and epistemological issues, and then challenged the learner's answers by raising another question that led to the asking of further questions. Underlying this type of discussion is the Socratic belief that truth is knowable, and that by setting a series of questions we may reach the truth and possess knowledge. Platonic dialectic stems from Socrates's method, as it is carried out through refutation: Person A makes an assertion such as 'Truthfulness is the best policy', and person B then asks person A questions until person A reaches a contradiction of the initial assertion.

Though Socrates and Plato used this dialectical method in real-life conversations, the process can be applied to ideas as well. Consider hermeneutic philosophy, in which philosophers try to answer the question of how understanding is possible. Their main idea is that understanding emerges within a slightly different form of dialectical discussion, between an interpreter and a text. For Gadamer (1976), the hermeneutic situation is by its nature dialectical, as it has a dialogical structure; it involves a movement from the interpreter's tradition-influenced prejudices (the interpreter's horizon) to the object of his or her interpretation, until he or she reaches an understanding ('fusion of horizons'). Similarly, Palmer (1969) uses Buber's (1971) terms to define this encounter as an I-Thou relationship in which the interpreter constructs a dialectical discussion with the text in order to gain understanding. While struggling to understand the text, the interpreter raises questions to the text and challenges its answers. At times he or she agrees with the text; at other times he or she doubts its claims. Nevertheless, this process of questioning and replying enables the interpreter to attribute meaning to the text.

Take, for example, Biesta's (2010) analysis of Dewey's (1916) theory of communication. By re-evaluating Dewey's theory in the light of Derrida's (1976) deconstruction, Biesta (2010) offers a solution for a philosophical problem that lies within Dewey's ideas. Biesta (2010:723) explains:

> *My purpose here is not to undermine and even less to destruct Dewey's philosophy of communication [...] What I am suggesting instead is that the only way in which Dewey's philosophy of communication can live up to its own ethos is if it embraces the deconstruction that follows from applying the communicative ethos onto itself [...]*

In other words, insofar as we read Dewey (1916) in a non-deconstructive way, the question emerges of whether this philosophy can indeed facilitate communication across difference (which is its ethos). However, reading Dewey's (1916) ideas within deconstruction, we shift from the metaphysics that caused this philosophical problem towards a deconstructivist metaphysics that allows for a genuine participation in the process of communication.

Another example is Alexander's (2006) work on the problem of acquiring knowledge within qualitative research, given its origin in the subjective experience of the participants. As a solution to this problem, Alexander (2006) suggests moving from the common view in educational research that holds two (or more) epistemological paradigms – positivism and constructivism – towards Dewey's (1916) pragmatism, in which this dichotomy collapses. Doing so, we face a new philosophical problem – strong relativism – that undermines the epistemic status of the researcher's findings. A possible way to avoid this relativism, argues Alexander (2006), is to read Dewey's (1916) ideas within Aristotle's (1994) distinction between *phronesis* and *sophia*. He writes:

> *How, one might ask, is it possible to decipher the degree to which one account of events is better than another, since each person brings her own conception of what it might mean to solve the problem at hand? An answer may be found by applying Aristotle's analysis of efficient and final causes to this Deweyan synthesis of theory with practice as least as its [sic] appears in the human sciences.* Alexander (2006:219)

These examples illustrate the technique of confronting different arguments, comparing counter-stances and contrasting various ideas in order to understand how it might be possible to rationally believe something, given certain conflicting or contrasting attitudes that also seem reasonable. This dialectical analysis allows us to consider the bearings of counter-ideas on our view, as it yields a vital dialogue that is being shaped by questions and answers that each view raises against the other. The task of the researcher is not just to 'hear' the different voices, but also to evaluate them. Relocating the central views in different contexts allows him or her to expand the scope of explanations he or she wishes to offer, and to form not only a plausible explanation but also an interesting one.

Implications of dialectical hermeneutics for educational theory and practice

The above analysis can benefit educators, educational researchers and philosophers in different ways. First, since teaching and learning are interpretive practices, it may be the case that the best way to learn would be by questioning, a process that puts at risk the learner's own possibilities and allows him or her to transcend the narrow confines of his or her opinions. As Gallagher (1992:165) points out:

> The essential moment in learning is an encounter between the student as learner and that which is to be learned [...] it is a meeting on the basis of a question so that the unfamiliar is made to stand out by the question itself and thereby gain the possibility of attaining objective status. The learner approaches the subject matter with a question built into his very approach. The question, framed within the tradition context of language, may, of course, be posed by a teacher in her attempt to facilitate the encounter with subject matter. Such a pedagogical question would be iterated in language that [...] would attempt to draw the student into questioning the subject matter for himself.

In this approach to learning, the interplay between learner and subject matter constitutes the educational experience, as the subject matter does not remain external to the learning situation; it is part of the interpretational process that challenges the learner to think for him- or herself or to project his or her own possibilities. We reach this encounter with subject matter (learning) by questioning. Evidently, both educator and learner within the learning situation are involved in questioning in a primary way. However, only genuine questioning – that is, questioning that is real and relevant for the learners – can bring about learning.

This idea dovetails with Dewey's (1938) pragmatic approach, which points to the fact that in our everyday life we encounter new experiences which entail questioning what we know, believe and think. These perplexities pave the way to knowing what we engage with, by putting into practice different hypotheses to resolve the questions/problematic situations. In the educational context, then, every situation of learning involves problem-solving. One way to resolve problematic situations is by the give-and-take process of trial and error. Within the dialectical play between the learner's own beliefs, knowledge and experiences and the problematic situation, new actions or ideas may emerge that are aimed at resolving it. Here, questioning (problematic situations) facilitates learning insofar as these questions are real and relevant to the learner, and yield ideas and thoughts that are explicitly tested in experimental situations. For Dewey (1916:157), the 'art of instruction lies in making the difficulty of new problems large enough to challenge thought and small enough' that helpful suggestions may arise. Thus, educators would prompt their learners to enter a dialectical conversation with the curriculum, tradition and subject matter by encouraging them to raise questions. The challenge is to think of ways to facilitate the learner's encounter with the subject matter, making the question relevant, real and interesting for the learner, so that learning may take place.

Secondly, educational researchers who study pedagogical phenomena within the qualitative paradigm need to bear in mind that they are engaging in two interpretive processes: understanding the participants' behaviour, and making their discourse understandable (that is, explaining their own interpretation to the reader). Dialectical analysis plays a dual role, as it allows researchers to engage in a genuine conversation with people to reveal the teloi that prompt them to behave in a certain way, and by so doing illuminate human practice. Communicating these understandings to the public through a text (in an article, for example) or a dialogue (in a conference or a class) also entails an interplay of interpretation, and as such involves dialectical processes. Researchers should therefore take into account the fact that research is governed not only by their understanding of the phenomena under investigation, but also by their understanding of how these interpretations can best be communicated to educators, policymakers, learners and parents.

Thirdly, dialectical analysis as presented here may be applied by philosophers of education in their investigations. This means adopting an eclectic position (Schwab 1978) in which they compare or contrast ideas or embed familiar ideas in rival conceptual frameworks – an activity that Biesta et al (2010:230) call 'making the familiar strange' – so as to reinforce their argument or form a philosophical explanation.

Conclusion and recommendations for future research

We have sought to forge a link between hermeneutics and educational practice, research and philosophy. We have seen that educational experience can be viewed as hermeneutic in nature since it involves communication (language) – the interchange of learners' and educator's interpretations. Viewed in this light, educational experience has a circular structure (taking the form of questioning) and it is constrained by tradition, personal experience, culture and so on.

The link between hermeneutics and educational research refers to qualitative research programmes in education that seek to understand the practice and behaviour of educators, learners and policymakers by offering teleological explanations which are interpretive in nature.

The relation between philosophy and hermeneutics as presented here is twofold: First, we have identified some educational theories that dovetail with critical and radical conceptions of hermeneutics. Secondly, we have argued that dialectical analysis in philosophical studies in education may be employed for the sake of forming philosophical explanations or justifying an argument. This method takes the form of questioning, as it entails embedding new ideas in familiar theoretical frameworks and letting the texts 'speak' to one another.

Future research may further explore the connection between hermeneutics and education, empirically rather than conceptually. It would be interesting to understand how philosophers of education engage in dialectical analysis in conducting their research. To this end, an empirical study is needed that examines philosophers' practical knowledge – that is, what they have come to know through their research experience. Since practical knowledge is very often tacit (Polanyi 1958), the task is to allow philosophers of education to articulate how they come to know and experience their knowledge, so as to shed light on the ways in which they undertake the Socratic form of dialectic during their investigations.

We hope that, coupled with examples of the role of dialectical analysis in philosophical research, the explication of the connection between hermeneutic philosophy and education delineated here will inform the perspectives of educators, practitioners and philosophers of education.

References

Alexander HA. 2006. A view from somewhere – Explaining the paradigms of educational research. *Journal of Philosophy of Education*, 40(2): 205–221.

Apple M. 1982. *Education and Power*. Boston: ARK.

Aristotle. 1994. *Metaphysics* [approx 360s BCE]. Translated by D Bostock. Oxford: Clarendon.

Biesta G. 2010. 'This is my truth, tell me yours'. Deconstructive pragmatism as a philosophy for education. *Educatinal Philosophy and Theory*, 42(7):710–727.

Biesta G, Allan J & Edwards R. 2010. The theory question in research capacity building in education: Towards an agenda for research and practice. *British Journal of Educational Studies*, 59(3):225–239.

Buber M. 1971. *I and Thou*. Translated by W Kaufman. New York: Scribner.

Davies B. 1989. *Frogs and Snails and Feminist Tales. Preschool Children and Gender*. Sydney: Allen & Unwin.

Derrida J. 1976. *Of Grammatology*. Translated by G Spivak. Baltimore: Johns Hopkins University Press.

Dewey J. 1916. *Democracy and Education: An Introduction to the Philosophy of Education*. New York: Macmillan.

Dewey J. 1938. *Logic: The Theory of Inquiry*. New York: Henry Holt.

Dilthey W. 1988. *Introduction to the Human Sciences: An Attempt to Lay a Foundation for the Study of Society and History*. Translated by RJ Betanzos. Detroit: Wayne State University Press.

Foucault M. 1977. *Discipline and punish: the birth of the prison*. New York: Pantheon Books.

Freire P. 1970. *Pedagogy of the Oppressed*. Translated by MB Ramos. New York: Herder and Herder.

Gadamer H-G. 1975. *Truth and Method*. London: Sheed and Ward.

Gadamer H-G. 1976. *Philosophical Hermeneutics*. Translated by D Linge. Berkley: University of California Press.

Gadamer H-G. 1992. *Truth and method*. 2nd ed. Translated by Joel Weinsheimer and David G. Marshall. New York: Crossroad.

Gallagher S. 1992. *Hermeneutics and Education*. Albany: SUNY.

Guba EG. 1990. The alternative paradigm dialog. In EG Guba. (ed). *The Paradigm Dialog*. Newbury Park: Sage. 17–27.

Gur-Ze'ev I. 2005. *Critical Theory and Critical Pedagogy Today: Toward a New Critical Language in Education*. Haifa: University of Haifa.

Gur-Ze'ev I. 2010. *The Possibility/Impossibility of a New Critical Language in Education*. Rotterdam: Sense.

Habermas J. 1971. *Knowledge and Human Interests*. Translated by JJ Shapiro. Boston: Beacon.

Heidegger M. 1962. *Being and Time*. Translated by J Macquarrie & E Robinson. New York: Harper & Row.

Hempel CG. 1966. *The Philosophy of Natural Science*. Englewood Cliffs: Prentice Hall.

Howe KR. 1988. Against the quantitative-qualitative incompatibility thesis or dogmas die hard. *Educational Researcher*, 17:10–16.

Lubeck S. 1996. Deconstructing child development knowledge and teacher preparation. *Early Childhood Research Quarterly*, 11(2):147–167.

MacNaughton G. 2005. *Doing Foucault in Early Childhood Studies: Applying Poststructural Ideas*. London: Routledge.

Nozick R. 1981. *Philosophical Explanations*. Cambridge: The Belknap Press of Harvard University Press.

Palmer ER. 1969. *Hermeneutics. Interpretation Theory in Schleiermacher, Dilthey, Heidegger, and Gadamer*. Evanston: Northwestern University Press.

Peters MA & Burbules NC. 2004. *Poststructuralism and Educational Research*. Lanham: Rowman & Littlefield.

Polanyi M. 1958. *Personal Knowledge: Towards a Post-critical Philosophy*. London: Routledge.

Ricoeur P. 1970. *Freud and Philosophy: An Essay on Interpretation*. New Haven: Yale University Press.

Ricoeur P. 1981. *Hermeneutics and the Human Sciences.* Edited and translated by JB Thompson. Cambridge: Cambridge University Press.

Ryan S & Grieshaber S. 2004. Research in review. It's more than child development: Critical theories, research, and teaching young children. *Young Children*, 59(6):44–52.

Schleiermacher FDE. 1977. *Hermeneutics: The Handwritten Manuscripts.* Translated by J Duke and J Forstman. (eds). Missoula: Scholars Press.

Schwab JJ. 1978. The practical: A language for curriculum [1969]. In I Westbury & NJ Wilkof. (eds). *Science, Curriculum, and Liberal Education: Selected Essays.* Chicago: University of Chicago Press. 287–321.

Smith NH. 2002. *Charles Taylor: Meaning, Morals and Modernity.* Cambridge: Polity.

Taylor C. 1964. *The Explanation of Behaviour.* London: Routledge & Kegan Paul.

Taylor C. 1989. *Sources of the Self: The Making of the Modern Identity.* Cambridge: Harvard University Press.

Von Wright G-H. 1981. *Explanation and Understanding.* Ithaca: Cornell University Press.

Systems theory and education:

A philosophical enquiry into educational systems theory

Alison Taysum

Introduction

This chapter focuses on a critical reading of the philosophical underpinnings of systems theory, chaos theory and complexity theory, as they pertain to the philosophy of education. The chapter describes and critiques how systems theory identifies particular elements of a system that function in a linear fashion. Standards are the master that the products, including the humans of the system(s), must satisfy, in order to conform to the demands of human capital made by an economy. The chapter then develops a critical reading of how innumerable systems are located within chaos theory. Chaos theory focuses on the current conditions in context, where structures are the policies and regulations, and agency is the power individuals have to operate within and over those structures, or the power to resist orders from the structures.

Shakespeare's (2001) character Hamlet suggests that with chaos a person suffers 'the slings and arrows of outrageous fortunes', which brings into sharp focus whether the person should 'be' or 'not be'. The critical reading explores how, with a moral compass that ensures the prevalence of an overarching ethical framework, the outrageous fortunes are regulated. Pring (2000:140) argues that morals deal with the right or wrong thing to do, while ethics is 'the philosophical enquiry into the basis of morals or moral judgement'. Ethics is the search for rules to guide human behaviour, and these rules may be in the form of prime principles that guide judgements about morals.

Systems theory and chaos theory have progressed the neoliberal project that is subject to de-regulation, which removes state intervention of a moral compass that ensures the prevalence of an ethical framework and the application of human rights. As such the neoliberal project is located within chaos, continually on the edge of falling, or collapse, or indeed has fallen, as evidenced by the global financial crisis of 2008. States have lost control of the neoliberal project (Watson 2001) and therefore cannot advocate for the rights of the child, or for human rights UN 1948, 1989/90), which are trumped by the logic of the market. To avoid system failure an ethos, or a moral compass, is required that assures the prevalence of an ethical framework and governance systems that prevent de-regulation of minimum labour wages, and assures social protection (Wacquant 1999).

Peck and Tickell (2002) argue new technological systems of governance and new institutions are emerging with the normalisation of the neoliberal economic technocratic management. The normalisation occurs using systems thinking and chaos theory, coupled with invasive social policies that affirm and extend market logics. The assumed chaos of neoliberalism assures that the general public remain disassociated from the economy and the politics of their nation state, and are therefore disempowered. Arguably, stability is possible only with intervention or regulation that creates an ethos where a shared moral compass assures the prevalence of an ethical framework, in which human rights are central. Williams (2016:1) cautions that 'manipulative, irrelevant anecdotal appeals to self-interest [are] a poor advertisement for [a] democratic process'. To counter such rhetoric, members of the masses need to be independent free thinkers and learners.

The public need time to stop and think, and engage in dialogue. The public need to have educated debate about resisting chaos and the constant fear of a fall, and develop peaceful community cohesion. Community cohesion is hallmarked by political engagement, and by regenerated local economies (Smith 1904) with vibrant cultures that celebrate diverse and intergenerational cultural heritages. Arendt (1981) proposes that war crimes were committed by those who did not stop to think when conforming to system orders. The question that we therefore address in this chapter is: In education, what is the ethos realised through a shared moral compass that assures the prevalence of an ethical framework based on human rights and responsibilities (UN 1948)?

Systems theory: Key issues

What is arguably missing in systems theory and chaos theory is how cognition and knowledge are construed and re-construed to empower citizens to learn to be participatory in their local communities. Passing high-stakes tests of prescribed curricula in a context of dualistic conformance and non-conformance does not recognise the ways in which young people learn to be co-creative social innovators for equity. Nor does it recognise renewal underpinned by values on which all can provisionally agree. When considering values connected with learning, the values of a higher education institution are seeking truth, being respectful and tolerant of diversity, being critical (that is, being open to all alternative viewpoints) and being committed to the generation of new knowledge (Barnett 2000).

Complexity theory includes cognition, and advocates for learning that takes place in a learning organisation which construes and re-construes (Senge 1997). Furthermore, the values bring stability, for as Perry and Szalavitz (2006) suggest, the currency of any system is trust. The need to build trust for human beings is essential for mental health, particularly for communities' most fragile people. In considering the rights of children in need in Norway, Vaage (2014) has found that the Convention of the Rights of the Child (UN 1989/90) were always obstructed by immigration regulations. One reason for immigration, and migration, is to escape the chaos of war, and people leave their homes and their livelihoods to avoid a fall. The immigrants who successfully fight the tides of change are faced with immigration regulations that put them back on the brink of a fall. The human experience that conforms to the declaration of human rights and the rights of the child, and that offers stability and social protection in a democracy, is ignored – which is dehumanising (Freire 1972).

A more democratic education system that seeks balance in the association between the public as a whole, an embedded economy and states' people is based on the complexity theory of a learning organisation. Such a system has the potential to become fully integrated and distinctive by being both functional and aesthetic, recognised through a standardised and creative system of education. This education system would have a moral compass that is systematically examined through an ethical framework, which is missing from what Hobbes calls a Leviathan-ruled system of chaos that protects the Leviathan. Potentially, a democratic education system can achieve economic growth or stability, healthy gross domestic product and the co-creation of democratised knowledge. The ethos of such a system focuses on values – that seek truth by hearing all voices in the argument; are inclusionary, respectful and tolerant; are critical; and are committed to the generation of new knowledge – which connect with Barnett's (2000) principles of a higher education institution. An education system with this kind of ethos offers the chance to acquire thinking tools for empowering all participants to be societal innovators and social entrepreneurs who can work for equity and renewal (Horizon 2020 2015).

The dehumanising effect of systems theory without an ethos

Von Bertalanffy (1968) argues that systems theory became fashionable because systems in engineering enable small units of power, for example steam or electricity, to turn small cogs, which by a linear mechanistic system increases capacity to move larger and larger cogs in automation. Von Bertalanffy (1968:3) comments that self-controlling machines which need to be switched on and off, for example the 'humble domestic thermostat', or the drones of today, need an operator. Thus, there needs to be a relationship between human beings and machines. However, for a drone to hit its target and conform to orders, it must be assembled from various components and using different technologies, such as 'mechanical, electronical, chemical, etc' (Von Bertalanffy 1968:4). A drone is therefore not the product of a single machine; rather, it is the product of systems of technologies, and machines in relationship with human beings.

These systems are located within the human context, which is in the natural world, and the nature of human beings is revealed through practice in relationship with the natural world. Therefore systems are located within a political, economic, financial, cultural and social global context, as well as in a nation state and localised context. A systems approach to production, commerce and in this case armaments is required that optimises efficiency at minimal cost. Von Bertalanffy (1968:4) argues that the problems of systems become too much for one 'mathematician' to control, which necessitates control through the use of computers. Computers can optimise efficiency and minimise costs of automated systems through a form of statistical control called 'cybernetics'. In cybernetics, Wiener (1954) argues, orders are given from machine to machine, orders are given from human to machine, and orders are given from machine to human through systems of compliance to maximise efficiency and eliminate non-compliance. There is no resistance to these orders.

Systems approaches are problematic because there are paradoxes within systems with the current scientific knowledge base. For example, integrating wave theory and particle theory reveals that we have many gaps in our knowledge about the atom, and its relationship to the other (atoms). We do not understand the conditions required for its mobility and its relationship to that which would stop it, such as gravity or 'little g'. We do not understand the wide gaps between atoms that seem to suggest matter is more not there than there, and we do not understand where 'not there' is. We cannot say if the associations between atoms are equitable over time, or how long a period of time atoms need in which to have equitable associations. We do not understand how atoms are subject to the discovery by William Thomson (also known as Lord Kelvin) (1852) of the thermodynamic second law that all matter will decay, and we do not understand how atoms might be renewed. We do not understand whether patterns of association exist between atoms, because currently they appear too random or simply too complex to be understood through current systems approaches.

Relating the paradoxes of systems thinking to society, Von Bertalanffy (1968) believes that, previously, atrocities could be blamed on dictators, or evil noble-people who gave orders. This connects with Hobbes's (2010) identification of the Leviathan. Von Bertalanffy (1968) argues that historical atrocities can be blamed on an individual, or the Leviathan taking a 'who did what' approach. Thus Leviathans such as Ceaser, Napoleon and Hitler have tried to take control of Europe, driven by a desire for power and the protection of their own interests regardless of the cost. Arendt (1981) suggests that those who committed war crimes against innocent people in the Holocaust were agents conforming to orders from Hitler without a moral compass or ethical framework, and they, in turn, did not stop to think or apply a moral compass or ethical framework to their actions. When obeying orders, these people operated within chaotic socio-cultural systems that support the mobilisation of low-power cogs to work together in systems to optimise economic efficiency, reduce waste and eliminate paying any price of non-conformance.

Doing the right thing or doing things right

Applying a systems theory without an ethos is dehumanising – it reduces human beings to respond to orders as machines. People's non-conformance in a system without an ethos can be defined as an element of a system that does not optimise efficiency in the goal. In 2008 the world financial crisis saw privatised banks being bailed out by the tax payer, with the UK tax payer paying 37 billion Pounds Sterling to banks (BBC News 2008). And the USA 'fronted $700bn in taxpayer funds to prop up the financial institutions that brought the economy to the brink' (Herbst 2013), demonstrating that privatisation does not work. The media inform citizens of the events of the chaotic socio-economic systems, but national leaders appear to be able to do little to address them. As Von Bertalanffy (1968:8) points out:

> *Events seem to involve more than just individual decisions and actions and to be determined more by socio-cultural "systems," be these prejudices, ideologies, pressure groups, social trends, growth and decay of civilizations, and what not. We know precisely and scientifically what the effects of pollution, waste of natural resources, the population explosion, the armaments race, etc., are going to be. [...] But neither national leaders nor society as a whole seems to be able to do anything about it.*

Von Bertalanffy (1968) suggests that we cannot take comfort in blaming the individual if he or she is not provided with an opportunity to develop thinking tools to resist orders that are without ethos and therefore immoral or unethical. In other words, we cannot blame citizens for doing things right when following orders if they have not learned how to engage with educated debate to discuss the moral and ethical underpinnings of the order. An alternative approach would be to develop a state of democracy for all, one that Dewey (1916) argues integrates diverse and conflicting interests and diverse and conflicting philosophies, where sufficient evidence of trustworthy warrants for the claims made is all that is required to bring certainty. 'Apart from inquiry, apart from the praxis,' Freire (1972:72) suggests, 'individuals cannot be truly human. Knowledge emerges only through invention and reinvention, through the restless, impatient, continuing, hopeful inquiry human beings pursue in the world, with the world, and with each other.'

A grand theory is arguably required to enable leaders of nations to work together with an ethos, or shared moral compass, that assures the prevalence of an ethical framework, to navigate through the complexity and chaos. Such a moral and ethical framework legitimises the resistance of orders when the orders are immoral.

Chaos theory: Key issues

Where is the good in chaos?

Lorenz (1995) suggests that the ancient meaning of the word 'chaos' was an absence of any kind of organisation. More recently, Lorenz (1995) continues, the word has come to mean disorganisation that acquires order. The conditions or state will determine the future, so chaos is deterministic (Lorenz 1995). However, predicting what this pre-determined future is, without hindsight, is not possible. This is because the state of the model varies with one or more dependent or independent variables. Independent variables cannot change, for example the birth date of participants in the model. Dependent variables can change, for example test scores that depend on the conditions before and during the test.

Models are therefore dynamic, deterministic and open to change, and are organised and ordered, while operating according to the thermodynamic rule that all things decay, which contradicts the notion that a chaotic system will fall into order. Perhaps through integrating systems theory and deterministic chaos theory, we can say that there may be an iterative process which moves from some sense of order to no sense of order, and that this very pattern of oscillation is, in a sense, an order. Therefore dynamic models may predict change in a chaotic deterministic oscillation of disorder and order, with system approaches that recognise independent and dependent variables. Thus, as physicists follow a body of knowledge that reconciles both wave and particle physics and the recognition of the backwash, nations' leaders may reconcile a systems theory approach and chaotic determinism oscillating from disorder to order.

Considering chaos theory, readers might have the idea that something is wrong here. Perhaps, as Dewey (1909) suggests, we are alerted to something being wrong on the personal, emotional level. Trees stand for hundreds of years; bees and butterflies facilitate pollination to enable the growth of blossoms and fruit. We are able to see systems everywhere in nature that are sustainable within patterns, if we have an overview of those patterns. Furthermore, trees sustain life – if they did not exchange carbon dioxide for oxygen, we would not live as we know living today. Therefore we might imagine that trees are good, and that bees and butterflies are good. Is it possible that the notion of 'good', or ethos in the form of a moral compass that assures the prevalence of an ethical framework, is missing from the innumerable linear mechanistic systems situated within chaos theory?

Complexity theory: Key issues

Where is the good in complexity?

Complexity theory takes a more integrated approach to innumerable systems and the decay of matter within a chaotic conceptual framework. It considers the development of cognition and the human experience. It adds principles that bring stability to our human condition and mental health. The principles consider the aesthetic that lifts human beings above the functionalism of Parsons (1967). The aesthetic and ethos raise us from the barbaric to the civilised, and human rights present clear lines between that which is barbaric, chaotic and unjust, and that which is civilised, complex and just. These principles include having respect and tolerance for difference where there is no harm done, generating new knowledge, and seeking out the truth by listening to and critically analysing all alternative arguments and voices (Barnett 2000). Stuart Mill (1859) proposes that seeking truths by hearing all voices of all groups enables current understandings to be verified, or replaced if they are found unsuitable.

Aristotle (1926) argues that addressing alternative rhetorics through critical engagement with the emotional and intuitive, or pathos, needs to be revealed with an ethos of making moral and ethical judgements. Orators may tap into the passions of the audience, and through empathy persuade them to agree with their interests, thus using pathos, Aristotle (1926) believes. Rather, Aristotle (1926) suggests that the listener is required to listen and make judgements based on experiential, empirical evidence, and the logic of the orator's knowledge of and advocacy for a particular regime. The regimes may be democratic, post-racial, oligarchic, aristocratic, monarchic, totalitarian or neoliberal, or have evolving gender relationships, or may be a combination of these (Green & Janmaat 2011; Rich 2013).

Listeners need to make logical discerning judgements using reasoned discourse, or logos, about how different regimes being advocated for relate to freedom, wealth and education. Aristotle (1926) proposes that the listener is therefore required to make judgements based on experiential empirical evidence, or pathos, and logical arguments, or logos, based on the epideictic nature of the orator, which means making judgements on his or her character and on his or her virtues in terms of justice, courage, self-control, magnificence, magnanimity, liberality, mildness and wisdom. The character and virtues connect with the orator's ethos. The listener is therefore required to rationalise and make forensic judgements that are experientially empirical, logical, moral and ethical, engaging with pathos, logos and ethos, on how the orator treats others and how his or her rhetoric aligns with his or her beliefs and practice.

According to Aristotle (1926), we cannot 'know' anything other than our beliefs, because the concrete world is experienced and each person experiences that world in a different way, which is entwined with his or her disposition shaped by his or her culture. Therefore, the listener needs to apply logic to the construction of arguments step by step, and needs to have the thinking tools to be able to do this successfully. A step-by-step construction of arguments is presented in Figure 6.1, adapted from Aberdein (2016:4).

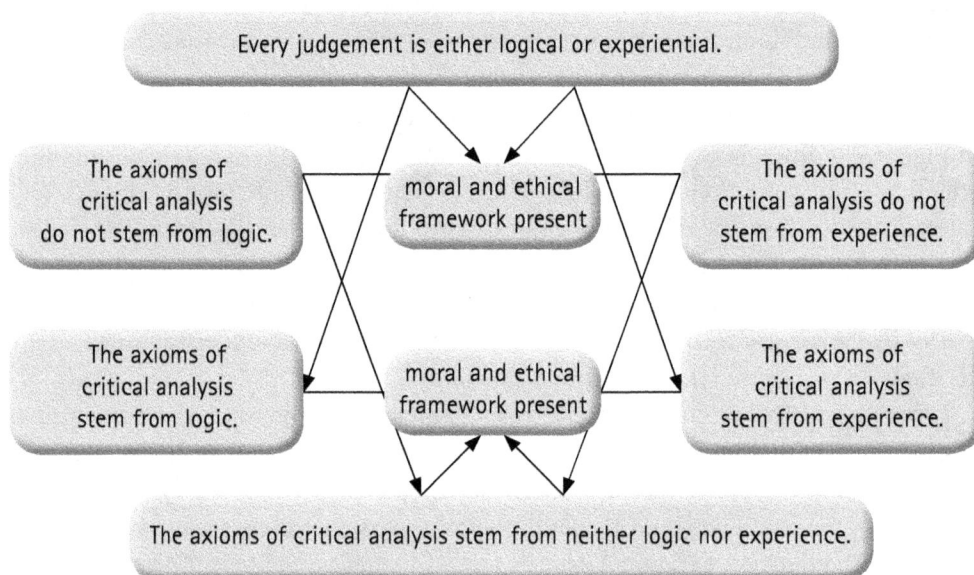

Figure 6.1 The logos, pathos and ethos in the construction of arguments (adapted from Nelson 2016:80)

There is not enough scope to discuss the Aristotelian Hexagon or the Kantian Hexagon in this chapter, nor how Figure 6.1 transforms the hexagon into an eight-pointed star. Neither is there scope to discuss the impact of modernism and dualisms of conformance or non-conformance on the orders of the system, which challenge the hexagon (Magnani 2016; Moretti 2012; Smessaert 2012) and octagon. This is the stuff of another paper that also recognises the body of work of Leonard Nelson, including the continuum revealed in Figure 6.1 of the axioms of critical analysis that stem from a combination of some logic (logos) and some experience (pathos) that include a moral and ethical dimension (ethos) in one judgement.

The continuums step has been added to this figure in order to begin to address Aristotle's (1926) notion that some axioms of critical analysis stem from experience (pathos) and others from logic (logos). Aristotle's (2009) golden mean along this continuum may be where the 'moral compass and ethical framework' or 'ethos' is located. The continuum provides an alternative to the 'conformance or non-conformance dichotomy' of 'The axioms of critical analysis stem from experience but do not stem from logic', or 'The axioms of critical analysis stem from logic but do not stem from experience'.

Aristotle (2009) believes that judgements made only on logos and pathos are dehumanising, and that ethos is essential in the equation, as also shown in Figure 6.1. Arguably, a paradigm shift is required that moves beyond the dualistic nature of conformance and non-conformance to a complex system of ethos, pathos and logos. And perhaps the greatest of these is ethos, with a shared moral compass and ethical framework within the education system. There is potential for provisional agreement on principles of a complex education system to take place at community and state levels. These principles can then be legislated for where the state controls the legislation or the regulation. In a complex system the state has the power to bring balance, by protecting the public from chaos through regulation that removes the fear of always being on the brink of collapse. Legislation guided by ethos assures the prevalence of an ethical framework underpinned by principles of inclusion, respect, critical thinking and the generation of new knowledge (Barnett 2000). The principles of an education system with such an ethos align with the declaration of human rights and the rights of the child (UN 1948, 1989/90), and are accompanied by responsibilities for the self and the other in association with the economy and the statesperson (Rousseau 1998). Therefore, this kind of ethos shifts a system from chaos to regulated complexity where the ethos, pathos and logos are transparent and understood by all.

Implications of these philosophies for philosophy of education

An education system built on chaos perpetuates fear

An education system is a societal system that percolates through and arguably drives all societal activities. An education system can be found in early years' settings and public and private schools; in the home; in further education; in apprenticeships; in 'on the job' training programmes; in professional development; in lifelong learning initiatives that seek to retrain individuals, particularly those not in education, employment or training (NEET); in higher education; at the University of the Third Age; at night school; in distance learning arenas where learners engage with an education system in one nation state, reside in another nation state and do not cross a physical border; in all aspects of a citizen's public life as a consumer; and for undocumented persons and the homeless, in whichever context they survive.

An education system that operates according to a linear, closed model, in which human capital is produced to meet the needs of a labour market like small units of power, or cogs, contributes to a giant machine that fuels the neoliberal chaos. The machine operates on the fear of being perpetually on the brink of collapse. A system without ethos, where human beings function in chaos, enslaves people, keeps them in the shadows and perpetuates their fear of the next change.

This may further reduce their participation in decisions of what happens in their neighbourhoods.

Furthermore, unemployment is as high as 50% in some European countries (Manos, Rabemiafara & Ward 2014), with the transition from education to work becoming ever more difficult. Young people are gaining only temporary contracts, for which they are over-qualified (Eurofound 2015). People living in fear have two responses – fight or flight – and neither is productive to society. DeGruy (2005:7–8) describes a scene in which an African American boy was threatening to 'beat up [her] son' because her son was staring at him. In response to DeGruy's request for the boy's reason, he replied, 'Wha' he think he lookin' at?' DeGruy continues:

> "He may have been looking at you because he was thinking of asking if you'd like to play with one of his video games in the house. He could have been looking at you because he thought that maybe you might want to walk down the street to the park." [The boy seemed] to buy it enough to agree not to beat up my son [...]. After the boys walked away it dawned on me that there was a stark contrast between this experience and the ones in South Africa where the young African males greeted each other with the common phrase, "I see you". I couldn't help feeling the emotional distance that separated the two statements: the friendly acknowledgement, "I see you" and the angry, menacing, "What you lookin' at?" The gap between African and the African American was suddenly stark and clear. Somewhere along the way African American children have become so emotionally fragile that they cannot often withstand the implications associated with a simple gaze.

The distinctiveness of an education system with ethos, pathos and logos empowers young people to see each other, empathise with each other and learn to care for each other. Where children find it normal to hold a gaze they are more likely to build community with a currency of trust (Perry & Szalavitz 2006). This is in line with Dewey's (1916) view that education prepares individuals for democratic engagement with the other, the state and the economy, where the media helps or hinders the associations between these groups.

The ethos of an education system built for equity and renewal

The ethos, shared moral compass and ethical framework of such an education system is more than an intellectual exercise. It demands theories in the classroom, suggests Dewey (1909), that are culturally relevant and that can be tested in practice, which moves towards ensuring the prevalence of an ethical framework.

Comenius (1896) argues that a universal education requires those of 'weaker dispositions' to receive more attention in the education system. These are learners whose rights are not protected. An education system that seeks to mitigate for those with weaker dispositions connects with Paulston's (2000) argument that comparative education should seek to understand the fragility of human beings and develop better theories in order to improve education systems. This aligns also with Senge's (1997) ideas of knowledge production and mobilisation through pedagogical relationships in education systems. These relationships exist between members of communities that are usually made up of learners and educators, with the aim of facilitating knowledge generation through language (Lee & Danby 2012). Such an approach may use Socratic dialogue (Leal & Saran 2004), in which core virtues as identified by Aristotle (1926) – kindness, politeness, integrity, effort, courage, resilience, gratitude and faith – may, by taking a Kantian (1900) approach, be rationalised. The rationalisation of core virtues in the classroom creates new knowledge under conditions of trust, respecting the self and the other, agreeing to disagree and recognising diversity through inclusive practices (Barnett 2000). A discerning, critical rationalisation of core virtues with a moral compass and ethical framework that includes all voices (Stuart Mill 1859) may underpin a commitment to societal equity and renewal.

The balance of power between traditional and popular cultures

Knowledge generation through such dialogues gives educators platforms and positions of power from which to influence the shaping of identities (Stenhouse 1983). Educators may intentionally or unintentionally expect marginalised groups to assimilate into the dominant culture and/or the educator's culture, which prevents people from being authentic and independent (Clayton 2014). Being independent means being able to pursue personal ambitions and interests regulated by principles that the community endorses. The issue is how free people are, within Comenius's (1896) notion of a universal education system for all, to choose to endorse regulations, particularly if these are developed by dominant cultures in an education system that does not recognise popular culture?

Educators may also transmit knowledge through dogma that might advocate one ideology and/or one political party over another, which denies all voices being heard in an educated debate in the classroom. Furthermore, education systems may have hierarchical approaches to knowledge mobilisation through prescribed curricula and even lesson plans to which educators make no contribution but are told to deliver. The educators become the tools and the downloaded materials become the toolbox that are disassociated from the practice and cultural heritage of the diverse learners in the classroom. Therefore, marginalised groups' participation, including educators' participation, may not be authentic in a standardised linear education system that seeks conformity to orders in a hierarchical approach.

In an education system that does not allow spaces for talking back to dominant masters, meaning that voices are not heard, individuals are misrecognised. This can cause internal angst and lead to fear, anger and conflict. Fear, anger and conflict are elements of destruction and therefore readily fit into a system of chaos. Angst may stand as a barrier to becoming independent in rationalising the conception of what counts as good, or what counts as virtues that guide behaviour. Thus, evaluative groupthink, or evaluative cultures, may be causing some groups to develop what the dominant group labels 'weak dispositions'. An education system with linear processes located within chaos that is always rapidly changing and on the brink of a fall is itself responsible for creating learners' weak dispositions. *Weak dispositions* are created because the learner becomes dependent on the master. *Strong dispositions* are created when learners are empowered as independent, autonomous, democratic young people with multicultural dispositions who are open to different worldviews and cultural heritages. Diverse groups need the opportunity to become community innovators by talking together and building cultural alignment on core principles of what counts as good, or just, in preparation for renewing communities in the real world built on equity.

Chaos, repetitive strain and human indignity

Aristotle (2009) suggests that we become just by performing just acts, and temperate by performing temperate acts. People who perform just and temperate acts are already just and temperate, and in turn they can induct people into performing just and temperate acts by requiring these people to copy them (Aristotle 2009). This is problematic, however, because different people have different dispositions and starting points when being inducted into becoming just and temperate, and they may have different ideas of what just and temperate acts are. DeGruy (2005) suggests that people in the USA who have a cultural heritage of slavery and segregation are vulnerable to replicating the acts of the dominant group, but without having developed the dominant group's dispositions, which is required for an understanding of the values underpinning the acts. Furthermore, those with post-traumatic slave syndrome have not developed the critical thinking tools required to expose dominant groups' potential acts of institutional racism and human indignity through educated debate (Collins Ayanlaja & Taysum 2016).

The problem of who decides what counts as just and temperate acts is compounded if evaluative groups or cultures are determining what the truth is, and whose cultural heritages are part of that truth, curricula and education system, and whose are not. Furthermore, DeGruy (2005) comments that when African Americans have a history of slavery that was executed through violent oppression by a dominant group, coupled with a history of segregation, they can experience low self-esteem, have trust issues and find it difficult to sustain loving relationships. Arguably this is because a slave is misrecognised by the master, who does not act towards slaves in just and temperate ways. The masters take away the slaves' freedom, deny them their human rights and economic independence, shackle them, emotionally and physically abuse them, refuse to trust or love them, and oppress them.

A history marked by misrecognition, mistrust and an absence of love can also negatively affect a person's future relationships, for example the relationship between a father and his child. In 2010, 72% of black children in the USA were raised in single-parent families (Carlson 2015). Children who come from a single-parent family with a cultural heritage of segregation and slavery do not have the same dispositions and starting points in schools as children from the dominant group. Therefore, acquiring just and temperate acts, when it is not clear what the starting points are for acquiring such acts, needs problematising (Haydon 2009; Peters 1966, 1981).

Drawing on particular empirical evidence to address these issues would be constraining. A large survey to test a model of the principles, values, virtues, and just and temperate acts that are inclusive and respect diverse groups would reveal the dominant culture's views that continue to develop marginalised groups' 'weaker dispositions'. Weaker dispositions, identified by Comenius (1896), will continue to exist, ostensibly because marginalised groups are subjected to the repeated indoctrination provided by the education system that created these dispositions. Therefore the chance to imagine alternative futures, and to create different life narratives within an education system, is limited.

Truth, freedom and human dignity

An education system that develops as a learning organisation (Senge 1997) may enable individuals to co-create, and mobilise knowledge with the other. Moving towards a balance between traditional knowledge, and starting where the child is, potentially enables transcendence beyond the limitations of evaluative traditional cultures revealed through practice. Seeking the truth by reimagining the forms through regressive abstraction may break the chains of repetitive linear systems and empower individuals to be independent and authentic. The regressive abstraction starts from a concrete example, perhaps of a moment of courage within a learner's cultural heritage, and seeks a general principle on which all can provisionally agree. Such an agreement might be that it takes courage to overcome the fear of asking questions when the questions challenge dominant societal structures that have traditionally offered social and physical preservation and protection. Education systems as learning organisations can give learners the confidence to ask questions, so that they can become community innovators and reimagine alternative futures.

The circular argument about reimagining alternative futures based on ideals is problematic, because these imagined futures are not founded in the concrete. Perhaps a way forward, taking a complexity theory approach, is to draw on

Kant's (1900) notion of rationalising morality. Rationalising morality provides individuals with an opportunity to engage with the philosophy of education. In turn, the philosophy of education empowers individuals to transcend the limits of indoctrination and the replication of inequalities and indignities in education systems. Open education systems empower human beings to learn practically, theoretically and morally so that they can be free, and masters of their own destiny.

Potentially the most important implication of the debates around the theory of education systems discussed in this chapter is for an education system to develop all learners' characters as free and independent thinkers. Free and independent thinkers can make discerning logical, emotional, intuitive, moral and ethical judgements that apply logos, pathos and ethos to their associations with the economy and with the statespeople for whom they voted to represent them. The judgements in Figure 6.1 on page 78 regarding virtues and their rationalisation can be developed in a step-by-step way using the learning to critically analyse and reflect for emancipation (CARE) framework (Taysum 2012). Interested readers are invited to read about the aims, methods and intended learning outcomes of the framework in Taysum (2012).

This framework connects with Arthur and Carr's (2013) important work on the development of character. The framework enables educational professionals to document how learners respond to being able to ask good questions; critically analyse the underpinning moral and ethical foundations of knowledge, the evidence, the logic, the rhetoric and the orator; and make discerning judgements about the warrants for the claims that are made. These judgements need to be nuanced or delicate, yet robust, and should not swing violently from one extreme to the other (Dewey 1909).

Curricula need to be designed to ensure comprehensive coverage of what virtues are and what virtuous acts are, and to recognise all members of multicultural intergenerational communities, evolving gender relationships, differing worldviews and differing cultural heritages. Refugees, immigrants, migrants, all minoritised groups and all dominant groups need to be recognised within the curricula, the framework of the rights of the child and the declaration of human rights (UN 1948, 1989/90) associated with responsibilities. Curricula also need to provide opportunities for the development of young people's skills and knowledge to rationalise and critique the virtues as independent learners who are seeking to conceptualise what counts as good, and why. A shift away from labelling learners as having 'weak' or 'strong' dispositions moves towards seeking to understand how education systems, educator education and continuing professional development might empower learners to become societal innovators for equity and renewal (Horizon 2020 2015).

Conclusion and recommendations for future research

Education: An ethos of empowerment for societal innovation, equity and renewal

Innumerable systems located within chaos theory are used to drive the neoliberal project, which is always on the brink of collapse. States have lost control of the neoliberal project (Watson 2001), and therefore cannot advocate for human responsibilities, human dignity, the rights of the child or human rights (UN 1948, 1989/90). Rights and responsibilities are trumped by the logic of the market. Regulating the market with an ethos realised through a shared moral compass assures the prevalence of an ethical framework. Regulating chaos may slow down change, and empower citizens to participate in education and the education of their children, and in educated societal debates about changes. An education system with ethos, pathos and logos has the chance to build communities that challenge the neoliberal project, while encouraging societal innovation, equity and renewal. Societal innovation is realised through the development of small and medium-sized enterprises built by entrepreneurs (Smith 1904) that offer genuine competition to public corporations. Education systems with ethos, pathos and logos may empower entrepreneurs to trust in the delicacy and robustness of their judgements based on critical analysis, giving them confidence to take more risks in the regeneration of local communities economically, culturally and politically.

The school is the hub for communities; it serves as a small democracy within larger education systems and has the potential to take a complexity theory approach with a transparent ethos, pathos and logos. Ethos, pathos and logos foreground the human experience in communities, and moves beyond accountability and grading citizenship to broader ambitions to empower societal innovators for equity and renewal (Horizon 2020 2015). Key to a system of ethos, pathos and logos is the critical analysis of the state of the system(s). A thinking tool to support this is the learning to CARE framework (Taysum 2012). Further research might be done into how learners can use this thinking tool to critically engage with orators and the rhetoric of the popular press, and other forms of media, social media and pictorial forms, and to assess how these shape identities and selfhood. Research also needs to be done, Paulston (2000) believes, into the fragility of the human condition, which DeGruy (2005) identifies as a consequence of the dehumanising experience of being enslaved.

Educational professionals, including educators and leaders, need to be thoroughly prepared for an education system with ethos, pathos and logos. The critical decision-making and participation in education policy as text and as discourse in education systems need to be informed by ethos, pathos and logos, as indicated in Figure 6.1 on page 78. Educational professionals need to be empowered in order to empower young people, to work with their families and to reclaim what it is to be human. Citizens need critical thinking tools to challenge and resist a neoliberal project that does not have an ethos. This connects with Comenius's (1896) view that education systems should pay more attention to humans with 'weaker dispositions'.

Through international comparative philosophical enquiries into differing education systems, new insights might be gained of what the ethos is in each case. The philosophical enquiry would also reveal which thinking tools are available in the education system to mobilise knowledge, as well as explore learners' starting points before engaging with knowledge. These starting points may be located in traditional and/or popular funds of knowledge. The philosophical enquiry aims to develop character and virtues, develop multicultural dispositions (Taysum & Slater 2014) that are tolerant of alternative worldviews and draw on thinking skills such as the learning to CARE framework (Taysum 2012). International comparative philosophical enquiries into education systems have the potential to provide refreshed insights into the possibility of a universal ethos, pathos and logos of these systems that empower every learner to lead a good life in a community, and into what that means to him or her.

Education systems arguably need a universal ethos, pathos and logos, where participation in policy as text and policy as discourse is located at Aristotle's (2009) point of a golden mean along the continuum of 'the axioms of critical analysis stem from logic' and 'the axioms of critical analysis stem from experience', with the presence of a moral compass that assures an ethical framework (see Figure 6.1 on page 78). The ethos, pathos and logos need to be underpinned by a search for truth by including all voices, the generation of new knowledge, innovation and entrepreneurialism, respect and tolerance for diversity, being critical, and having the critical thinking skills to resist unregulated chaos. An education system with ethos, pathos and logos is therefore distinctive, because it empowers and mobilises young people to become societal innovators and entrepreneurs for equity and renewal. Equity and renewal may be located in the framework of the rights of the child (UN 1989/90) and the declaration of human rights (UN 1948), coupled with societal responsibilities.

References

Aristotle. 1926. *The 'Art' of Rhetoric* [367–322 BC]. Translated by JH Freese. London: William Heinemann.

Aristotle. 2009. *The Nicomachean Ethics* [approx 340 BC]. Translated by D Ross. Oxford: Oxford University Press.

Arthur J & Carr D. 2013. Character in learning for life: A virtue-ethical rationale for recent research on moral and values driven education. *Journal of Beliefs and Values*, 34(1):26–35.

Barnett R. 2000. *Higher Education: A Critical Business*. Buckingham: The Society for Research into Higher Education & Open University Press.

BBC News. 2008. UK Banks receive £37bn bail-out. Monday, 13 October. Available: http://news.bbc.co.uk/2/hi/business/7666570.stm. (Accessed 11 February 2017.)

Carlson MJ. 2015. Fathers unequal: US men as partners and parents in an era of rapid family change. OECD Employment, Labour and Social Affairs Seminar, 28 May. Available: https://www.oecd.org/els/emp/OECD-ESL-Seminars-Carlson-fathers-unequal-May2015.pdf. (Accessed 12 February 2017.)

Clayton M. 2014. Anti-perfectionist childrearing. In A Bagattini & C Macleod. (eds). *The Nature of Children's Well-Being*. Dordrecht: Springer. 123–140.

Collins Ayanlaja C & Taysum A. 2016. A Bourdieusian analysis of institutional racism: The case of a US secondary school. Paper presented at the World Education Research Association Focal Meeting, 8–12 April, Washington DC.

Comenius J. 1896. *The Great Didactic* [1632]. London: Adam and Charles Black. Available: https://archive.org/details/greatdidacticofj00come. (Accessed 11 February 2017.)

DeGruy J. 2005. *Post Traumatic Slave Syndrome: America's Legacy of Enduring Injury and Healing*. Portland: Joy DeGruy Publications.

Dewey J. 1909. *Moral Principles in Education*. Cambridge: Riverside.

Dewey J. 1916. *Democracy and Education: An Introduction to the Philosophy of Education*. New York: Macmillan.

Eurofound. 2015. Youth entrepreneurship in the EU – values, attitudes, policies. 7 May. Available: https://www.eurofound.europa.eu/youth-entrepreneurship-in-the-eu-values-attitudes-policies. (Accessed 11 February 2017).

Freire P. 1972. *Pedagogy of the Oppressed*. Harmondsworth: Penguin.

Green A & Janmaat J. 2011. *Regimes of Social Cohesion. Societies and the Crisis of Globalization*. Basingstoke: Palgrave Macmillan.

Haydon G. 2009. Reason and virtues: The paradox of RS Peters on moral education. *Journal of Philosophy of Education*, 43(s1):173–188.

Herbst M. 2013. The bank bailout cost US taxpayers nothing? Think again. The Guardian Online, 28 May. Available: https://www.theguardian.com/commentisfree/2013/may/28/bank-bailout-cost-taxpayers. (Accessed 11 February 2017.)

Hobbes T. 2010. *Leviathan* [1651]. Edited by I Shapiro. London: Yale University Press.

Horizon 2020. 2015. CO-CREATION-01-2017: Education and skills: Empowering Europe's young innovators. Available: https://ec.europa.eu/research/participants/portal/desktop/en/opportunities/h2020/topics/co-creation-01-2017.html. (Accessed 30 May 2017.)

Kant I. 1900. *Kant on Education* [1803]. Translated by A Churton. Online Library of Liberty. Available: http://oll.libertyfund.org/titles/kant-kant-on-education-uber-padagogik. (Accessed 30 May 2017.)

Leal F & Saran R. 2004. A dialogue on the Socratic dialogue, Act Two. In P Shipley. (ed). *Occasional Working Papers in Ethical and Critical Philosophy*, 3:35–42.

Lee A & Danby S. 2012. *Reshaping Doctoral Education: International Approaches and Pedagogies*. London: Routledge.

Lorenz E. 1995. *The Essence of Chaos*. Washington: University of Washington Press.

Magnani L. 2016. Violence hexagon. *Logica Universalis*, 10(1):359–371.

Manos M, Rabemiafara N & Ward T. 2014. Young people and temporary employment in Europe. Available: https://www.eurofound.europa.eu/observatories/emcc/comparative-information/young-people-and-temporary-employment-in-europe. (Accessed 12 February 2017.)

Moretti A. 2012. Why the logical hexagon? *Logica Universalis*, 6(1):69–107.

Nelson L. 2016. A Theory of Philosophical Fallacies. *Argumentation Library*, Volume 26: 73–81. Switzerland: Springer International Publishing.

Parsons T. 1967. *The Structure of Social Action*. New York: Free Press.

Paulston R. 2000. Imagining comparative education: Past, present and future. *Compare: A Journal of Comparative and International Education*, 30(3):353–367.

Peck J & Tickell A. 2002. Neoliberalizing space. *Antipode*, 34(3):380–404.

Perry B & Szalavitz M. 2006. *The Boy Who Was Raised as a Dog: And Other Stories from a Child Psychiatrist's Notebook: What Traumatized Children Can Teach Us about Loss, Love, and Healing*. New York: Basic Books.

Peters RS. 1966. *Ethics and Education*. London: Allen & Unwin.

Peters RS. 1981. *Moral Development and Moral Education*. London: George Allen & Unwin.

Pring R. 2000. *The Philosophy of Educational Research*. London: Continuum.

Rich W. 2013. *The Post-Racial Society is Here. Recognition, Critics and the Nation State*. London: Routledge.

Rousseau J-J. 1998. *The Social Contract, or Principles of Political Thought* [1762]. Translated by HJ Tozer. Hertfordshire: Wordsworth.

Senge P. 1997. *The Fifth Discipline: Art and Practice to Self-training Organization*. Moscow: Olympus Business.

Shakespeare W. 2001. *The Tragedy of Hamlet Prince of Denmark*. Vol XLVI, Part 2. The Harvard Classics. New York: PF Collier & Son, 1909–14; Bartleby.com. Available: http://www.bartleby.com/br/04602.html. (Accessed 23 February 2017.)

Smessaert H. 2012. The classical Aristotelian hexagon versus the modern duality hexagon. *Logica Universalis*, 6(1):171–199.

Smith A. 1904. *An Inquiry into the Nature and Causes of the Wealth of Nations* [1776]. Available: http://www.econlib.org/library/Smith/smWN.html. (Accessed 12 February 2017.)

Stenhouse L. 1983. The relevance of practice to theory in curriculum change. *Promise and Practice*, 22(3):211–215.

Stuart Mill J. 1859. *On Liberty*. Available: http://www.utilitarianism.com/ol/two.html. (Accessed 12 February 2017.)

Taysum A. 2012. *Evidence Informed Leadership in Education*. London: Continuum.

Taysum A & Slater C. 2014. The education doctorate EdD and educational leader dispositions and values in England and the United States. In A Taysum & S Rayner. (eds). *Investing in Our Education? Leading, Learning, Researching and the Doctorate*. Scarborough: Emerald. 149–170.

Thomson W. 1852. On the dynamical theory of heat, with numerical results deduced from Mr. Joule's equivalent of a thermal unit, and M Regnault's observations on steam. *The London, Edinburgh, and Dublin Philosophical Magazine and Journal of Science*, 4(XXII):8–12. Available: https://archive.org/stream/londonedinburghp04maga#page/8/mode/2up. (Accessed 12 February 2017.)

UN (United Nations). 1948. The Universal Declaration of Human Rights. Available: http://www.un.org/en/universal-declaration-human-rights/. (Accessed 12 February 2017.)

UN (United Nations). 1989/1990. Convention on the Rights of the Child. Available: http://www.ohchr.org/EN/ProfessionalInterest/Pages/CRC.aspx. (Accessed 12 February 2017.)

Vaage AB. 2014. Asylum-seeking children, mental health and child psychiatry services: Reflections from a project in south-western Norway. In G Overland, E Guribye & B Lie. (eds). *Nordic Work with Traumatised Refugees: Do We Really Care.* Newcastle upon Tyne: Cambridge Scholars. 71–87.

Von Bertalanffy L. 1968. *General System Theory: Foundations, Development, Applications* [1905]. New York: George Braziller.

Wacquant L. 1999. How penal common sense comes to Europeans: Notes on the transatlantic diffusion of the neoliberal doxa. *European Societies*, 1:319–352.

Watson K. 2001. Introduction: Rethinking the role of comparative education. In K Watson. (ed). *Doing Comparative Education Research: Issues and Problems.* Oxford: Symposium Books. 23–42.

Wiener N. 1954. *The Human Use of Human Beings: Cybernetics and Society.* Oxford: Da Capo.

Williams R. 2016. In S Stephens. (ed). After Brexit? The referendum and its discontents. Available: http://www.abc.net.au/religion/articles/2016/06/24/4488874.htm. (Accessed 11 February 2017.)

African feminist perspectives and education

Rachel Shanyanana and Joseph Divala

Introduction

This chapter provides a theoretical exploration of feminism and feminist education on the African continent. Our main argument is that, in many cases, forms of feminism that have been offered in Africa are greatly limited in bringing about true educational transformation. These approaches, as we evaluate them below, are single-focused and tend to be poorly developed to suit or speak to the conditions of life on the continent. In this regard, we explore conceptually each of these positions as we search for an approach that stands a better chance of representing the African conception of life, as well as respecting the identity of women and men as co-dependents.

Given our own positioning in the higher education system in Africa, we propose that a conception of ubuntu feminism, with particular slants of nego-feminism (which we discuss in more detail below), has the potential to realise the ideals of emancipation for women and children without alienating the women themselves or the men who need to be part of the transformative process as equals with women. We also argue that only when there is a deeper understanding of feminism and its subtle power can education become transformative and promote humaneness. In order to do this, we first discuss the conceptual underpinnings of general feminism before examining the various positions on African feminism. At the end of this chapter, we offer a blended understanding of African feminism and argue for its relevance in promoting transformative education on the continent.

The conceptual underpinnings of feminism

The term 'feminism' is complex and has become topical in contemporary discourses, both in the political domain and in academic circles. The concept of feminism can be traced back to the 1880s in France. It is argued that the term was coined by merging the French word *'femme'*, which means 'woman', with 'ism' as representing a belief system (Moses 2012:763). Other scholars suggest that the term 'feminism' first emerged in the English language or dictionaries in the 18th century, evoked by the historical activities of women's movements in the USA demanding the right to vote. In the 19th century, more feminist groups joined hands to deal with the appalling and gross social injustices that characterised their daily experiences (Heugh 2011; Norwood 2013:225).

Although the concept has been the centre of public debate since the 18th century, it still has no single, clear and universally accepted meaning. Various scholars around the world continue to present feminism differently. For instance, some perceive it as a consciousness, while others view it as an activity or a set of activities. Such variation demands critique and further interrogation if the meaning of the concept is not to be lost. While this chapter attempts to explore underlying philosophies driving the deeper conception of feminism, in terms of its diversity, its differences and its specificity, we caution against adopting a 'one size fits all' definition, which is rampant in popular discourse or at first mention of the concept.

Central to the meanings of feminism is the call for the equality of all in opportunities, treatment and respect, affecting the social, economic and political spheres of life. Some scholars see feminism as a political and philosophical framework, whereas others regard it as made up of strategies that underlie women's practices/activism throughout history. Watson (2014) proposes that feminism is 'the theory of the political, economic and social equalities of the sexes', which constitutes the liberation, freedom and self-determination of both women and men (Tong 2009).

Alkali et al (2013:248) argue that feminism is anchored in the problems of inequality and unfairness in the treatment of women that many people through the ages have assumed to be normal. These experiences indicate that women have long been treated as second-class citizens – they have traditionally been ascribed inferior roles compared to their male counterparts, and womanhood has been objectified in society.

In reaction to these entrenched perceptions, feminism is associated with the key task of 'breaking down and deconstructing [...] sexist ideologies that devalue their humanity', Norwood (2013:225) tells us. Feminism takes as its starting point the idea of 'transforming societies through both intellectual and pragmatic approaches. Across [all spheres of society], [...] women share a rich and powerful history of resistance, despite attempts to silence and make them invisible' (Norwood 2013:225).

Although most academic discourses have tried to present and defend a rational conception of feminism and its associated movements, other perspectives have considered feminism as a move by women and other sympathisers to make women 'be like men', 'look like men' and 'act like men' (Alkali et al 2013:239, citing Kolawole 1997). This perception is often conflated with Western feminism. In this regard, Alkali et al (2013:239) depict Western feminism as a 'radical approach [equated with] rebelliousness, fearlessness, political awareness of sexism and a [...] drive for equality of the sexes'. Alkali et al (2013:240) further indicate that such an approach, which aligns feminism with 'violent confrontation, militancy and aggression', has resulted in a backlash. This characterisation of feminism is remiss: It presents feminism as seeking recognition by male hegemonic structures and approaches to life. In a typical sense, the idea that feminism is driven by the feeling of being, looking and acting like a man already endorses the man as the 'being and existence par excellence' that the woman has to emulate. This thinking puts the man at a level of assumed natural privilege and superiority, which begs its very question.

Numerous scholars have explored feminism from differing theoretical traditions and standpoints. Tong (2009), for example, identifies four major varieties of feminism: liberal feminism, Marxist feminism, radical feminism and socialist feminism. Motta et al (2011:5) add to this list black/African feminism and postmodern/post-structuralist feminism. Lorber (1997) perceives three broad categories that reflect particular theories and political strategies with regard to the gendered social order. This categorisation of feminism is close to what can be referred to as 'standpoint feminism'.

In a sense, these are all different *forms* of feminism, since scholars consider the feminist perspective from various standpoints. For instance, it is not unusual to see that *gender-reform feminisms* include liberal, Marxist, social and development feminism. Similarly, *gender-resistant feminisms* include radical, lesbian, psychoanalytic and standpoint feminism, while *gender-revolution feminisms* include multi-ethnic, men's, social constructivism and postmodern feminism, as well as queer theory. In other words, the many variants of feminism are associated with a variety of philosophical and political outlooks. Thus, these traditions are sketched in certain epochs by diverse theorists and are underpinned by specific ideologies and purposes. We now examine the list provided by Motta et al (2011).

Liberal feminism

Originating as a wave in the 1960s, liberal feminism rests on the call for equality in the legal, educational and public spheres. Its underlying tenets are that individuals are autonomous beings and ought to be afforded the same freedom to exercise their rights to law, attain an education and engage in political activities (see Benhabib 1992; Enslin 2003; Nussbaum 2000; Okin 1999). Liberal feminists believe that oppression exists because of the way in which men and women are socialised. Such socialisation supports patriarchy and keeps men in power positions. Liberal feminists see women as having the same mental capacity as men, and thus they believe that women should be given the same opportunities in the political, economic and social spheres. Women should have the right to choose, just like their male counterparts, rather than have their life chosen for them because of their sex.

In contrast to this broader perspective, liberal feminism has been known to concentrate on the legislation aspect in the fight against patriarchy. It has been criticised for not breaking down the deeper ideologies of society and patriarchy, and for ignoring race and class issues, particularly for women from the working classes.

Radical feminism

Rooted in the 1970s, radical feminism has been associated with a challenge to patriarchy as the fundamental system of power that perpetuates all other forms of injustice. This tradition is seen to promote differences between women and men under the umbrella of lesbianism and global sisterhood (Butler 1990; Daly 1979). Radical feminists want to free both men and women from the rigid gender roles that society has imposed upon them. This sex–gender system has created oppression, the radical feminists believe, and they see their mission as being to overthrow the system by any possible means. Such feminists highlight the importance of individual feelings, experiences and relationships.

Marxist/socialist feminism

Founded within the Marxist tradition, this theory suggests that gender oppression could be mitigated with the end of capitalism and class society. Scholars within this strand – such as Barrett (2014), Flax (1987) and MacKinnon (1989) – assert that as long as society is classified based on class and controlled by capitalist rules, gender oppression will thrive. Similar to Marxism, socialist feminism advocates for the alliances between women's movements and working class struggles with the aim of overcoming both patriarchy and capitalism (Cornell 1998). Jaggar (1983) postulates that socialist feminists reject the idea of biology predetermining gender. They argue that social roles are not inherent and women's status must change in both the public and private spheres. Similar to radical feminists, socialist feminists consider that although women are divided by class, race, ethnicity and religion, they all experience the same oppression simply by being women.

Black/African feminism

Feminism in this strand entails the representation of both black and African women in their struggle against gender oppression and marginalisation alongside their challenge to racism, capitalism and patriarchy (Mohanty 2003; Tamale 2011). In the struggle for recognition and against marginalisation, black/African women champion the recognition of their oppressed and subaltern experiences in the feminist discourses that are at the centre of this theory. The assumption is that other strands have not addressed their distinctive narratives, so there is a call for a particular approach that is aligned with black/African ways of life.

In view of these arguments, Assié-Lumumba (2007:477–479) proposes that efforts should be made to provide learning opportunities which would bridge the gap of gender inequality. She further suggests that, since schools and higher education institutions play a major educational role, they must also organise activities that can contribute to the promotion of people's well-being in all areas of expertise in which women are shown to be powerful and positive, and in which they are acknowledged for their potential contributions to development (Assié-Lumumba 2007:477–479).

Postmodern/post-structuralist feminism

The demand for feminism theory to transcend the 'essentialisms of gendered binaries and fixed identities towards a queering of our practices of self and other' is central to this tradition (Motta et al 2011:5). Numerous scholars, such as Butler (1990) and Tamale (2011), call for an ungendered approach to the practice beyond heterosexuality and recognition of the other, such as homosexuals, if equality is to be attained. While the queer feminist wave demands recognition for homosexuals' lived experiences within the feminist discourse, most societies – specifically in Africa – see these experiences as unfamiliar and at odds with their lived reality.

We now highlight some of the tensions and misconceptions in feminism.

Misconceptions in feminism

Arguably, the prevalence of conceptions in feminism is itself a recipe for *mis*conception. Misconceptions seem to have emerged from a lack of critical analysis and understanding of particular feminist concepts.

One of the central misconceptions is that feminism intends to create a divide between men and women whereby women claim power that is assumed to belong to men. Heugh (2011) attests that black women who publicly express discontent with black men's patriarchal 'African' customs are characterised as being disloyal to African traditions. Feminism is also problematically equated with womanism – a thinking that expects only women to defend feminism and that sees men who happen to support this ideology as either homosexual or cowardly (Tamale 2011).

Another misconception is the belief that feminism, by demystifying marriage and motherhood, evokes danger in emerging generations, who will become radical and develop immoral traits.

By contrast, this chapter argues that the demand for women's rights and an equal position in society should be regarded as a call for social justice. We suggest that not only women but also men have the obligation to do so. While attempting to dismantle the negative myths around feminism alongside the associated pessimism, this chapter proceeds with a critical interrogation of Western feminism. We call for a reconceptualisation of African feminism as a way of constructing a more plausible framework that is analogous with African values and experiences, particularly the plight of women on the continent, who bear the brunt of domestic violence, gender-based violence, rape and so on.

These social ills are reported in daily papers across the continent, but especially in countries such as Namibia, South Africa and Malawi, with which we have first-hand experience. In view of these challenges and the demand for the creation of transformative education, we consider whether there is an authentic and unique approach that may assist Namibia, Malawi, South Africa and other African societies, particularly their educational institutions, to nurture gender-sensitive citizens who are capable of meaningfully interrogating the prevailing feminist discourses in an effort to break the scourge of violent power relations between women and men.

We argue that it is the ambivalent perceptions of feminism, and the prevalence of relativism when approaching critical debates on this topic in our time, which compel us to revisit the prevailing thinking on feminism. In this regard we begin to ask whether a conception can be drawn out from the various conceptions that is close to African forms of life. If so, we wonder what this conception would look like, and whether feminism considered from an African perspective can contribute to the development of a transformative higher education system in Africa.

Feminism on the African continent

Just as feminist thinking is evolving over time in socio-political settings, we anticipate that such a scenario may not be much different when we begin to examine feminism on the African continent. Before we proceed, however, we need to clarify an issue raised above on the assumed characteristics of Western feminism. For some scholars, all other forms of feminism resemble Western feminism in the sense that they have to speak to the core of feminism if they are to be worthy of the name. This is a generalisation, but there are characteristics of the Western worldview that affect what people have labelled 'Western feminism'. Arguably, the discussed distinction between Western feminism and African feminism is really a distinction between the Western worldview and the African worldview. For instance, most of what is called feminism, which is in fact Western feminism, stems from an individualised conception of being that looks at a person as one with agency and whose agencies it is incumbent upon the self to execute. In this regard, the woman is encouraged to exercise agency and be an equal actor with all other actors.

Stromquist (2015:59) suggests that realising feminism involves 'changing social mentalities [...] unlearn[ing] old beliefs and challeng[ing] ingrained values and practices'. The individual should seek to promote and attain social change by confronting the conditions of limitation that have for years obstructed such liberation. Stromquist (2015:69) talks about the process of empowering women as 'the process of acquiring more egalitarian gender perspectives as well as the confidence to mobilize to solve problems, [through which] women learn important knowledge and skills for further political engagement'. Similarly, the envisaged woman's identity in Western feminism is not located 'primarily within the domestic sphere and in reproductive functions', because this woman has 'to assume economic and political roles and to engage in autonomous social advancement' (Stromquist 2015:70), enabling her to attain economic and social mobility necessary in a globalised world.

Heugh (2011:93) argues that the concept of feminism, among others, has been extended to Africa as a means of 'opportunistic agents from the contemporary socio-political and economic contexts'. This is because African people (particularly women) are perceived as being inarticulate and illiterate, and therefore dependent on feminists from developed countries to speak for them. While some African women indeed lack voice and agency, Western women regard it as their role to speak for them. Some African feminists seek to debunk such a view and express their rights through their African voice. They argue that African women's interests and aspirations can be sustainably represented and articulated by those whose lived experiences are akin to Africa's socialisation and way of life. Early African feminist scholars who have championed feminism towards social justice for all include Assié-Lumumba (2007), Gouws (2008), Mama (2007), Mikell (1997), Mohanty (2003) and Oyewumi (1997, 2003), to mention just a few.

We suggest that it is limiting to see feminism merely as practised by Western females rather than as an idea and consciousness exercised by scholars who seek social justice. The term 'feminism' thus needs to be reconceptualised if it is to serve as a potential answer to the gender-violated nature of contemporary societies. Evidence of emerging studies criticising Western feminist literature on behalf of African women includes Benson (2009:110), citing Lorraine Heunis, a participant in a workshop of South African feminist activists: 'We are poor, but we are not stupid. We don't need you to take decisions for us just because we live in informal settlements and you have skills and resources. But we can use your help. It is better to raise these issues here today, instead of sitting here and then we leave and have a lot to say'.

As a central medium of transferring Western cultures and way of life, Heugh (2011:89) asserts that education in Africa is frequently couched 'within the discourses of deficiency or cast in the "no-win" scenario of playing "catch-up"' with Western culture, curricula and languages, among others. As such the African woman becomes one who has to be spoken for, given that traditional systems are repressive. Western education has indeed brought learning materials and teacher education. But African feminists argue that Western feminism is not as innocent as it presents itself to be, because it is a product of the neoliberal economic framework with accompanying structural adjustment programmes (SAPs) of the 1980s that inevitably brought about an adjustment of African cultures and philosophy of life (Desai 2002). The main argument here is that Western educational strategies have not attempted to synchronise with the central socio-economic gender practices of the continent (Heugh 2011:89; Mazrui & Mazrui 1998:195). It is within the foregoing conclusion that African scholars criticise the Western perspective of feminism and demand a standpoint that takes into account local beliefs and practices.

Evidently, tension exists between Western and African feminist studies. For example, Norwood (2013:225) posits that 'African feminism is an intellectual and pragmatic movement, born out of the experiences and conditions of colonialism, slavery, and patriarchy'. This movement 'strives to end interlocking systems of multiple oppressions', as also opposed by African scholars who argue that 'western and White feminism has historically been problematical' (Norwood 2013:225). Despite that, feminism in general struggles to 'dismantle patriarchal social systems that prioritize men's interest and authority over women's' through different movements or waves (Norwood 2013:225). The 'first (1840s–1920s) and second (1960s–1970s) wave feminists tended to normalize middle-class, White, and Western experiences' (Norwood 2013:225). To attest to the above claim, Heugh (2011:93, citing Salo and Magona) point out that 'a lot was being written about us but not written by us. We may not be for example a professor of anthropology or history, but there is value in those like me writing about our experiences, who did not study apartheid but lived it'. Consequently, 'as third (1990s to present) wave and "third world" feminists charge', the first and second wave feminists 'failed to recognize and appreciate the extent to which race, class, and sexuality, and citizenry intersect and further deepen oppression' (Norwood 2013:225).

In addition, in constructing a 'legacy of resistance to western hegemonic forces, African feminists charged western feminist theories with overemphasizing biological differences between the sexes' and perceived men and women as being naturally conflicting (Norwood 2013:227). Not surprisingly, 'western feminists' also portray 'African women as helpless victims' and overstate 'women's sexuality and/or sexual orientation' (Norwood 2013:227). 'African feminists, in collaboration with other "third-world" feminists, critiqued Western feminists for homogenizing them and disregarding their agency and achievement' (Norwood 2013:227, citing Morell & Ouzgane 2005).

Scholars such as Arndt (2002:27), Mikell (1997) and Tamale (2011) argue that in the African context, the concept of feminism is misconstrued and mostly associated with the Western radical form of feminism, which is non-African and promotes a man-hating ideology that rejects marriage and motherhood. This misconstruction is considered to be inconsistent with African traditional values. Thus we support the argument of Heugh (2011:100–101), and of Mohanty (2003) and Mohanty, Russo and Torres (1991), that a debate (in this case feminism) conceptualised elsewhere and brought to the African context without undergoing reinterpretation 'may constitute unintentional but, nevertheless, aggressive acts of delegitimizing the linguistic citizenship of women in Africa'.

We now further explore notions of African feminism and its characteristics, commenting on variants such as state feminism, womanism, nego-feminism, stiwanism and motherism.

State feminism

Okeke-Ihejirika and Franceschet (2002) present state feminism not as a notion that has a distinct ideological or theoretical basis, but as the idea that the feminist agenda is propelled by the state. All efforts, mechanisms and programmes that the state puts in place to promote the identity and place of the woman in society are thus considered as state feminism. State feminism seeks to ensure that there are officially recognised avenues through which women can legitimately make political demands in order to open up access and avenues of influence for and by women – in other words, putting the necessary procedural tools in place for women's voices to be heard in public life. No mention is made, however, of the philosophical position or theoretical standpoint that gives a unique identity to the cause for an equal status.

In many ways, most of the approaches to feminism that are anchored on mere policy change within nation states are reminiscent of this brand of feminism. Here, feminism is promoted as just a matter of access to political and economic activities in the public space. Beyond access to influential positions, everyone is left to their own devices with regard to the unique identity of the woman in society in relation to the hegemonic patriarchal system that has long been entrenched in many African states.

In our view, state feminism is a top-down imperative that risks losing the gains in promoting the equal identity of women in society in the face of weak governance structures, a phenomenon common to emerging democracies in Africa. The rampant ethnic mindset, greatly influencing African governance structures, is one such example that can easily undermine state feminism, and fundamentally render matters of gender justice meaningless.

Womanism and motherism

Alkali et al (2013:239) introduce womanism as a particular brand of feminism whereby the African woman depicts a mindset characteristic of an African woman who does not seek to be like a man or act like a man. This position is said to have been developed in opposition to radical feminism, which alienates and instils fear in men. What is not evident is the uniqueness of this standpoint. Among other things, we wonder how it is possible to fearlessly attack traditionally entrenched inequalities in African societies without at the same time being understood as intending to upset the traditional perception of what womanhood means. Perhaps the main problem in wanting to do this lies in the fact that it would be difficult to stand on both sides of the raging river without being swept away by the very current that is being weathered.

According to the concept of motherism, the mother–child relationship of love and care is used to highlight the emancipation of women. Womanhood is anchored in nurturing and respect for humanity in the same way as a woman lives for her child in Africa. Thus the idea of motherism suggests that there is hope for this continent even with its many ills, such as civil war, disease and hunger.

Problematic in this version of feminism is the apparent disregard of what a man or manhood becomes. While the ethic of care is positive, there is no guarantee that by practising this kind of feminism, say in education, the attitudes and practices of dominating men will themselves be changed.

Stiwanism

The term 'stiwanism' is argued to be derived from STIWA, the acronym for 'social transformation including women in Africa' (Alkali et al 2013:242). The thinking behind this philosophy is that all social transformation on the African continent can meaningfully take place if the woman and womanhood are considered in equal partnership with men. This thinking also acknowledges that although the woman's lived experiences ought to be grounded in what it means to be a woman on the continent, her aspirations are a critical component in building a sustainable harmonious society of equals. In other words, the woman and womanhood ought not be considered as an object of charity as far as imagining social transformation is concerned.

In our view, the concept of stiwanism implies a democratic deliberative space where equal voice and equal right to introduce matters for public discourse are the norm. Furthermore, this space can begin to identify historical inequalities between the sexes by virtue of its educative nature (Benhabib 1992; Young 2000).

Nego-feminism

Alkali et al (2013) borrow the concept of 'nego-feminism' from Nnaemeka (2004). Nego-feminism is presented as a feminist stance centred on peace, conflict management and resolution, negotiation, complementarity, collaboration and a 'give and take' approach to life when it comes to relations between women and men in society. Similar to stiwanism's focus on social transformation, as discussed above, nego-feminism highlights the collaborative and complementary nature of the way in which women and men have to co-exist. The position argues that man as solitary is an incomplete existence, as it would be for the woman. Cruz (2015:28) argues that in nego-feminism, 'groups interact with each other and intuit their social links to others such that the emergent relationships are guaranteed by the harmony and well-being of the social group'. Nego-feminism thus has no winners and losers. Instead, a man's success in life is seen as depending on the cooperation of women, as much as the success of a woman depends on the cooperation of men, without the two sides positioning themselves as rivals in the development of society.

If we relate nego-feminism to the promotion of social justice through education, the position teaches us to strive for a good, meaningful life that can be achieved in the interests of everyone in society. Alkali et al (2013:248) further argue that the question of men's ethic as 'characterized by autonomy and laws ought always to be complemented by women's ethic of care with its emphasis on empathy and supportive relationships'. This position demands that education on the African continent cultivate dispositions which recognise the vulnerability of the human condition, and which understand that this human condition can be enhanced only by a collaborative effort on the part of both women and men. Societal role models cannot only be men; women also have a high stake in being beacons of hope for the future of society.

Common features in African feminism

The discussion above begs the question of whether there are specific features that can hold together feminist thinking on the African continent. Is this feminist thinking unique to Africa? Cornell and Van Marle (2015) propose 'ubuntu feminism'. Here we use the concept of ubuntu as an emblem of the communitarian character of personhood on the African continent, where being is primarily defined by belonging. Cornell and Van Marle (2015) introduce ubuntu feminism in order to highlight the idea of an ethic of care, whereby a society would seek its own destruction if relations within it were purely intended for the advancement of the individual and the individual's rights.

Other than ubuntu feminism being considered as a branch of ubuntu philosophy, what should be central to feminist thinking that is representative of the African is that which typifies African forms of life. Holism, collectivism and situational positioning are thus central to an African perspective.

The concept of *holism* represents the embedded forms of life on the African continent that continually diminish the lines between private and public. The communal forms of life characteristic of an African life are such that practical knowledge and theoretical knowledge are largely considered as giving meaning to each other. On matters of identity, work and family life are not considered to be separate and distinct forms of life, for these are lived through each other (Cruz 2015:26). A woman's lived experiences and expectations in the workplace cannot be meaningful if her womanhood and possible role as a mother are not taken into consideration. Holism essentially rejects dualist forms of life that are capable of tearing families and institutions apart. In terms of reimagining educational interventions for equal educational outcomes, it would be naïve to consider that once a young woman enters university, the burdens of excelling and fulfilling her potential are similar to those of a young man.

African feminism is understood as operating within African thought, where being is defined more by its belonging than its individual existence. The group is the primary unit of analysis, and thus paramount in the redefinition of feminism is the relationship between women, children and men. Similarly, although the notion of motherhood discussed earlier epitomises the bond that a mother has with her child, it is equally true that every adult in African culture is a parent to every child and the child can be reprimanded by any adult in society, not just the biological parent. The sanctity or dignity of a woman in African feminism is not an individualised issue – it is *collective*.

Lastly, African feminism is characterised by *situational positioning*. In a way, this idea directly responds to the critique that early forms of Western feminism neglected the lived experiences and contextual backgrounds of women of colour and blacks (Brady-Amoon 2011). The idea of situational positioning does not seek to relativise the objectives of feminism, as some may argue. This concept is largely a caution that we cannot advocate forms of life which fail to take into account forms of life that may undermine the emancipatory agenda if we do not attempt to understand the structure of society and how meanings in life are generated in these conditions.

In particular, situational positioning demands that we recognise that despite being born a man or a woman, some of these individuals operate in opposite roles. Specifically, there are women who are revered for their manly character in holding families together, and men who display caring characteristics in contexts where everyone expects them to display a traditional manly character. Nnaemeka (1998) and others argue that framings of gender within the African context are not as rigid and absolute as many traditional literatures on the topic want us to believe.

In problematising feminism, Motta et al (2011:2) call for a revisiting and reinvention of feminist theorising and practice that synchronises critical understanding of the past with contemporary struggles. The reconstructed theorisation may concomitantly create approaches that inform both internal and external practices in academia to support women's movements. For them, feminist theorising in academia ought to aid better practices exercised elsewhere in society. Failure to do so may lead to feminists' marginalisation due to their tendency to privilege essentialism and ignore the voices of people who belong to silenced and marginalised groups: black and working-class women. Thus, the above-discussed misconceptions and tensions manifest a disconnection between traditions and activities among feminists, which prompts our call towards consolidated efforts among feminists if authentic emancipation is to be engendered.

The implications of feminist discourse for education in Africa

In this reflective section, we propose to suggest some of the things of which education on the continent should be mindful in order for appropriate forms of feminism to be cultivated. Before we proceed, we wish to reiterate and clarify the conceptual underpinnings of feminism with which we are working. In the previous section we rounded off the discussion by briefly exploring some of the common features of an African worldview that many scholars have associated with African feminism. The concepts of holism, collectivism and situational positioning appeared prominently as characteristics of an African feminism. Two brands of feminism discussed above summarily represent our standpoint as well as being the central tenets of an African worldview. We argue that ubuntu feminism and nego-feminism have many things in common, and the two together generally present a better version of African feminism. Below we indicate what education from an African feminist perspective should involve.

An African feminism and a feminist approach to education on the continent should be capable of representing the African identity that speaks to women, men and children without unfairly excluding any of these groups. This education system should prioritise values such as the element of 'give and take' that nego-feminism proposes. The system would also need to continually uphold the value of co-dependence between women and men in developing communities and shared forms of life on the continent.

In this way, African feminism comes to understand and promote the holistic nature of life for all members of society. This feminism cannot be 'one size fits all', because existential conditions on the continent are not stuck in rigid forms. Critical in making African feminism work on the continent is the role that both women and men can play in addressing gender-based injustices and their ramifications in society, particularly reflecting on ascribed gender roles and identities. This thinking also calls for humane education.

Humane education is rooted in the affective qualities of the human being. These include empathy and care towards the other, irrespective of their gender or class or other differentiating conditions. Humane education focuses on the troubled histories of women in different cultural settings where, to a large extent, women have been alienated and oppressed in defence of cultural integrity. In addition, Brady-Amoon (2011:142–143) proposes that a feminist African education ought to be centred on people's experiences and how they make meaning in life amid their weaknesses, strengths and potentials. We have argued that the conception of life in this sense is shared and collective. This implies that such an education system should focus not only on the self but on how the self is developing a greater awareness of the other, and how the collective is moving forward together to create societies that are meaningful and liberating for everyone. A feminist African education would similarly envisage educational programmes that are rooted in the different contexts and reflective of these lived experiences.

A feminist pedagogy hinged on central elements of ubuntu feminism and nego-feminism has great potential to confront gender-based violence, which in many cases has ended in so-called 'passionate' or 'intimate killings'. We consider passionate killing to be murder like any other form of murder, and that framing the murder as 'passionate killing' shows a misunderstanding of how women and men ought to be equal co-developers of African society. This in itself shows a complete absence of the 'give and take' attitude that an African feminist education should be cultivating.

While it is true that African traditional systems have used the idea of communitarianism to suppress women's aspirations, promote subjugation and the male dependency syndrome, nego-feminism and ubuntu feminism put a premium on the fact that women and men cannot exist and flourish in exclusion of each other. This understanding demands a reconceptualisation of the notion of community that has been constructed to women's disadvantage. The idea of community per se is not oppressive, we argue; what is oppressive is the way in which power relations within traditional communities have been manipulated and legitimised as being essential to the idea of community itself. Ubuntu feminism and nego-feminism call for a fresh understanding of the idea of community such that values of equality, co-dependence, collaboration and a true sense of being human are shared and practised equally.

Thus we believe that it is not feminism which is alien to African education. Rather, the driving ideological positions adopted within a specific brand of feminism may militate against African systems and ultimately undermine the development of a unique and genuine form of African feminist education.

The blended form of African feminism in education, combining ubuntu feminism and nego-feminism, is in our view an apt approach, since it considers human beings as individuals with potentials and equal intelligence who will equally contribute to the well-being of all in society.

Given the challenges confronting Namibia, Malawi and South Africa, a reconceptualisation of ubuntu feminism and nego-feminism stands a better chance of developing positive gender relations, as much as upholding the true identity of both women and men, whose identities do not depend on feelings of superiority, humiliation and exploitation in the name of culture. Africa's other contextual conditions, those of developing forms of democratic life, stand a chance of being enhanced through forms of African feminism that are conditioned by reciprocity, agency and equality for the development of its people.

Finally, a feminist African education, we propose, cannot avoid being the foundation for the ethical professional development of its own educators, both male and female. This approach holds the promise of moving the current gender and feminist thinking beyond a 'numbers game' towards realistic transformation that is reflected in the education system.

Conclusion and recommendations for future research

The above discussion has settled on the adoption of a reconceptualised form of African feminism that combines ubuntu feminism and nego-feminism. The proposed approach requires African education systems to revise the salient acquired forms of education that are in many ways riddled with Western assumptions of feminism not consciously reflective of the situations in which such forms are meant to operate – that is, the communal, humane expectations placed on individuals in the African context. The African feminist education we have put forward has great potential for addressing entrenched male privileges, the oppression of women and the creation of an enabling and just system of education.

In recommending prospective research, we accede that our argument may seem limited by having left untouched the debate of the postmodern feminist wave, specifically queer feminism. Clearly, the queer feminist wave is new to feminist discourse, particularly on the African continent, and it is a champion for homosexuality as a suitable categorisation beyond the currently assumed heterosexual gender binary. Many African feminist proponents regard queer feminism as being radically influenced by Western feminism and at odds with African feminism. While acknowledging the relevance of the queer feminist conception, we have not considered this strand of feminism in this chapter due to its apparent contradictions with African feminist thought. Nevertheless, queer feminism is an evolving area of concern. More time is required to conceptualise and thoroughly interrogate it. Our position, therefore, is that to do justice to this critical idea, future research could investigate the tension between African feminism and the queer feminist wave towards the creation of a harmonious connection for a better transformative and inclusive feminist education.

References

Alkali M, Talif R, Wan Yahya WR & Jan JM. 2013. Dwelling or duelling in possibilities: How (ir)relevant are African feminisms? *Journal of Language Studies*, 13(3):237–253.

Arndt S. 2002. *The Dynamics of African Feminism: Defining and Classifying African Feminist Literatures*. Trenton, NJ: Africa World Press.

Assié-Lumumba N. (ed). 2007. *Women and Higher Education in Africa: Reconceptualizing Genderbased Human Capabilities and Upgrading Human Rights to Knowledge*. Abidjan: CEPARRED.

Barrett M. 2014. *Women's Oppression Today: The Marxist Feminist Encounter*. London: Verso.

Benhabib S. 1992. *Situating the Self*. New York: Routledge.

Benson K. 2009. Collaborative research in conversation. *Feminist Africa*, 13:107–116.

Brady-Amoon P. 2011. Humanism, feminism, and multiculturalism: Essential elements of social justice in counseling, education, and advocacy. *Journal of Humanistic Counseling*, 50(2):135–148.

Butler J. 1990. *Gender Trouble: Feminism and the Subversion of Identity*. New York: Routledge.

Cornell D. 1998. *At the Heart of Freedom: Feminism, Sex, and Equality*. Princeton: Princeton University Press.

Cornell D & Van Marle K. 2015. Ubuntu feminism: Tentative reflections. *Verbum et Ecclesia*, 36(2). Available: http://dx.doi.org/10.4102/ve.v36i2.1444. (Accessed 13 February 2017.)

Cruz JM. 2015. Reimagining feminist organizing in global times: Lessons from African feminist communication. *Women & Language*, 38(1):23–41.

Daly M. 1979. *Gyn/Ecology: The Metaethics of Radical Feminism*. London: The Women's Press.

Desai M. 2002. Transnational solidarity – women's agency, structural adjustment, and globalization. In N Naples & M Desai. (eds). *Women's Activism and Globalization: Linking Local Struggles and Global Politics*. New York: Routledge.

Enslin P. 2003. Liberal feminism, diversity and education. *Theory and Research in Education*, 1(1):73–87.

Flax J. 1987. Postmodernism and gender relations in feminist theory. *Signs: Journal of Women in Culture and Society*, 12(4):621–643.

Gouws A. 2008. Changing women's exclusion from politics: Examples from southern Africa. *African and Asian Studies*, 7(4):537–563.

Heugh K. 2011. Discourses from without, discourses from within: Women, feminism and voice in Africa. *Current Issues in Language Planning*, 12(1):89–104.

Jaggar A. 1983. *Feminist Politics and Human Nature*. Oxford: Rowman & Littlefield.

Lorber J. 1997. The variety of feminisms and their contributions to gender equality. *Oldenburger Universitätsreden*, 97:7–45. Oldenburg: *Bibliotheks- und Informationssystem der Univ. Oldenburg*.

MacKinnon CA. 1989. *Toward a Feminist Theory of the State*. Cambridge: Harvard University Press.

Mama A. 2007. Critical connections: Feminist studies in African contexts. In A Cornwall, E Harrison & A Whitehead. (eds). *Feminisms in Development: Contradictions, Contestations and Challenges*. New York: Zed Books. 150–160.

Mazrui A & Mazrui AA. 1998. The linguist balance sheet: Post-Cold war, post-apartheid & beyond structural adjustment. In AA Mazrui & AM Mazrui. (eds). *The Power of Babel. Language and Governance in the African Experience*. Oxford: James Currey; Nairobi: East African Educational; New York: State University of New York; Cape Town: David Phillip. 192–211.

Mikell G. 1997. *African Feminism. The Politics of Survival in Sub-Saharan Africa*. Philadelphia: University of Pennsylvania Press.

Mohanty C. 2003. 'Under Western Eyes' revisited: Feminist solidarity through anticapitalist struggles. *Signs: Journal of Women in Culture and Society*, 28(2):499–535.

Mohanty CT, Russo A & Torres L. (eds). 1991. *Third World Women and the Politics of Feminism*. Bloomington: Indiana University Press.

Moses CG. 2012. 'What's in a name?' On writing the history of feminism. *Feminist Studies*, 38(3):757–779.

Motta S, Flesher Fominaya C, Eschle C & Cox L. 2011. Feminism, women's movements and women in movement. *Interface: A Journal for and about Social Movements*, 3(2):1–32.

Nnaemeka O. 1998. Mapping African feminisms. In A Cornwell. (ed). *Readings in Gender in Africa*. Bloomington: Indiana University Press. 31–41.

Nnaemeka O. 2004. Nego-feminism: Theorizing, practicing, and pruning Africa's way. *Signs: Journal of Women in Culture and Society*, 29(2):357–385.

Norwood C. 2013. Perspective in Africana feminism; Exploring expressions of black feminism/womanism in the African diaspora. *Sociology Compass*, 7(3):225–236.

Nussbaum MC. 2000. The future of feminist liberalism. *Proceedings and Addresses of the American Philosophical Association*, 74(2):47–79.

Okeke-Ihejirika PE & Franceschet S. 2002. Democratization and state feminism: Gender politics in Africa and Latin America. *Development and Change*, 33(3):439–466.

Okin S. 1999. *Is Multiculturalism Bad for Women?* Princeton: Princeton University Press.

Oyewumi O. 1997. *Invention of Women: Making an African Sense of Western Gender Discourse.* Minneapolis: University of Minnesota Press.

Oyewumi O. (ed). 2003. *African Women and Feminism: Reflecting on the Politics of Sisterhood.* Trenton: Africa World Press.

Stromquist NP. 2015. Gender structure and women's agency: Toward greater theoretical understanding of education for transformation. *International Journal of Lifelong Education*, 34(1):59–75.

Tamale S. (ed). 2011. *African Sexualities: A Reader.* Cape Town: Pambazuka Press.

Tong R. 2009. *Feminist Thought: A More Comprehensive Introduction.* 3rd ed. University of North Carolina: Westview Press.

Watson E. 2014. Gender equality is your issue too. Speech given at a special event for the HeForShe campaign, 20 September. United Nations Headquarters, New York. Available: http://www.unwomen.org/en/news/stories/2014/9/emma-watson-gender-equality-is-your-issue-too. (Accessed 13 February 2017.)

Young IM. 2000. *Inclusion and Democracy.* Princeton: Princeton University Press.

The place of critical theory in understanding education in Africa

Chapter

8

Joseph Divala and Joseph Hungwe

Introduction

In this chapter, we examine the nature of critical theory and its role in understanding education. In an attempt to locate the relevance of critical theory on the African continent, the chapter proposes decolonisation of the (higher) education system as a unique format of doing critical theory. First, we explore the historical beginnings of critical theory and its conceptual underpinnings. Then we discuss the centrality of emancipation and the different forms that debates on emancipation have taken. In trying to ground the implications of critical theory in education in contemporary South Africa, we examine issues of decolonisation of higher education as a manifestation of a particular brand of critical theory relevant to African (higher) education systems.

Critical theory

Critical theory as we know it today exists in many varieties, strands and models, and is similarly interpreted in many ways. Thus, over time, it has become difficult to concisely define critical theory. Rasmussen (2015), for instance, observes that critical theory is rather general and has become meaningless. According to this critique, feminism, postcolonialism, critical discourse analysis and critical race theory, among others, claim to be critical theories, yet their subjects of focus are different. Critical theory has taken differing forms in accordance with the social issues pertinent at the time. Rasmussen's (2015) view is debatable, perhaps even easily dismissed, as we show below.

Is critical theory a subject-specific matter, or is it much more of an approach? While there is a relationship between a subject matter and an orientation, or an approach, we suggest that critical theory is an approach, an outlook, a methodological frame that can be used to analyse issues whose end is the emancipation of the person and the human condition. Whether the approach can be used to understand and consider the place of women in society, or how racial interactions need to be reconsidered and reconstituted, is in our view inconsequential to the *nature* of critical theory.

If we are correct, then critical theory must have essential features that can be used in any strand of the theory, such as critical race theory, feminism, postcolonialism and many others. A way of learning more about these features is by understanding where this theory comes from, and how it was used in the context in which it developed. We are not simply doing a heuristic exercise here – we locate the exercise and our very function within the practice of education. Thus the discussion of critical theory has a bearing on education. We will extend this discussion to assess what 'doing' critical theory implies under the conditions of education, and particularly higher education, in South Africa and the greater African region. The debate focuses on the decolonisation of the education system.

Critical theory and its goals in society

Critical theory originated in the Frankfurt School in the 1920s. Despite its diverse traditions and social emphasis, this social theory can be attributed to figures such as Max Horkheimer (1895–1973), Theodor Adorno (1903–1969) and Herbert Marcuse (1898–1979) as the founders. Jürgen Habermas is associated with the later versions of critical theory espoused in philosophy and sociology (Watson & Watson 2011). According to Kellner (1990), the social and political conditions of the time informed the discourses and dimensions that critical theory took.

Critical theory developed as a kind of socialist thinking advocating 'equality and community action in public policy and education' (McKernan 2013:417). The critical theorists confronted these challenges by introducing dedicated schools, such as the London School of Economics, to focus on the study of reform strategies for the eradication of social injustice. The strategies were consolidated around the following ideas: Higher education should focus on everyday social problems, economics should grow as industrialisation develops, systems should work properly, everyone should be equal, and life should be lived according to the standards of the time (McKernan 2013:417–418). Such schools upheld the notion that 'knowledge was power and in the hands of key policy-makers [this knowledge] guaranteed social reforms' (McKernan 2013:423).

According to Marx, critical theory came about through the realisation of the magnitude of the prevailing exploitation and oppression (Kellner 1990). While Marxism reduced society in terms of economic disparities between classes, critical theory claims to encompass the social, psychological, cultural and political aspects of the individual as he or she relates to the broader society (Kellner 1990). Horkheimer (2002:242), by contrast, as well as Adorno, Marcuse, Fromm and many others, argues that critical theory is effective less because it seeks to explain, understand and interpret society, and more because it seeks to change and liberate human beings from circumstances that enslave them.

When these ideas are translated into education, they form the hub of critical pedagogy as advocated by Freire (see Leonard & McLaren 1993). Critical theory becomes a systematic approach by which we can perform ideological critique that should help in eliminating false consciousness and allow us as individuals and communities to resist oppressive ways of life. Removing false consciousness, developing critical thinking and openly, critically perceiving the forces that enslave the human being are central to any educational project. An education system that does not attempt to free the human mind from the shackles of society and its dominating agents is an education that falls short of its very name. The process of developing people through education is essential critical work, given that it is through education that human beings come to recognise and develop their potential and begin to attain higher forms of life. Such enlightenment of the mind is unique to the process of educating a person, irrespective of the tradition at stake.

Despite this apparently single and distinct perspective on transforming ways of life and people's lived experiences, critical theory is not a seamless single front in terms of what it focuses on. As McKernan (2013:426) notes, 'the first generation of critical theorists [...] rejected rationalism, or the positivist understanding of research' in favour of an understanding of such knowledge that changed the way people dealt with the challenges that confronted their living conditions and experiences. This is why McKernan (2013:426) emphasises that the idea of 'kritik' as used by the first-generation critical theorists denoted 'inquiry and action' that challenged political and social policies, including educational policies.

The second generation of critical theorists saw critical theory as being primarily concerned with a 'critical and reflective evaluation of society, culture and institutions through a Marxist social class lens at the outset although it later departed from this perspective' (McKernan 2013:426–427). Habermas (1985, 1990) is now known for introducing 'discourse ethics' and 'communicative action'. These do not indicate a move away from critical theory, but rather are inherent in it. Discourse ethics is concerned with the norms of conversation that influence how human beings realise their common goals. The expression of views in deliberation can eliminate or entrench forms of inequality among people.

The concept of *critique* is indispensable to critical theory. Critique entails a shift from positivism, where knowledge is claimed to be attained through some causal relation and verified as matters of fact. Critique enables the researcher to reflect on conditions such as poverty, crime, racism, xenophobia and many other social ills (Watson & Watson 2011). The researcher explores the values and theories that are behind dominant and popular cultures. Essentially, critique as constituted in critical theory is an analysis or a review or an assessment of the social order. Using critical theory, we can question assumptions that account for practices such as colonisation, Afrophobia (the fear of foreigners of African descent in any context), international migration and competition over economic resources, as well as for the ways in which race or nationality affect higher education practices.

The concept of *emancipation* is also pivotal to critical theory. Emancipation, we believe, comprises universal human interactions in which sources of unfair and judgemental prejudices are addressed. Watson & Watson (2011:68) suggest that 'emancipatory values are especially important when considering social systems wherein inequality of power exists in relation to opportunity, authority and control'. A critical theory researcher can initiate emancipation by identifying obstacles to human social freedom.

As noted, critical theory not only attempts to explain society, but also seeks social transformation in situations of social inequality. 'A critical theory wants to explain a social order in such a way that it becomes itself the catalyst which leads to the transformation of this social order' (Brookfield 2005:7, citing Fay 1987). In this regard, critical theory attempts to bring about positive change, and is therefore essentially transformative. Critical theory induces social transformation through the identification and isolation of underlying causes that give rise to social inequalities. Albury (2005:257, citing Bohman 2005) notes that critical theory attempts to clarify 'what is wrong with the current social reality, identify actors to change it, provide clear norms for criticism and achievable practical goals for social transformation'.

Critical theory underscores the significance of challenging norms that account for hegemonic ideologies. This supports the claim that norms or values are intricately linked with action. Roach (2008) believes that critical theory expounds underlying values as being accountable for ideological orientations. We could employ this tenet to advance the argument that there are underlying values in society which lead to the practice of Afrophobia, for instance.

According to critical theory, all political and social structures are ultimately and inevitably alterable. Critical theory thus disputes the notion of immutability of social and political structures (Roach 2008). It can be argued then that the difficulties societies face in bringing about just conditions of life to many disenfranchised communities in Africa, and South Africa in particular, result from the thinking that social, political and economic structures should continue to be run as they currently are because dismantling them 'could' result in untold suffering for the very people we want to emancipate. 'Critical theory judges social arrangements by their capacity to embrace open dialogue with others,' Linklater (2007:46) observes, 'and envisages new forms of political community that break with unjustified exclusion.'

Critical theory's primary focus is on social structures, arrangements and institutions, with the aim of exposing the powers giving shape to such social orders. Sinnerbrink (2012) suggests that critical theory takes up the role of analysing historical and social conditions of crisis occurring within society. This position evidently aligns with the early critical theory position of the Frankfurt School of material conditions being seen as indispensable to human freedom. Human existence and its material conditions are not equated with freedom – they are necessary for the *realisation* of freedom. To this end, Ivkovic (2014:29) asserts that critical theory 'aims to articulate an evaluation of a given social order by theorising a gap between the normative potentiality that this order harbours and the still deficient actuality of the current state of development'. Kellner (1990) also points out that the word 'critic' contained in this theory is meant to emphasise the aspect of denouncing all forms of oppression and exploitation, as well as the resultant inequalities between people.

Critical theory identifies the existence of power relations in ideologies and themes that inform social arrangements. Such relations need to be dismantled if human beings are to realise their freedom. Social ideologies give shape to reality, it is believed. These power relations reveal that there are subjects who dominate and those who are dominated (Creswell 2014). If that is the case, the work of emancipating people requires 'ideology critique' and a re-examination of the social arrangements at the centre of human practice.

Within critical theory there is a view that societies maintain repressive structures by advancing popular ways of thinking which inevitably become dominant (Freeman & Vasconcelos 2010). Values, beliefs, assumptions, misconceptions and stereotypes of one society are promoted over those of other social groups. For Dryzek (1987:657), this theory is 'confidently directed against particular repressive or exploitative social relations based on class, gender, race and spatial location'. Societies thus tend to render other social groups invisible. Invisibility does not imply that a given social group is not existent, but it is silent and marginalised and regards itself as socially excluded to the extent that it considers itself irrelevant. It is in such contexts that critical theory enables the exposition of the binaries of the powerful and the powerless, the dominant and the marginalised.

Clearly, critical theory offers society possibilities that can lead to emancipation (Sinnerbrink 2012). Critical theory's procedure here is through critically questioning the political structures that lead to social realities. Such questioning reveals that 'the priority given to members of a political community often gives rise to injustice to non-members and non-citizens', as Bohman (2012:98) observes. Critical theory interrogates both the beneficiaries and the deprived of a given social system by viewing all its beliefs, assumptions, (mis)perceptions and values. In so doing, there is an assertion that such social values and beliefs are indeed the production of the given social context.

Critical theory in education

The original thinking around critical theory evidently takes Freire's critical pedagogy, which is concerned with teaching for emancipation and enhanced modes of human liberation, as making up the goals of education. There are schools of thought that still entertain certain forms of indoctrination as forms of education. Such matters, we propose, can best be referred to as 'forms of schooling' or 'training' rather than 'education' per se. In its proper context education centres on the development of the mind, and the capacity of the mind to think critically and creatively. Such an understanding of education has emancipatory characteristics.

As McKernan (2013:425) argues,

> *history indeed repeats itself. It is this repetition of dominion and submission that must be halted, and halting it presupposes knowledge of its genesis and of the ways in which it is reproduced: critical thinking. For both critical theorists and critical educators, then, the development of this critical lens is the goal of education, but it also is a tool that must be brought to bear on educational systems and the ways that they perpetuate unequal divisions of power and social injustices. [...] Only by critiquing "common sense" notions that pass themselves off as value free can individuals discern whose interests they serve and who might benefit if such notions and social structures are disrupted and transformed.*

Given that the process of educating human beings is a universal call embedded in the nature of what it means to be human, this chapter contends that critical theory applies to African higher education systems just as it applies to any other education system. Africa is a complex continent, with multiple and divergent cultural, political, socio-economic and historical circumstances which shape and determine higher education systems. But we take the uniform African experience of colonialism as the basis or point of convergence in this chapter.

Apart from a few states, Africa's history is that of being colonised at some point. A critique on colonialism thus becomes a common denominator for African higher education. 'People should be able to rationally analyse and criticize the different ideological discourses imposed on them,' Jacobs (2014:303) comments. If this is the case, applying critical theory to higher education discourse, especially the question of colonisation, means that we should interrogate the framework within which the African higher education system is operating. Can the higher education system today be considered to facilitate rational engagement and the seeking of solutions for the many predicaments that African society, its government and economic system face owing to its past colonial life?

According to Jacobs (2014:297), 'critical theory is an emancipatory approach that enables us to dig beneath the surface of social life and uncover assumptions that keep us from fully understanding how the world works'. Such structures could be in the form of values, norms, symbols and languages that have been externally imposed. In the case of African universities and the general education band, this could imply that critical work in education should not shy away from a critical engagement of the practices, norms and standards of knowledge, and of the success, which operate within our systems. In view of this quest, Morreira (2015) observes that universities in Africa generally preserve and thereby sustain colonialism both through what they teach and aspire to. Higgs (2012) further notes that the research methodologies which are usually prescribed and employed in African higher education tend to be dismissive of African contexts and cultural values. This is not to deny that knowledge has universalistic elements, but to take note of the significance of particular circumstances and cultural values that inform researchers within a given context. These research methodologies are often Eurocentric and designed to promote European value systems.

If we concur with McKernan (2013) and many others who suggest that the framework of critical theory in education should be used as a tool for seeing things differently and ultimately changing these things, then we need to reframe our discourse on higher education such that a resultant change of operation – that is itself liberating – becomes inevitable. So the debate on the discourse on decolonisation, and the intellectual engagement with ways of changing the patterns of behaviour within African higher education institutions, should continue, to the benefit of African people.

Africa's decolonisation project as African critical theory work

The material conditions within which critical theory developed are not those in which most African systems find themselves today. This position seems to partly justify the idea that critical theory is self-contradictory and has no single referent. Despite the apparent endorsement of its self-disintegration, we argue that particular schools of critical theory may, of course, be products of their unique material conditions, but the methodological underpinnings of critical theory speak to the same core issues.

If critical theory's quest is to challenge and alter structures and values that deny human beings their basic freedom (McKernan 2013:417, citing Horkheimer 1937), then Africa's decolonisation project is essentially critical theory work. Craggs (2014, citing Lee 2010) suggests that decolonisation's objective is to examine the unequal social and economic power relations that have been entrenched by the colonial systems. Other scholars, by contrast, such as Hwami (2016, citing Hobson 2016), dismiss critical theory–as framed within Marxism–as an ideology that is not related to oppressed black people under colonialism. We think that Hwami's (2016, citing Hobson 2016) reading of critical theory is problematic given what critical theory seeks to achieve within any human condition.

Decolonisation can be associated with descriptors such as independence, complete sovereignty, empowerment, economic transformation, indigenisation and self-determination (Hebie 2015; Hwami 2016). In some instances, decolonisation has entailed putting in place drastic measures and economic and cultural policies that can almost be considered as anti-European. For instance, this clearly applies in the context of Zimbabwe, currently, where decolonisation has been touted as an approach that enhances sovereignty through the empowerment of black people (Hwami 2016). The antipathy towards colonisation in Zimbabwe is often popularised in political slogans such as 'Zimbabwe will never be a colony again',

'Land to the people' and many more. For South Africa, the narrative of previously disadvantaged groups of the population is advanced as a way of redressing the injustice of apartheid. This narrative is part of the decolonisation project and is at the heart of what critical theory seeks to do.

Craggs (2014:40) points out that 'decolonisation is often seen in retrospect in a cloud of disappointment, the failure of development projects, neo-colonial economic and political relationships, continued violence, the ultimate dissolution of alternative and radical forms of geopolitical organisation'. In the same vein, Craggs (2014, citing Blunt 2005) proposes that as part of the process of decolonisation, there is a need to critically review the inextricable link between the past and the present, and the relationship between the coloniser and the colonised. In a way, Craggs's (2014, citing Blunt 2005) assertion indicates that colonialism has continued to exist in the previously colonised countries and states, though in different forms.

In the African context, decolonisation can be considered from the political, economic, social and educational spheres. Mamdani (2016) categorises decolonisation into themes such as the political, economic and epistemological. According to this thinking, *political* decolonisation involves not only gaining independence from external control, but also challenging the internal and external processes that are responsible for the reproduction of racial and ethnic colonial legacies. Decolonisation from an *economic* point of view extends beyond local ownership of local resources to a critical examination of foreign, 'remote' control. The *epistemological* theme addresses 'categories, with which we make, unmake and remake and thereby apprehend the world. These categories are intimately linked to our notions of what is human, what is particular and what is universal' (Mamdani 2016:79). The epistemological perspective implies, among other things, reflection on the underlying values that inform a person's worldview, perceptions and forms of social interaction; critical examination of privileged forms of knowledge; and re-conceptualisation of knowledge that is relevant to the context and conditions of Africa.

Decolonisation is a complex, multifaceted process, and therefore includes all three categorisations. The political, economic and epistemological are interwoven to the extent that it is only through their aggregation that decolonisation can be viewed. Decolonisation is not an event that can be confined to one historical moment, but rather a continuous process. It entails a re-engagement with the political, social and economic environments of a particular group of people.

Decolonisation seeks the social, political and economic emancipation of the formerly colonised masses. We concur with Barnsley and Bleiker's (2008) argument that decolonisation is a right for freedom from imperialism and illegal occupation of countries and territories. But from an educational perspective, decolonisation is not simply a matter of occupying geographical spaces. It is more a matter of occupying epistemic spaces and framing epistemic bodies that superimpose on African thought systems as they are understood in contemporary spaces. Thus Higgs (2012:37) clarifies that 'the marginalisation of African values in African education has resulted in the general Westernisation of education theory and practice'.

Power relations are assumed by decolonisation in which there is a group of colonised people and the colonisers. Often the colonisers impose structures, values and norms that seek to maintain their dominance and control over those whom they have colonised. We contend therefore that attempting to appropriate critical theory in its Western form is wrong, in the sense that the approach of content critical theory, with its constitutive elements, is rather alien and incompatible with the African higher education landscape. Decolonisation should instead be understood as another version of critical theory, as are feminism and critical race theory.

We are aware that Africa has not been alone in experiencing colonisation and its associated political, social and economic ramifications. But the African experience of colonialism was brutal and entrenched a system that has remained embedded in the social and political psyche of Africans. According to Pepinsky (2015), colonialism was underlined by the objective of creating colonies that in turn become vehicles for imparting the cultural values of the colonisers. To that end, education was not neutral but tailored to reproduce colonialism. The vestiges of colonialism are still in evidence in Africa to the extent that Africans have remained colonised even in the colonisers' absence. The decolonisation of education, particularly higher education, is a crucial part of doing critical theory in Africa.

The centrality of African higher education systems in the decolonisation project

Education is not a neutral process, but involves the inculcation of a given people's norms and beliefs. According to Assié-Lumumba (2016), education provides a worldview, ethos and social representation. In this view the decolonisation of higher education is a central and urgent issue in Africa. The acknowledgement that Africa is not a homogeneous cultural group of people equally implies that higher education is confronted by different social problems. Nevertheless, the generic experience of colonialism remains a common factor at postcolonial African universities. Prinsloo (2016:165) notes that 'decolonising universities is essential if we are to rethink ourselves and cultivate African epistemologies'. This is not to suggest that the primary and secondary education levels should be left out of decolonisation debates.

Decolonisation is premised on the notion that although the political dispensation of colonialism was officially brought to an end, colonialism has taken new forms. Prinsloo (2016, citing Pillay 2015) argues that most African universities are Westernised. The Westernisation of universities is seen in the curricula as well as the institutional cultures. There is a perception that because African universities are so Westernised, the graduates they produce are Africans who are foreign to African ways of life, as they disassociate themselves from anything African.

For Shockley & Frederick (2010:1216, citing Asante 1998), decolonisation implies 'placing African ideals at the center of any analysis that involves African culture and behavior'. In many ways this process involves challenging the remnants of colonialism in whatever form they manifest themselves, as Ciccariello-Maher (2014) argues. The implication is that educators, researchers, policymakers and university learners should be critically exploring colonialism within their various environments.

Similarly, decolonisation demands that 'academics confront the epistemic violence inherent in these knowledges which "authorizes thinking about Others in ways that enables political and economic violence to be enacted on the bodies of subject men and especially women"' (Prinsloo 2016:165, citing Pillay 2015). Decolonisation thus involves the rejection of Western university ideals in which Eurocentric epistemologies that are embedded within African universities will need to be unravelled.

For Prinsloo (2016), decolonisation in university spaces requires questioning the underlying assumptions, norms and dominant discourses that inform the practices, aims and objectives of higher education in Africa. Assié-Lumumba (2016) similarly suggests that education in Africa needs to be designed by Africans, who would presumably take into account the relevant social, political and economic circumstances. Ochwa-Echel (2013) lists HIV/AIDS, perennial drought, debt and human rights abuses, especially by the political elites, as the immediate challenges that African higher education should address from a decolonisation perspective.

Conclusion and recommendations for future research

Let us reflect on some of the misconceptions surrounding decolonisation as a way of foregrounding the place of decolonisation in critical theory. We focus on the charges that decolonisation is imbued with violence, involves certain assumed binaries and seeks the erasure of universal forms of knowledge. By counteracting these narratives, we also attempt to propose why the decolonisation project ought to be given legitimacy.

Is decolonisation synonymous with violence?

Given the historical circumstances of struggle under colonialism in Africa, there is always a misconception about the instrumental value of violence in the process of decolonisation. Political philosophers such as Fanon saw violence as an indispensable instrument in the total liberation (decolonisation) of the colonised people (Hwami 2016). In the struggle for African political independence, armed military action or rebellion was put in place to confront an unjust and oppressive system. The enemy to be destroyed was the white colonisers, as well as every value that they represented. Insofar as violence achieved the desired goal of political decolonisation, it was canonised as an effective method, and as the 'only' language that an oppressor could understand or at least with which the oppressor could be forced to the negotiating table.

Apparently the canonisation of violence is still embedded in African social and political institutions. The militant approach to protests, as can be traced in the #RhodesMustFall and #FeesMustFall movements in South Africa, and the land invasions in Zimbabwe and parts of South Africa, all seem to place violence within the decolonisation project, although the acts of violence themselves are momentary and not representative of the core arguments in the movements. Unintentionally, such action may lead to a vicious cycle of violence, where some people and their value systems are dethroned and replaced by others who could be even more ruthless.

We suggest that employing decolonisation as a critical theory within higher education in Africa could instil an academic approach to social issues characterised by a robust exchange of ideas. Despite Africa's many instances of social and political strife, from a decolonisation perspective higher education can champion new ideas of coexistence, tolerance of social diversity and the general upliftment of Africans.

On decolonisation as a binary of dominators and subordinates

The discourse on decolonisation begs the question of the rightful agents of decolonisation. Who are the correct 'owners' of the struggle? Who should champion the cause? To the extent that decolonisation is contested terrain, we consider these questions to be very important in the process of outlining the discourse. The significance of these questions becomes apparent when consideration is given to the historical and contemporary fact that decolonisation appears to be a contestation between races, and thus, in the context of Africa, between the white and black populations. There is a perception that white learners and white educators in particular cannot or should not participate in dialogues of decolonisation, since they continue to represent the interests of yesterday's enemies. The narrative seems to suggest that black people are the rightful actors and agents of decolonisation, while white people embody the remnants of colonialism.

At times in this context we encounter insinuations that, while white people may present commentary, they should not research and write on issues such as ubuntu, or anything related to African philosophy, in a way that positions them within these worldviews. Such narrative squarely places the black person as the rightful owner of what being African means. We once attended a symposium on decolonisation in which some black learners explicitly expressed their reservations about the presence of white educators and learners. One participant clearly articulated his objections by noting that 'you cannot plot the downfall of your enemies in their presence'. We contend that decolonisation framed in racial markers is misdirected and does not take into account the current social composition of Africa. Thus, a key function of decolonisation from a critical theory perspective within higher education in Africa is to combat social ills such as racism and tribalism.

On decolonisation misunderstood as a quest for particularisation of knowledge

Decolonisation is often accused of being designed for the particularisation of knowledge in the context of African universities. Horsthemke (2009:4, citing Ekong & Cloete 1997:11, Ntuli 2004, Masehela 2004) dismisses the notion of 'tak[ing] culture and identity to be the "central determinants of which knowledge to get into the curriculum"'. Furthermore, contentious questions such as 'Who is an African?' and 'What does it mean to be regarded as an African?' are all raised in the debates concerning the decolonisation of knowledge systems. In response to such misconceptions, we argue that colonialism resulted in hierarchies of knowledge systems and continues to determine whose ideas are dominant in academic discourses in Africa. A cursory glance at the reference lists of master's and PhD theses produced in Africa uncovers the fact that few African scholars are cited. This raises questions about whose epistemologies, theoretical frameworks and methodologies are employed.

While we acknowledge that African scholarship is comparatively lower than that of Europe and the USA, the dominance of Western epistemologies at universities is, from a critical theory perspective, highly problematic. While decolonisation does not imply getting rid of anything associated with European civilisation, systems of knowledge and colonial languages, decolonisation cannot work if we do not institute a process in which common humanity is recognised, acknowledged and affirmed. The disruption of hierarchies of knowledge systems and the dominance of Western epistemologies is essential.

References

Albury NJ. 2015. Objectives at the crossroads: Critical theory and self-determination in indigenous language revitalization. *Critical Inquiry in Language Studies*, 12(4): 256–282.

Assié-Lumumba NT. 2016. Evolving African attitudes to European education: Resistance, pervert effects of the single system paradox, and the *ubuntu* framework for renewal. *International Review of Education*, 62(1):11–27.

Barnsley I & Bleiker R. 2008. Self-determination: From decolonization to deterritorialization. *Global Change Peace and Security*, 20(2):121–136.

Bohman J. 2012. Critical theory, republicanism, and the priority of injustice: Transnational republicanism as a nonideal theory. *Journal of Social Philosophy*, 43(2):97–112.

Brookfield SD. 2005. *The Power of Critical Theory: Liberating Adult Learning and Teaching.* San Francisco: Jossey-Bass.

Ciccariello-Maher G. 2014. Decolonial realism: Ethics, politics and dialectics in Fanon and Dussel. *Contemporary Political Theory*, 13(1):2–22.

Craggs R. 2014. Postcolonial geographies, decolonization, and the performance of geopolitics at Commonwealth conferences. *Singapore Journal of Tropical Geography*, 35(1):39–55.

Creswell JW. 2014. *Research Design: Qualitative, Quantitative, and Mixed Methods Approaches.* Los Angeles: Sage.

Dryzek JS. 1987. Discursive designs: Critical theory and political institutions. *American Journal of Political Science*, 31(3):656–679.

Freeman M & Vasconcelos EFS. 2010. Critical social theory: Core tenets, inherent issues. *New Directions for Evaluation*, 127:7–19.

Habermas J. 1985. *The Theory of Communicative Action.* Volume 2: *Lifeworld and System: A Critique of Functionalist Reason.* Translated by T McCarthy. Boston: Beacon.

Habermas J. 1990. Discourse ethics: Notes on a program of philosophical justification. In J Habermas. *Moral Consciousness and Communicative Action.* Translated by C Lenhardt & S Weber Nicholsen. Cambridge: The MIT Press. 43–115.

Hebie M. 2015. Was there something missing in the decolonization process in Africa?: The territorial dimension. *Leiden Journal of International Law*, 28(3):529–556.

Higgs P. 2012. African philosophy and the decolonisation of education in Africa: Some critical reflections. *Educational Philosophy and Theory*, 44(s2):37–57.

Horkheimer M. 2002. Traditional and critical theory [1937]. In M O'Connell. (ed). *Critical Theory: Selected Essays.* New York: Continuum. 188–243.

Horsthemke K. 2009. The South African higher education transformation debate: Culture, identity and 'African ways of knowing'. *London Review of Education*, 7(1):3–15.

Hwami M. 2016. Frantz Fanon and the problematic of decolonization: Perspectives on Zimbabwe. *African Identities*, 14(1):19–37.

Ivkovic M. 2014. Two attempts at grounding social critique in 'ordinary' actors' perspective: The critical theories of Nancy Fraser and Alex Honneth. *Filozofija i Društvo*, 25(3): 29–50.

Jacobs AHM. 2014. Critical hermeneutics and higher education: A perspective on texts, meaning and institutional culture. *South African Journal of Philosophy*, 33(3):297–310.

Kellner D. 1990. Critical theory and the crisis of social theory. *Sociological Perspectives*, 33(1):11–33.

Leonard P & McLaren P. (eds). 1993. *Paulo Freire: A Critical Encounter.* London: Routledge.

Linklater A. 2007. *Critical Theory and World Politics: Citizenship, Sovereignty and Humanity.* Oxfordshire: Routledge.

Mamdani M. 2016. Between the public intellectual and the scholar: Decolonization and some post-independence initiatives in African higher education. *Inter-Asia Cultural Studies*, 17(1):68–83.

McKernan JA. 2013. The origins of critical theory in education: Fabian socialism as social reconstructionism in nineteenth-century Britain. *British Journal of Educational Studies*, 61(4):417–433.

Morreira S. 2015. Steps towards decolonial higher education in southern Africa? Epistemic disobedience in the humanities. *Journal of Asian and African Studies*, 1–15.

Ochwa-Echel JR. 2013. Neoliberalism and university education in sub-Saharan Africa. *SAGE Open*, July–September:1–8.

Pepinsky TB. 2015. Trade competition and American decolonization. *World Politics*, 67(3):387–422.

Prinsloo EH. 2016. The role of the humanities in decolonising the academy. *Arts & Humanities in Higher Education*, 15(1):164–168.

Rasmussen ML. 2015. 'Cruel optimism' and contemporary Australian critical theory in educational research. *Educational Philosophy and Theory*, 47(2):192–206.

Roach SC. (ed). 2008. *Critical Theory and International Relations: A Reader*. New York and Abingdon: Routledge.

Shockley KG & Frederick RM. 2010. Constructs and dimensions of Afrocentric education. *Journal of Black Studies*, 40(6):1212–1233.

Sinnerbrink R. 2012. Critical theory as disclosing critique: A response to Kompridis. *Constellations*, 19(3):369–383.

Watson SL & Watson WR. 2011. Critical, emancipatory, and pluralistic research for education: A review of critical systems theory. *Journal of Thought*, 46(3/4):63.

Realism and education:

A philosophical examination of the 'realness' of the university

Søren Bengtsen and Ronald Barnett

Introduction

Over the last 50 years or so, the philosophy of education has developed into a substantial field in its own right, with a global reach. However, for the most part we find the field to be ontologically rather thin, having tended to focus on the excavation of concepts, especially in the hands of major philosophers, and to avoid considerations of education in its more realist moments. If we are right, this is grave neglect, since education has its place, ontologically, in the world as a social institution, and has aspects that are independent of human conceptualisations. Consequently, a philosophy of education that lacks a realist dimension would undersell its emancipatory possibilities.

This chapter, then, challenges understandings of the university as being primarily a socio-cultural and socio-political institution. We argue against post-structural reductions of the university to being an institution that can in essence be moulded according to the demands of the market, wider national and regional economic interests and social politics. Such approaches, we claim, have a much too narrow conception of how a university is real, or really is. Even though the university is occupied with state socio-political agendas and initiatives, its realness extends far beyond immediate institutional and national policies.

In this chapter, we seek to assist in redressing this general situation by bringing out some of that potential – of a realist approach to the philosophy of education – and we do so by focusing on the university and on higher education. The fundamental point of the chapter, and the potential for future higher education, lies in an ontological rethinking of the university and its implications for being and learning. By exploring the ontology of the university, we argue, the ontological nature of not only being but also learning becomes evident. We aim to show that when an understanding of the university is informed by contemporary realist philosophies, it has weighty implications for higher education. Drawing on Harman's (2002, 2005) and Bhaskar's (2008) avowedly realist philosophies, we show that a widened understanding of the ontology of the university reveals that higher education is not just tied to present state socio-political and socio-economic interests, but is also embedded in even deeper and more strange and unsettling ontological layers. This, we go on to argue in a thesis of our own, makes higher education depend on three often overlooked parameters for learning: the unknown, the impure and the imaginative strands of higher education reality.

New realisms: A point of departure

Today, the terms 'realism' and 'the real' are being explored anew in many ways. During the last decade various strands of realism have emerged, united in the task of reclaiming what Shaviro (2014) calls 'the universe of things', involving the attempt to rebel against the claimed anthropocentrism found in most philosophies after Kant, the disavowal of relativism and the apparent cul-de-sac of much of postmodernism, and the resistance of the venture – in the so-called 'Anthropocene' (which some see as the current geological age) – of understanding the world in purely human terms and judging the nature of things and events merely on the basis of what they mean to us as human beings. Terms have recently emerged such as 'continental realism' (Ennis 2011), 'new realism' (Ferraris 2014), 'positive realism' (Ferraris 2015) and even 'realist magic' (Morton 2013), together with the notorious movement of 'speculative realism' (Bryant, Srnicek & Harman 2011; Gratton 2014; Harman 2010). These forms of realism have fostered differing forms of ontological philosophies, such as Bennett's *Vibrant Matter: A Political Ecology of Things* (2010), Bogost's *Alien Phenomenology – Or What It's Like to Be a Thing* (2012) and Bryant's *The Democracy of Objects* (2011) and *Onto-Cartography: An Ontology of Machines and Media* (2014).

Two contemporary approaches to realism seem to stand out. One is that of the American philosopher Graham Harman (1968–), who disturbed the waters with his early books *Tool-Being: Heidegger and the Metaphysics of Objects* (2002) and *Guerrilla Metaphysics: Phenomenology and the Carpentry of Things* (2005). Harman (2002, 2005) encourages in us a sensualism that delights in seeing new kinds of strangeness in familiar entities or activities. The other realist approach, already becoming influential in educational research, is that of Roy Bhaskar (1944–2014), whose efforts to re-establish an ontological basis for philosophy stretched over nearly 40 years. Bhaskar (2008) points to deep ontological layers that not only may not coincide with our perceptions of the world, but which may have profound effects on the ways in which we are in the world. There are yet other 'realisms', but we cannot go deeply into them here. We focus on Harman's and Bhaskar's philosophies of the real as being particularly significant representatives of the genre. The generic aim in all of these forms of realism, which have many points of disagreement between them, is philosophically to delve into the realness of entities standing independently of human perception and cognition.

So as to give this chapter focus within the very broad field of education, we shall look especially at the university. And we suggest that in order to understand the university and its claims of validated knowledge seriously, the university should be critically explored and discussed in the context of the new philosophical realisms. This way, urgent philosophical questions arise concerning the 'realness' of the university and higher education: What is the university? Is the university real, or is it an ideological construction? (And does this make it any less real?)

Or is it a socio-political imagination, or utopia? Fundamentally, we interpret the 'real' perspective as an interest in the intersection between different planes of being, which we see as opening possibilities for new understandings of the university.

Critical realism and criticality in higher education

Criticality has long been a favoured theme in Western philosophy, conjuring a concern with valid reason and right knowing. In other words, criticality has been understood as an epistemological concept.

Moving beyond the lifeworlds of human beings

In the work of Bhaskar, however, the idea of criticality shifts from epistemology to ontology. Bhaskar (2008:49, 58ff) identifies three ontological domains – the empirical, the actual and the real (see further below) – which he aligns with 'generative mechanisms' that have 'causal' properties. In contrast to post-structuralist versions of the real, critical realism points to the need to locate ontologies outside the socio-cultural realm. For Bhaskar (2008), critical realism lays bare a much more varied, but also alien, form of ontology, in which large parts of what is real may never relate to the lifeworlds of human beings, although they may still be exerting their powers.

Bhaskar (2008:44) challenges what he describes as the 'strong anthropocentric current in classical and subsequent philosophy', a current which has sought 'to rephrase questions about the world as questions about the nature and behaviour of men'. Essentially, he wants us to disconnect from the radical and 'barely concealed anthropomorphism' of social constructivism (Bhaskar 2008:16), where the world is understood as a socio-cultural projection. Bhaskar (2008:17) calls this the 'transitive dimension', where the object of knowledge is being determined through the shape of socio-material knowledge production. In fact, Bhaskar (2008:17) argues, it is the other way around. It is the 'intransitive dimension', namely 'the real structure or mechanism that exists [which] acts quite independently of men and the conditions which allow men access to it' (Bhaskar 2008:17). This 'independence approach' saves ontology from becoming absorbed into the socio-cultural workings of power as often presented in postmodern theories.

According to Bhaskar (2008:116), science exists because the world is ontologically structured in a way that invites scientific discovery. He explains: '[I]t is because the world is open that science, whether or not (and for how long) it actually occurs, is possible' (Bhaskar 2008:116). For the sake of the argument here, we shall substitute Bhaskar's term 'science' with the term 'higher education'. Higher education is a response, a reaction, to the deep structures of the world and not merely a world-constructing activity. This may be seen when, for example, the reality of events in the practice of schools, hospitals or social welfare works, over time, to influence and even change the learning goals and preferred methods of study in higher education programmes, as new enactments of pedagogy, care and social service suddenly emerge from depths unfathomable to traditional understandings of these areas of work. Or when a highly idiosyncratic and untraditional reading and analysis of a canon work in English literature emerges in response to deeper ontological layers within the text and context of study. Thus, deep changes in the literary world may alter the way we see our cultural heritage and engage with classical texts.

Transcendental realism and higher education

The epistemological endeavour of higher education is creative and critical at its core because it is responding to a multilayered reality that demands and invites such ingenious methods. This way, our knowledge is based on what Bhaskar (2008:56) calls 'transcendental realism'. As mentioned, Bhaskar (2008:58ff) distinguishes between three main ontological domains, namely:

1. the *empirical*, including the experiences and perceptions of individuals and groups of, for example, educators and learners within higher education
2. the *actual*, including events in which the forces of things act in union to manifest various natural, social and political phenomena that may or may not be observed
3. the *real*, including mechanisms beyond our grasp – the deep inner workings of the forces of things.

These three ontological domains sometimes overlap. As Bhaskar (2008:49) points out: '[G]enerative mechanisms [within the domain of the real] endure even when inactive and act even where [...] there is no one-to-one relationship between [these mechanisms] and the particular sequence of events that occurs'. Drawing on Bhaskar (2008), we emphasise that through the activity of higher education, learners and educators are linked to the various levels of the real, and that even though some levels are beyond our grasp they are not unknowable in principle. In this way, Bhaskar (2008) presents an understanding of academic activity that positions epistemology alongside ontology, and we suggest epistemology as being 'ontologically sensitive'.

This flips the traditional understanding around. For instance, it is not only through changing the higher education curriculum that we change our understandings of what universities are. On the contrary, it is because universities sometimes reveal hidden and deep layers of reality that higher education changes. As Bhaskar (2008:47) explains: 'The world consists of mechanisms not events. Such mechanisms combine to generate the flux of phenomena that constitute the actual states and happenings of the world. They may be said to be real, though it is rarely that they are actually manifest and rarer still that they are empirically identified by men'.

Thus, Bhaskar draws out an entire ontological realm extending beyond the realm of the human and human beings. He elaborates that these mechanisms:

> *are quite independent of men – as thinkers, causal agents and perceivers. They are not unknowable, although knowledge of them depends upon a rare blending of intellectual, practico-technical and perceptual skills. They are not artificial constructs. But neither are they Platonic forms. For they can become manifest to men in experience.* (Bhaskar 2008:47)

Thus, the generative mechanisms may be unknown, but they are not unknowable per se. At the deep level they might or might not intersect with our reality. In the field of higher education, and in the university, we give these mechanisms names such as 'globalisation', 'neoliberalism', 'cognitive capitalism' and 'marketisation'. Such large and global forces cannot be immediately seen nor straightforwardly examined – their form and their features remain hazy and can only be speculated upon. The names we use are simply cyphers, literary efforts to refer to features in the world that are largely hidden from the immediate gaze, but which here have genuine and indeed massive effects. We might even say that global university rankings were originally epistemological in offering understandings and interpretations of universities, but have now acquired ontological status, having attained an independence and acting with causal powers on universities and their peoples (often without their knowledge).

Significantly, knowledge activity, or epistemology, becomes critical and creative because of, and as a response to, the deep, multilayered and open ontology in which it is embedded. In this way, we suggest, critical realism prompts a critical ontology and a critical epistemology, inextricably linked. The ontology is critical in its pluralism. Several ontological realms co-exist, but without merging into a whole, and holistic, monism (the theory that denies the existence of a distinction in a particular sphere). Higher education practice has to be critical because it is responsive to an ontology, which is ever changing, opening itself up to us and sometimes withdrawing from our grasp. The implications for higher education are far-ranging indeed.

In this way the notion of criticality, often celebrated as the mark of good academic practice and scholarship, holds a much deeper and alien meaning. It is a response to a deep and hidden reality of the university that adds to the higher education curriculum of today. It asks strange and unsettling questions for critical thinking: Is there more to the pedagogical situation than higher education? What may lie hidden in the world beyond the scope of educational programmes and approved curricula? What more is there to be learned other than what programme designers and even political and intellectual leaders want learners to learn?

The deep structures of the university

We suggest that Bhaskar's (2008) three domains of the real may be usefully transferred to an understanding of the realness of the university, for Bhaskar's (2008) theory of science may be extended to a philosophical analysis of higher education: The *domain of the empirical* and the experience of the university may be seen within higher education in the daily teaching and learning experiences of educators and learners. In this domain, the university is experienced as being real in the unfolding of higher education arenas and activities, be they in the classroom, in the library, in the cafeteria, at the examination session or through laborious research work carried out alone, behind the closed doors of the office or the laboratory.

Furthermore, the *domain of the actual* becomes present in the events that surround and condition the daily experiences of higher education teaching and learning. The domain of the actual is enacted by the national policies and international and global drivers that influence higher education leadership and institutional practice. These 'patterns of events' (Bhaskar 2008:14) influence the domain of the empirical, as discussed by Barnett (1994, 2000), Canaan and Shumar (2010), Readings (1996) and Shumar (1997) in their studies on how social discourse and national policy influence higher education practice at an institutional level as well as at the level of learning and teaching practice.

However, the 'enduring powers of things' (Bhaskar 2008:164), or of the university in this analogy, also play out within the *domain of the real*. In this domain higher education practice links to a deeper ontological level, or 'deep structures' in Bhaskar's (2008:110) terminology. In this perspective, and because of the deep structures of the reality of the university, higher education is not only something we experience and enact as individuals and groups (the domain of the empirical) or something that is being framed and conditioned by policies and socio-political drivers (the domain of the actual); it is also very much something that unfolds partly beyond our comprehension in the deep structures of the university itself. These deep structures have real effects and play themselves out in institutional and personal stress in university life.

More optimistically, higher education today has the potential to explore aspects of the reality of the university that at first glance may seem very odd, but may hold potential for learning unparalleled in our present-day curricula. For example, it can be considered to what degree formation in higher education should include maturation of the soul and spiritual growth, as it did in medieval universities. Higher education could also be seen as an open-ended task, extending beyond the obtainment of a degree, instead being a place (world) to be entered several times during a lifetime or a career, when needed, for reasons other than gaining a qualification. Such aspects of learning and formation may seem difficult to align with contemporary demands of direct transfer between knowledge and material production and financial gain. But education may be said to be real in many ways that are not necessarily actualised in society today.

Within the domain of the real, higher education should thus be considered an ontological feature of the world unfolding the university's deep structures, as also alluded to by Barnett (2016:26) in his foregrounding of the 'presence of "generative mechanisms" [...] embedded in the deep layers beneath and within the university'. At this deep structured level of the university, higher education could be described as 'depth rationality' (Bhaskar 2008:107ff). As Bhaskar (2011:113) comments: 'The object of the depth-investigation is emancipation. [...] Now if the emancipation is to be *of* the human species, then the powers of the emancipated human being and community must already exist (although perhaps only as powers to acquire or develop powers) in an unactualized state'.

At this deep level of the real, the project of a philosophy of higher education as emancipation should be seen not only as a contingent socio-political power struggle, but also as an ontological enterprise. Ontologically, emancipation cannot be obtained through higher education unless this educational practice moves beyond the present-day ideas of emancipation accessible in political discourses and in society more generally. It does not mean that the deep academic 'stratum of reality' is more or less real than other 'strata' (Bhaskar 2008:169). It does mean that the higher education practice of searching for the deep structures of the university is real and not reducible to socio-cultural constructs (even though these are also real, but unfold within other domains).

Recently interest has grown in the ontological aspects of learners and their learning, especially their personal and existential experience within higher education, evident for example in Batchelor's (2008, 2014) work on the ontological dimension of learner voice, and in Barnett's (2004, 2007) and Hansen's (2010) work on the ontological levels of teaching and learning in higher education. Also, there has been a renewed focus on the domain of the actual seen in the discussions concerning academic virtues and citizenship (Macfarlane 2007; Nixon 2008; Watson 2014) and the new public good of the university (Filippakou & Williams 2015), and in debates on how policies and organisational structures influence the higher education system (Gibbs & Barnett 2014; Gibbs et al 2015). However, only a few have engaged with the domain of the real in relation to universities and delved into the deep structures of the university's realness (Barnett 2011, 2016; Bengtsen & Barnett 2017). Based on Bhaskar's (2008) domain of the real, we suggest that a renewed discussion of deeper and more alien layers of the university should take place, and should consider what an ontological acknowledgement of such layers may imply for higher education practice and curriculum design.

Speculative realism and the need for speculation in higher education

Today, speculative realism and kindred realisms cover the work of several philosophers. In this section, we base our discussion on Harman (2002, 2005, 2010, 2013).

Guerrilla realism

In Harman's speculative realism, we find a different, but in other ways also strikingly similar, kind of realism to that of Bhaskar (2008) – a point also argued in Bryant (2011:34ff) on the earlier philosophical influences on Harman's work. Harman (2010:182) himself foregrounds as well the influence and importance of Bhaskar's work on his own understanding of the real, and stresses that '[f]or Bhaskar [...] each emergent entity creates a new "real" at its own scale, and each of these reals belongs only to the entity in question rather than being partly shared in a continuum with all other things'.

To Harman (2010:183), Bhaskar is 'a philosopher of the much maligned "deep and hidden"', and he notes that for Bhaskar, 'the deep and hidden is speckled throughout every layer of our universe'. However, Harman's object-orientated ontology differs from that of Bhaskar in two ways. The first contrast is as follows: While Bhaskar's (2008) critical realism can be described as a structural ontology dealing with the levels and structures of the real, Harman's speculative realism is an aesthetic, sensual, 'carnal' (Harman 2005:76) and celebrative form of ontology, evoking the dramatic and mesmerising character of the world.

He may not be as focused on the sensual (and erotic) bodily imperatives that are to be found in the work of his former mentor Lingis (1998), but Harman (2002:238) is still orientated towards aesthetic-ontological phenomena such as the being of 'the life of every good sensualist who savors a night of amaretto and pearls, or every child who relishes the combat of plastic dinosaurs in a sandbox'. In contrast to Bhaskar, Harman's ontology holds within itself the 'aesthetic-ontological imperative' to enjoy the real. This 'guerilla realism' (Harman 2002:216), where the objects of the world and reality itself become vibrant and animated, is a reaction to the ontologically 'tiresome' and 'boring' philosophy of earlier realisms (Harman 2005:170, 2009:149 respectively), where tedious and dull thinking and writing styles deny the drama and energy of the world.

Harman's realism is not naïve or foolishly jubilant, but aesthetic and dramatic, perhaps even dramaturgic. These qualities, however, do not redeem humankind or hold within them an ethical imperative, because even though the 'world is filled with roulette tables, electrical grids, and the smell of freshly picked berries or buckets of ammonia', it is also the reality in which 'meteorites incinerate forests and gouge craters in villages near our homes' (Harman 2005:76). Sensuality, here, also includes an ontology of darker and more dangerous things, such as the realness of 'repulsive places' such as 'libertine dungeons, Nibelung underworlds, fields of chemical warfare, or outright slaughterhouses' (Harman 2005:141). If Bhaskar's (2008) ontological realism is printed in the metaphors of the combinations of biochemistry, quantum physics and geology, Harman's ontological realism is one of literature, film and mainstream popular culture.

Speculation in higher education

We come now to the second contrast between Harman's and Bhaskar's object-orientated ontologies. Where Bhaskar (2008) works with a deep-structured ontology, Harman (2010:180) works with a 'flat ontology' in which everything must be seen to be ontologically on the same footing. This is what Bryant (2011) calls the 'democracy of objects', according to which the most mundane and trivial object or event is just as real as the world's most fundamental structures. It is 'impossible to single out an elite cadre of substances', Harman (2005:85) explains, 'at the expense of all other entities. We find substances neither in the really, really tiny things, nor in the really, really natural things, nor in the really, really divine things. Substances are everywhere'. This relates to what he calls ontological 'sincerity' in which every object is 'obsessed' with being exactly what it is (Harman 2005:142, 139 respectively), just like platinum behaves 'as though it were obsessed with being platinum – which, of course, it is' (Harman 2008:139). This sincerity and obsession in each thing is what makes reality strange, because every object is, fundamentally, completely alien to other objects.

Here the term 'speculative' becomes central. According to Harman (2010), as philosophers we are obliged to strive for an understanding of alien phenomena. He stresses that by 'speculative', he means that 'none' of the speculative realist philosophies 'merely defend a dull and commonsense realism of genuine trees and billiard balls existing outside the mind, but a darker form of "weird realism" bearing little resemblance to the presuppositions of everyday life' (Harman 2010:2). 'Speculation in this sense,' Harman and his colleagues (Bryant et al 2011:3) elaborate, 'aims at something "beyond" the critical and linguistic turns [so constituting] a speculative wager on the possible returns from a renewed attention to reality itself.' Our epistemological endeavours, including philosophy and higher education teaching and learning, should aim at making use of a 'language appropriate to the strange layer of sensuous reality' (Harman 2005:45).

We exist, and think, constantly on the verge of what is alien and yet not necessarily beyond our daily lives. Harman (2005) evokes a lifeworld gone awry through its integration of the alien and the trivial – not unlike the experience often reported by learners of higher education and struggling educators. This disturbance and sometimes unsettling thought-upheaval should not be hastily dismissed as learners labouring to comprehend the standard curriculum, or as learners being unwilling to endure the demands of academic life. We argue that such academic struggle in learners and educators alike may arise because they acknowledge the deeper reality of the university: They acknowledge that the knowledge they build up may be only partially real. Much more troubling and strange forms of knowledge await in the deeper layers of the university's being, as for example when what should have been a course taken to improve a learner's understanding of elementary theories of learning changes the learner's conception of his or her educational project and leaves him or her to reconsider his or her career path, maybe even path in life. This may also occur when an advanced course in the political history of certain Western countries discloses a darker version of a country's actions, which may be difficult to reconcile and may lead to political activism.

When speculation, as a particular form of academic thinking, moves between the levels of the empirical, the actual and the real, it gains ontological power. When learners in their knowledge enquiry realise that what they experience in their higher education environment and specific disciplinary curriculum is connected to much wider socio-political and cultural movements and events, they move from the empirical level to the actual level. However, when they speculate, in Harman's (2010) sense of the word, they also begin to realise that their personal knowledge does not merely relate back to socio-political and cultural events and meanings, but also derives from much deeper ontological reservoirs within the university itself.

The real university: Unknown, impure and imaginative

We propose that the real university, the university within the domain of the real, can be disclosed through three deep structures of academic practice within higher education: the unknown, the impure and the imaginative. These forms of deep being, we believe, are ontological layers that influence higher education practice even without being acknowledged as doing so.

The unknown

As we have found with regard to Bhaskar's (2008) critical realism, the deep structures of the university are basically unknown (not least in their interactions), and because the deep level of higher education transcends our present-day socio-political concerns about the future of the university, as educators and learners within higher education we must also learn and teach for the unknown (Barnett 2004). We must integrate the domain of the real into our higher education practice in order to reach into the deeper structures of the university. As Barnett (2004:257) argues, '[a]t the heart of such a curriculum [for the unknown] will be an exposure to dilemmas and uncertainties'.

When we move into the deep structures of higher education reality, we realise that learning and teaching in higher education implies an 'ontological risk' (Barnett 2004:252) of our empirical and actual social selves and realities being disturbed and challenged. This may happen when learners realise that the university holds other avenues than sheer educational purposes. Exposure to alien forms of knowledge and unexpected, and sometimes unwanted, learning experiences may take place when learners and educators, perhaps unintentionally, engage with deeper structures of the reality of the university. For example, what should have been a rather formal and traditional series of lectures might turn into a succession of meetings between educator and learners in which they become personally and existentially exposed, as they lose themselves in the knowledge enquiry and critical debate. Or newly employed educators may discover that the liberal and tolerant institution they work for indirectly disfavours and marginalises working parents and young mothers in the planning and scheduling of their academic programmes.

Thus, higher education platforms within the university may sometimes seem to be surrounded by a vast sea of unknown, and maybe even darker (Bengtsen & Barnett 2017), structures of reality. As Bhaskar (2008) points out, the openness of the world demands a critical attitude towards it, which higher education can offer. However, this means that '[t]he openness of the pedagogical frames is not just epistemological but it is ontological in nature' and that 'a pedagogy for an unknown future becomes a pedagogy with the unknown built into it as living principles of educational exchanges and accomplishments' (Barnett 2004:258, 260).

Higher education practice, accordingly, is not or need not merely be about reproducing familiar and politically validated forms of knowledge that might be applied in a given social context. At the level of the deep structuring mechanisms, higher education responds to the openness of the world – it does not only produce reality, it responds to reality and may even attempt to modify it. This may happen when the learning processes of learners take on ontological form, when their learning transforms from an epistemologically and educationally vivid and applicable learning process to an ontological upheaval of world and thought. For example, they may discover that what they have held to be unquestionable truths about the physical or social reality of which they are part are in fact rough, lumped-together generalisations that help to maintain a common sense understanding of a phenomenon or events in the world, but are also reductionist and somewhat misleading. Or they may start speculating about dimensions of their disciplinary field, be it physics, theology or economy, that let them see into strata of their own social, political and cultural worlds in new ways, but which may also lay bare new ontological aspects.

The impure

From Bhaskar's (2008) and Harman's (2002, 2005) realisms, we may consider the element of growth and personal development in higher education. Emancipation through knowledge work and intellectual-existential efforts does not hinge on contemplative meditation alone, but is filled with challenging encounters of the social and personal reality. An example of this is given by Gibbs et al (2015) in their discussion of the many-sided and kaleidoscopic meaning of the element of time in higher education, and how our personal experiences with temporality and our individual and institutional 'relationship to time [within higher education] is thus crucial in how we conceive our activities and our responsibility for them' (Ylijoki 2015:106). After all, learners need to become adept at living in multiple timeframes all at once – in the immediate present, in the examinations to come and in the future as career plans are laid.

In a similar vein, Rømer, Tanggaard and Brinkmann (2011) argue that pedagogy at the deepest level is always an 'impure pedagogy'. When engaging with the unknown, higher education practice becomes impure because '[a] bit bleakly put you may say that no guarantees are given when you enter higher education. Just as it does not guarantee any happy ending' (Bengtsen 2014:81, our translation). The real forces at work are such that bringing a new kind of university or even a new kind of teaching and learning into being is threatened by the unforeseen, and is necessarily a set of negotiations and even compromises. Contrary to the usual expectation, our argument is that 'education is not necessarily a ticket to a more advanced or sophisticated level of knowledge and insight' (Bengtsen 2014:81, our translation). Instead of leading to a sense of personal and social clarification and growth, education 'may just as well lead through the door to a pancake house [a witch's hut], which is not necessarily a pleasant place to be, when the early phase of enchantment has subsided' (Bengtsen 2014:81, our translation; see also Bengtsen & Barnett 2017).

Attempting seriously to acknowledge the deep and real nature of the university is not a matter to engage in lightly. There is the attendant pedagogical responsibility, as an impure pedagogy for higher education advises us, of educators not to turn away from learners having a difficult time, but to stay with them through 'the dirt and the waste' (Bengtsen 2014:83, our translation) of their learning processes, where it is not pleasant to be, but where the heart of the matter often lies. To understand why learners fail to complete their higher education programmes, it is 'necessary to let this understanding emerge from within the learner's withdrawal process and powerlessness itself, in order to be able to better and more efficiently detect similar challenges in the future' (Bengtsen 2014:83, our translation).

When engaging ontologically with understanding and practices we have a 'drunken alchemy' (Harman 2005:170), an intellectual power that is not easy to control and use for our own benefit. Emancipation, in our sense of the term, should be understood in an impure form. It implies not just that we become free, but also that we become submerged within the deeper levels of reality as well as ready to engage with the real at every layer and in all forms of strangeness. As Harman (2005:141) disturbingly points out, academic freedom itself 'is never an absolute good, and is often a troubling void filled with addiction, hopelessness, confusion, or fantasies of triumph and revenge'. Higher education is thus none other than a space in which we encounter and live with impurity.

The imaginative

Based on Harman's (2010) understanding of speculation, we endorse the importance of imagination in higher education. Because the deepest levels of higher education are fundamentally unknown though not unknowable, and because higher education practice at the deep level is impure, we practitioners must be imaginative in order to make contact with these deep structures of the real university. We must meet with 'a deeper ontological substrate' of higher education through the use of imagination, because '[t]he imagination has a power to see into things, to feel into things, to be at one with things anew, so as to produce a new understanding of the object of the imagination' (Barnett 2013:53, 25 respectively). It is difficult to articulate such deep imagination; it must 'leap out, [and] leap beyond the familiar and redescribe it in strange terms' (Barnett 2013:15).

Within the domain of the real, such a form of the imagination transcends the ideological thinking in the domain of the actual. Seen in this way, higher education is not only under the imperatives of social policy made visible in, for example, entrepreneurially orientated knowledge production, but it must also heed the slower and more far-sighted orientation where its deep imagination 'may be transformed and sedimented over time (perhaps decades) into collective imaginaries' (Barnett 2013:15).

This is not to argue against ideology understood as constructive and positive socio-political strategies for higher education, but to argue for 'speciological' (our term, derived from 'speculation') agendas for higher education practice. Where ideological higher education planning is goal-orientated, and socially, morally and economically motivated, speciological planning is void of clear and immediate goals, and may have no visible or direct links to either social relevance, moral custom or financial benefit. Speciological planning, however, is orientated to learning phenomena on the fringes of what we may even consider worth knowing and knowing about from where we stand presently. The term 'speciological' is closely related to Barnett's (2013:160) notion of 'hopeful fictions' within higher education, meaning strategies that may never be fully achieved, but that are 'nevertheless invested with hope, energising the university in the direction of desirable journeys'.

Papastephanou (2014:31) adds another dimension – an ethical one – commenting that '[w]ithout losing their distinctiveness, ontology, epistemology and ethics find a unity as parts of an inextricable whole whose synergy is indispensable to re-thinking academia'. Such re-thinking includes reclaiming the space and pausing for deep thought and reasoning. Papastephanou (2014:34) underlines the importance of the 'ethical imagination' and its immunity to 'anti-utopian [and ideological] attacks'.

Through the imagination, the ontological and epistemological dimensions of higher education are interwoven, and the intellectual activity of higher education teaching and learning becomes an engagement not only with knowledge but also with reality itself. This certainly challenges the understanding of universities as institutions for higher education that feed almost directly into the production apparatus and employment market of our present societies and cultures. This is not to say that universities should not do that. But if imperatives about imagination and speculation are woven into the curriculum, the learning moves beyond 'merely' educational purposes, and becomes a transformation of the real, and of our personal and social realities, but also realities that lie within the institution itself.

Conclusion and recommendations for future research

Based on these philosophical reflections from the perspective of realism, we conclude that the university today is more real than presumed, more powerful in its own right than expected and, hence, more important than has been understood until now. The university is *more real* than presumed since it is grounded in generative mechanisms, deep structures and strata that we have argued constitute the 'real' domain of the university, a domain that is usually downplayed in today's debates. The university is *more powerful* in its own right because of the powers of the deep structures and the ontological engagement that emerges in their wake. This, however, does not make it any easier to be a member of higher education practice, as this domain may be seen to be of an impure and troublesome nature. The university is *more important* than hitherto understood because of the speculative and imaginative powers that can be turned upon it, and because it is possible for us to be speculative and imaginative about the university as a real institution. In turn, in part because of its strong and unmatched imaginative powers, the university occupies a privileged position.

The real(ism) of higher education must in this way become a speculative realism, a form of realism that pulls thinking into the unknown. Thinking here is not a mere mental construction but a movement of criticality within being. The realness of the university consists in the fact that it challenges its own reality – not by losing or risking it, but by using it as a way of coming into contact with what is beyond its own, presently conceived, reality. Recognising the presence of a deep reality may offer a way of meeting with what is external to our currently conceived reality of the university. However, such an encounter may move beyond what we presently define as higher education. Expanding and transforming how we conceive of the ontology of the university does not substitute or in any other way do away with a contemporary higher education curriculum, but it may surpass such a curriculum and thus also challenge traditional understandings of teaching and learning.

At work here are a social ontology and a social epistemology. Both are widening, and each influences the other – ideas of the university influence its being in the world, *and* changes to the university's social ontology affect ways in which we think about the university. These reflections lead to a renewed discussion about how the real university is the practice not only of epistemology but also of ontology. This double practice even introduces the prospect of an emancipation of the real university. There is surely much here for future scholarship on learning, and on being a learner in higher education.

References

Barnett R. 1994. *The Limits of Competence. Knowledge, Higher Education, and Society.* Buckingham: The Society for Research into Higher Education and Open University Press.

Barnett R. 2000. *Realizing the University – in an Age of Supercomplexity.* Buckingham: Open University Press.

Barnett R. 2004. Learning for an unknown future. *Higher Education Research & Development,* 23(3):247–260.

Barnett R. 2007. *A Will to Learn. Being a Student in an Age of Uncertainty.* Berkshire: Open University Press.

Barnett R. 2011. *Being a University.* London and New York: Routledge.

Barnett R. 2013. *Imagining the University.* London and New York: Routledge.

Barnett R. 2016. *Understanding the University. Institution, Idea, Possibilities.* London and New York: Routledge.

Batchelor D. 2008. Have students got a voice? In R Barnett & R di Napoli. (eds). *Changing Identities in Higher Education. Voicing Perspectives.* London and New York: Routledge. 40–54.

Batchelor D. 2014. Finding a voice as a student. In P Gibbs & R Barnett. (eds). *Thinking about Higher Education.* Switzerland: Springer. 157–174.

Bengtsen S. 2014. *Dannelse i overflod: Om universitetspædagogikkens luksusproblem.* In L Tanggaard, T Rømer & S Brinkmann. (eds). *Uren Pædagogik 2.* Aarhus: Klim. 73–92.

Bengtsen S & Barnett R. 2017. Confronting the dark side of higher education. *Journal of Philosophy of Education,* 51:1. DOI: 10.1111/1467-9752.12190.

Bennett J. 2010. *Vibrant Matter: A Political Ecology of Things.* Durham and London: Duke University Press.

Bhaskar R. 2008. *A Realist Theory of Science.* London: Verso.

Bhaskar R. 2011. *Reclaiming Reality: A Critical Introduction to Contemporary Philosophy.* London and New York: Routledge.

Bogost I. 2012. *Alien Phenomenology – Or What It's Like to Be a Thing.* Minneapolis: University of Minnesota Press.

Bryant LR. 2011. *The Democracy of Objects.* London: Open Humanities Press.

Bryant LR. 2014. *Onto-Cartography: An Ontology of Machines and Media.* Edinburgh: Edinburgh University Press.

Bryant LR, Srnicek N & Harman G. 2011. *The Speculative Turn: Continental Materialism and Realism.* Victoria, Australia: Re.press.

Canaan JE & Shumar W. (eds). 2010. *Structure and Agency in the Neoliberal University.* New York and London: Routledge.

Ennis PJ. 2011. *Continental Realism.* Winchester and Washington: Zero Books.

Ferraris M. 2014. *Introduction to New Realism.* Translated by S de Sanctis. London and New York: Bloomsbury Academic.

Ferraris M. 2015. *Positive Realism.* Winchester and Washington: Zero Books.

Filippakou O & Williams G. (eds). 2015. *Higher Education as a Public Good. Critical Perspectives on Theory, Policy and Practice.* New York: Peter Lang.

Gibbs P & Barnett R. (eds). 2014. *Thinking about Higher Education.* Switzerland: Springer.

Gibbs P, Ylijoki O-H, Guzmán-Valenzuela C & Barnett R. 2015. *Universities in the Flux of Time: An Exploration of Time and Temporality in University Life.* London and New York: Routledge.

Gratton P. 2014. *Speculative Realism: Problems and Prospects.* London and New York: Bloomsbury Academic.

Hansen FT. 2010. The phenomenology of wonder in higher education. In M Brinkmann. (ed). *Erziehung. Phänomenologische Perspektiven.* Würzburg: Königshausen & Neumann. 161–177.

Harman G. 2002. *Tool-Being: Heidegger and the Metaphysics of Objects.* Chicago and La Salle: Open Court.

Harman G. 2005. *Guerrilla Metaphysics: Phenomenology and the Carpentry of Things.* Chicago and La Salle: Open Court.

Harman G. 2009. *Prince of Networks: Bruno Latour and Metaphysics.* Victoria, Australia: Re.press.

Harman G. 2010. *Towards Speculative Realism: Essays and Lectures.* Winchester and Washington: Zero Books.

Harman G. 2013. *Bells and Whistles: More Speculative Realism.* Winchester and Washington: Zero Books.

Lingis A. 1998. *The Imperative.* Bloomington: Indiana University Press.

Macfarlane B. 2007. *The Academic Citizen: The Virtue of Service in University Life.* London and New York: Routledge.

Morton T. 2013. *Realist Magic: Objects, Ontology, Causality.* London: Open Humanities Press.

Nixon J. 2008. *Towards the Virtuous University: The Moral Bases of Academic Practice.* New York and London: Routledge.

Papastephanou M. 2014. Higher education and ethical imagination. In P Gibbs & R Barnett. (eds). *Thinking about Higher Education.* Switzerland: Springer. 23–36.

Readings B. 1996. *The University in Ruins.* Harvard: Harvard University Press.

Rømer T, Tanggaard L & Brinkmann S. (eds). 2011. *Uren Pædagogik.* Aarhus: Klim.

Shaviro S. 2014. *The Universe of Things: On Speculative Realism.* Minneapolis and London: University of Minnesota Press.

Shumar W. 1997. *College for Sale: A Critique of the Commodification of Higher Education.* London and New York: Routledge Falmer.

Watson D. 2014. *The Question of Conscience: Higher Education and Personal Responsibility.* London: IOE Press.

Ylijoki O-H. 2015. Conquered by project time? In P Gibbs, O-H Ylijoki, C Guzmán-Valenzuela & R Barnett. (eds). *Universities in the Flux of Time: An Exploration of Time and Temporality in University Life.* London and New York: Routledge. 94–107.

Islam and education:
Towards a post-structuralist understanding of Islamic education

Yusef Waghid and Nuraan Davids

Introduction

Let us begin by raising an immediate concern often instigated by events in the Middle East: Education as practised in the Arab and Muslim world – in the sense of countries with dominant Muslim populations – is representative of Islam. Because many countries in the Arab and Muslim world seem to repress their communities, their education systems are presumed to be inherently dogmatic and opposed to diversity of thought and practice. In this chapter, we do not deny that several governments in the Arab and Muslim world are repressive, patriarchal and exclusive, as confirmed by the fairly recent revolts in the name of the 'Arab Spring'. But we are concerned with the claim that education in Islam is incommensurate with criticality, diversity and openness to the new and the unexpected. Instead, in this chapter, we suggest that education as informed by one of the primary sources of knowledge for Muslims – the Qur'an – is aligned with post-structuralist thinking.

Towards a continuum of minimalist and maximalist philosophy of Islamic education

We use the term 'philosophy of Islamic education' to indicate thought that constitutes Islamic education – that is, what makes this form of education what it is. In examining the concept, we find that Islamic education is connected to at least three important action words: *tarbiyyah* (socialisation), *ta'lim* (individualisation) and *ta'dib* (social activism) (Waghid 2011).

First, to *socialise* learners to an inherited body of knowledge, as articulated in the Qur'an (the Word of God) and the Hadith (messages that confirm the life experiences of Islam's last prophet, Prophet Muhammad), is to initiate them into what is familiar to generations of Muslims since the demise of their prophet. The Qur'an and Hadith have been subjected to (re)interpretations that culminated in several juristic, theological and ethical texts that have gained prominence in the Arab and Muslim world since Prophet Muhammad's death. Prominent jurists such as Imam al-Shafi'i (767–820 CE), Abu Hanifah (699–767 CE), Ahmad ibn Hanbal (780–855 CE) and Imam Malik (711–795 CE), together with the theologian Jalal al-Din al-Suyuti (1445–1505) and ethicist and prominent Muslim philosopher al-Ghazali (1056–1111), are among the Muslim luminaries whose scholarly works have indelibly inspired understandings of the primary sources.

The socialisation of Muslims to these sources of knowledge has often taken the path of memorisation, especially of the Qur'an and several Hadith texts. In addition, understandings of these sources have also been along the line of Muslim sectarianism, of which Sunnism and Shi'ism are the most dominant sects. Sunnis represent the majority of Muslims, while the minority are Shi'is. Shi'is claim that following the Prophet's demise, the Islamic caliphate should have been assigned to Caliph Ali first, because he was a member of the Prophet's household, having been married to the Prophet's daughter Fatimah. But the majority of Sunni Muslims claim that Abubakr, Umar and Uthman had rightfully assumed the leadership of the caliphate, respectively, after the Prophet Muhammad and that Ali was instead fourth in line for the caliphate. This kind of political and religious sectarianism is still rife today, as is evident in the ongoing conflict between supporters of Shi'i-dominated Iran and those of Sunni-orientated Iraq.

Nevertheless, the sectarianism between the Sunnis and the Shi'is has mistakenly been considered as a justification for conflict, whereas, following the Qur'an, sectarianism is no reason for marginalisation and exclusion. It is instead a reason for diversity of knowledge, as aptly stated in the Qur'an (al-Hujurāt 49:13): 'I [God] have created you in tribes and nations in order that you know one another'. When people present their particular understandings and knowledge(s) in their encounters with one another, they do so in order to engage with one another. The basis of the engagement is 'to know one another', and so differences and sectarianism cannot be presumed to justify religious exclusion. It follows that socialisation (tarbiyyah) involves initiating Muslims into familiar understandings and differences about knowledge in relation to the primary sources of Islamic education.

Secondly, individualisation (ta'lim) is based on an understanding that Muslims who have been socialised to knowledge of the Islamic primary sources are encouraged to ask questions and reflect on their learning. As the Qur'an (al-Nahl 16:44) states, 'And we have revealed to you the message so that you make it clear to people and that they may give thought.' This is a plain indication that uncritical acceptance of things is discouraged, and that Islamic education obliges Muslims to reflect on, contemplate and question understandings. In other words, Muslims are encouraged to challenge and think about what they encounter rather than uncritically accept 'truths' at face value. Put differently, Muslims' learning depends on how they engage critically with texts and how they contemplate new understandings of their education. By implication, the assumption that Islamic education merely fosters doctrinaire thinking, whereby knowledge should be internalised unquestioningly, is indefensible. In any case interpretations of the Qur'an and Hadith are varied, which confirms the plurality of understanding that has characterised Islamic education.

The notion of critical questioning through *ta'lim* is based on the view that human experience, and therefore understanding, is flexible and cannot be assumed to be absolute and unchallengeable. Rather, interpretations are varied, and individualisation helps Muslims to look at their understandings with openness and to recognise the possibility that things could be otherwise. Thus, *ta'lim* is at variance with rigid and inflexible thought. Such critical learning is often associated with *ijtihād*, or intellectual striving. This makes sense because openness and reflectiveness are activities that require intellectual exertion. However, the notion of *jihad* (striving), which is linked with *ijtihād* (intellectual striving), is often erroneously associated with holy war, as if the pursuit of knowledge in Islam is an act of violence and terror. Instead, the Qur'an clearly advocates reasonableness against the eradication of ignorance and misunderstanding (Waghid 2011:35).

Thirdly, *ta'dib* (*social activism*) is linked to a philosophy of Islamic education on the grounds that memorisation, reflection and openness to the unexpected cannot only be associated with such a practice. Put differently, knowledge of Islamic content, and the ways in which such knowledge should be enacted, cannot remain confined to the level of cognition – that is, contemplation and reflection – and other forms of critical scrutiny. Rather, the Qur'an (*al-Asr* 103:1–3) insists that belief and contemplation should be accompanied by just action: 'By the token of time. Verily humankind is in loss, except those who believe (and contemplate) and do righteous deeds (or just acts)'.

A leading Muslim intellectual, Naquib al-Attas (1931–) (1991), suggests that '*ta'dib*' is the most appropriate term to denote Islamic education on the grounds that it involves the quest to cultivate truthful and just human action in relation to knowledge. More specifically, al-Attas (1991:34) contends that knowledge of Islam should be accompanied by 'right and proper action' (or just action) in a Muslim community so that a person's 'proper' understanding of knowledge directs him or her to act with truth and justice in that community. In other words, Islamic education has a socially just orientation whereby Muslims are urged to enact justice in their daily lives.

This philosophy of Islamic education, which depicts interrelated actions in the form of acquisition of knowledge, reflection about knowledge and application of knowledge, presents the possibility for Muslims to enact Islamic education in various ways:

- Socialisation can be privileged when knowledge is acquired.
- Reflective action takes place when Muslims contemplate the knowledge they have acquired.
- Just action can be practised when knowledge acquisition and contemplation are extended towards acts that can engender change in individuals and communities.

If Muslims practise only socialisation, they would have enacted a *minimalist* understanding of Islamic education. If their socialisation is complemented by reflective action, Islamic education would be practised in a richer way. But when they practise socialisation, contemplation and justice within themselves and their communities, Muslims can be said to have enacted a *maximalist* view of Islamic education.

Some Muslims consider the acquisition of knowledge to be a priority, with reflective action not being required of them because the interpretation of the primary sources has been the work of influential Muslim scholars. These Muslims may for example renounce further explication of knowledge 'truths' and rely on existing 'truth claims'. Such a view of Islamic education is associated with *taqlid* (imitation) of the Islamic canons. But blind imitation of Islamic texts can lead to a doctrinaire perspective of Islamic education, as such persons do not believe that knowledge 'truth claims' can be modified or even rejected.

Parochial interpretations of Islamic education tend to ensue that seem to be out of line with ever-evolving human change. Such rigidity is often assumed to exist in the interests of preserving tradition, as if nothing changes and things would remain fixed. In fact, more recently, interpretations of the Qur'an by proponents of violence, war and extermination of the enemy have been associated with 'truth claims' made by groups such as the Islamic State of Syria and Iraq (ISIS), who, in the name of establishing a caliphate, use archaic understandings of the primary sources to justify their acts of terror. Thus, socialisation alone can only result in injustice that is at variance with just action.

In sum, a philosophy of Islamic education comprises concepts that exist along a continuum of socialisation, reflective action and just action. But if these concepts are not enacted together, a distorted view of Islamic education could be pursued.

On the plausibility of a post-structuralist view of a philosophy of Islamic education

Let us examine whether the above-discussed philosophy of Islamic education is compatible with a post-structuralist view of education, while consulting the work of the Harvard philosopher Stanley Cavell (1926–). According to Cavell (1979:431), education is sceptical in the sense that human encounters occur 'in the face of doubt', where nothing is certain and human action remains in becoming, in other words inconclusive and open. Islamic education as depicted in the Qur'an is about acknowledging certainty without having to doubt the word of God (*al-Baqarah* 2:2): 'This is the Book (Qur'an), in it is guidance sure without doubt for the believers'. Muslims are urged to believe in the guidance of Allah (God), which is different from an understanding that guidance can have multiple interpretations. As the Qur'an states (*Ali Imran* 3:6–7):

> *It is He Who has sent down to you (Muhammad) the Book (this Qur'an). In it are verses that are entirely clear [al-muhkamat], they are the foundations of the Book; and others not entirely clear. So as for those in whose hearts there is a deviation (from the truth) they follow that which is not entirely clear thereof, seeking polytheism and trials, and seeking for its hidden meanings,* but none knows its hidden meanings save Allah. *And those who are firmly grounded in knowledge say: "We believe in it; the whole of it (clear and unclear verses) are from our Lord." And none receive admonition except [wo]men of understanding.*

If the Qur'an emphatically announces that 'none knows its hidden meanings save Allah', then interpretations can be different as there cannot be absolute certainty about the meanings of the verses. And even though the guidance of the Qur'an is certain for Muslims, its interpretation is not certain, as Muslims cannot completely know the meanings of Qur'anic guidance, which reside only with Allah. In this way, the unclear or allegorical (*al-mutashabihat*) do not always present themselves with certainty, as interpretations thereof might differ. Islamic education – or, more specifically, guidance from the Qur'an – is thus not entirely incongruent with uncertainty because there is always more to know and to understand. Islamic education is therefore in line with post-structuralist thought.

Cavell (2004:6) claims, moreover, that when human beings act upon the world, they do so with risk. They act upon their potential, such as desiring change of the world and changing it themselves (Cavell 2004:18). This view of education agrees with the Qur'an's insistence that humans should set about changing the world by themselves, and that change starts with people themselves – that is, 'changing within themselves'. For Muslims to embark on such a form of education involves taking some risk, as risk-taking is about opening themselves up to others and being prepared to carry out change. Considering such a view of Islamic education as showing bias towards taking risks, we can deduce that Islamic education is commensurate with post-structuralist thought.

A post-structuralist view of education is also pointed out by Cavell (1979:441) as lending itself to being just or humane towards others. This implies that people (Muslims) are urged to talk with others, listen to them, interact with them in deliberative ways and treat them with justice – a matter of acknowledging or conceiving the other from the other's point of view. In this regard the Qur'an (*al-Shūrā* 42:38) encourages Muslims to resort to *shūrā*, or mutual engagement, in conducting societal matters. In other words, engaging in *shūrā* involves deliberation whereby people express their willingness to listen to one another, and to disagree on matters. Alibasic (1999:243) suggests that *shūrā* is synonymous with oppositional engagement in the sense that Muslims are invited to talk back to one another, which prompts them to see things differently or anew – a matter of conducting *shūrā* in the quest for 're-beginnings'. By implication, *shūrā* is compatible with post-structuralist thought.

Pedagogical implications of a post-structuralist view of Islamic education

There are two perspectives worth taking into account when considering some of the pedagogical implications of a post-structuralist view of Islamic education. The first perspective is embedded in the very process of how notions of Islamic education have been and continue to be constructed. It is well established that Islamic education derives its premises, principles and objectives from both the Qur'an and the Sunnah (the life actions of the Prophet Muhammad). So the paradigmatic foundations of Islamic education are based, on the one hand, on the divine word of God as encountered in the text of the Qur'an, and on the other hand on the teachings and example of an individual: the Prophet Muhammad.

Following on this, and in terms of the second perspective, even if we decide not to look at the Qur'an from a theological standpoint, its message cannot be dislodged from its social historicity, in much the same way that scholars such as Abu Zayd (2004:43), maintain that 'the Qurān is in need of the Sunna more than the Sunna is in need of the Qurān'. Abu Zayd (2010:283) further argues that, as is the case with every other religion, Islam is the result of the interpretation and experiences of real people. And because Islam necessarily came into contact with other communities and other ways of thinking and being, Abu Zayd (2010:286) contends that 'one cannot find the meaning of a religion in the text but in the interaction between the text and the historical process, in the interaction between the believer(s)/the communities with their holy texts'.

One of the primary pedagogical implications of a post-structuralist view of Islamic education is thus not only to take into account other sources of meaning – as might be encountered in the socio-politico-cultural milieu of Islam – but also to recognise that the text (of Islam) can find meaning only in relation to lived experiences. Implicit in such a recognition is the acknowledgement of diverse interpretations – and, more importantly, *contested* interpretations. Certainly, from a post-structuralist perspective, the argument that meaning is constructed in and through lived experiences hints at the idea that the text is necessarily secondary to the one who reads, interprets and lives it. As Barthes (1988:171) asserts:

Thus is revealed the total existence of writing: a text is made up of multiple writings, drawn from many cultures and entering into mutual relations of dialogue, parody, contestation, but there is one place where this multiplicity is focused and that place is the reader, not, as was hitherto said, the author. The reader is the space on which all the quotations that make up a writing are inscribed without any of them being lost; a text's unity lies not in its origin but in its destination.

As a text comprising 6 000 verses without any obvious chronology, the Qur'an by its nature and purpose, explains Hourani (1985:25), is not a book of theology and therefore does not take an explicit position on a number of questions. Rather, the Quran is *hudā al-nās* (a guidance for humanity): '[T]his Qur'an is (nothing but) lights from your Lord, and Guidance and Mercy, for any who have faith' (*al-A'raf* 2:203, *al-Jasiya* 45:20). To Abu Zayd (1998:49), the Qur'an is a literary text that has human characteristics, which in turn are necessary for human comprehension.

Significantly, the Qur'an projects its meaning onto the reader or believer, thereby offering explicit credence to two of its paradigmatic premises. First, in recognising individual autonomy or *ijtihād* (intellectual striving or independent critical judgement), the Qur'an acknowledges an individual's capacity to reflect critically and to make judgements not only in relation to the self, but also in relation to all others: 'Why do they not reflect on themselves?' (*al-Rūm* 30:8). Secondly, because of its propagation of *ijtihād*, the language and engagement offered by the Qur'an is counter-intuitive to any form of compulsion, whether in matters of faith, knowledge or practice: 'There shall be no compulsion in religion' (*al-Baqarah* 2:256).

In imploring the reader to think about and to reflect on its text, the Qur'an invites him or her into a textual *shūrā* (mutual consultation or engagement) that cannot be divorced from the context of history, place and, indeed, others. The idea of *shūrā* between the text and its reader is derived from the revelatory origin of the Qur'an in which the archangel Gabriel instructs the unlettered Prophet Muhammad to 'Read!' (*al-Alaq* 96:1), thereby not only underscoring the criticality of engagement, but putting in place a conception of Islamic education that is essentially dialectical in nature. The instruction to read is thematically and consistently repeated throughout the Qur'an in its appeal to its believers or readers to contemplate, think, reflect, engage and deliberate. In this regard Arkoun (2002:181) describes the Qur'an as a composition of signs and symbols that affords all meanings and is open to everyone, and suggests that no interpretation can exhaust its text.

As a pedagogical encounter, the Qur'an offers two implications. First, learning is by nature an active encounter and, at times, a disruptive encounter. Secondly, in inviting the believer or reader into the language of its text, the Qur'an confirms that its teaching and knowledge are unlimited. Islamic education lends itself to a dialectical engagement by virtue of its recognition of the interrelatedness between *ijtihād* (intellectual striving or independent critical judgement) and *shūrā* (mutual consultation or engagement). This conceptualisation resonates with a linear conceptualisation of a philosophy of Islamic education as constituted by the notions of *tarbiyyah* (socialisation), *ta'lim* (individualisation and reflective action) and *ta'dib* (social activism or just action). While *tarbiyyah* involves initiating Muslims into familiar understandings and differences, *ta'lim* entails extending knowledge through reflecting on what we know and who we encounter, and *ta'dib* – as we shall discuss next – is made visible in how understandings and reflections are enacted in relation to others and communities. This brings us to a discussion of Islamic education in relation to deliberative encounters.

Deliberative encounters and respect

Implicit in our understandings of deliberative encounters is the possibility that something new or unfamiliar might emerge – that is, something that has not yet occurred or has not yet been encountered. Often, such things have always been present, they have simply not been deliberated upon or encountered. There are many complex reasons for the silences that might submerge particular deliberations or deliberative encounters. Barlas (2002:3), for example, maintains that without understanding the liberatory aspects of Qur'anic teachings – and thereby unquestioningly accepting its patriarchal exegesis – Muslim women 'cannot contest the association, falsely constructed by misreading scripture, between sacred and sexual oppression'. Arkoun (2002) refers to this uncritical acceptance of notions in Islam – whether couched in patriarchy or hierarchy – as the 'unthought'. Arkoun (2002:308) defines the 'unthought' as the power employed by the traditional *ulama'* – manifested in what might be understood as normative (predetermined) Islam. The repression, and at times marginalisation, of the 'unthought' ensures not only that particular dogmas continue to dominate understandings in Islam, but that these understandings are never scrutinised. How, then, do we propagate this scrutiny so that the 'unthought' becomes not only the 'thought' but the deliberation itself?

To our minds, the idea of a deliberative encounter offers a counter-argument to the idea of the Qur'an as an instrumentalist tool. Instead, what the Qur'an, and hence Islamic education, insists upon is self-scrutiny, as constituted through *ijtihād* (intellectual striving or independent critical judgement), contemplation and critical reflection in relation to the text. Deliberative encounters are thus given shape through a curiosity and willingness to encounter the texts, and the understandings of others through unconstrained practices of deliberation. And while a conception of a deliberative encounter relies heavily on being open to the not-yet-considered and the 'unthought', such a conception provides a dialectical avenue for engaging with the text of the Qur'an, as well as for living with the message that the text propagates, as encapsulated in this verse: 'O humankind, indeed We have created you from male and female and made you peoples and tribes that you may know one another. Indeed the most noble of you in the sight of Allah is the most righteous of you. Indeed Allah is Knowing and Acquainted' (*al-Hujurāt* 49:13).

The idea of a deliberative encounter brings into contestation practices of rote learning and memorisation, which are seemingly devoid of critical engagement, debate and disagreement. Islamic education is often accused of doctrinaire practices of teaching and learning, with the madrassah, in particular, becoming increasingly seen as a dogmatic breeding ground for intolerance and violence. Indeed, as Pohl (2009:20) notes, the allegations levelled at madrassahs have most frequently focused on the religious nature of the curriculum and instructional techniques, such as rote learning and memorisation, which are considered inadequate for preparing learners for life in the modern world and for becoming productive members of their countries' workforces.

The latter is a common yet ironic accusation. The response to these accusations lies in Islam's historical propagation. History reveals that the *halaqat* (from the singular '*halaqah*'), meaning 'a gathering of people seated in a circle' or 'a gathering of learners around an educator', were spaces where learners were encouraged to challenge the knowledge of their educators (Makdisi 1981). The pedagogical implications of these *halaqat* were deliberations not only on commonalities and differences, but also informed by mutual respect. The call, then, for new forms of Islamic education is not external to this education's conceptual basis. In fact, it is inherent in the way that the language, form and content of Islamic education have taken shape as a codified expression of a way of life. Scholars such as Arkoun (1991) therefore maintain that there exists an important hermeneutical (interpretational) question as to how a text (the Qur'an) revealed 1 400 years ago might continue to address an audience who find themselves, often as minorities, in pluralist societies.

Willingness to engage in a deliberative encounter with another in order to bring our own views under scrutiny, and to be prepared to engage from the perspective of the other, implies a measure of respect for the other and for the encounter. In fact, we suggest that recognition of the self involves recognition of the other. This is because the type of self-reflection that ought to accompany recognition of the self as an autonomous being, who holds particular understandings and perspectives, would have to mean affording similar understandings to the other. The self cannot be understood without taking others into account. Wan Daud (2009), for example, explains that an individual 'is only so when he [or she] realizes simultaneously his [or her] unique individuality and the commonality between him [or her] and other persons close to him [or her] and surrounding him [or her]'. It is within such a construction of the interconnectedness between individuals that we argue for deliberative encounters that are characterised by respect.

The conception of respect (*adab*) in Islamic education is implicit in notions of virtuous conduct. To this end respect is not only reflected in social constructions of decency and desirable etiquette, but is also constitutive of what it means to act with humaneness. The essence of acting humanely and recognising the responsibility that connects humanity in our humaneness is aptly reflected in the

Qur'anic dictum '*Inna hathihil ummah ummatul wahidah*' ('Indeed this community [of humans] is but a single community'). It is worth considering that the description of a community as singular is not premised on a view that all humans should be the same or act in the same way, but rather that every human bears an internal connection to any other human on account of his or her humaneness, in other words, the very act of accountability towards someone else.

Cavell's (1979) point that being human requires acknowledging accountability towards others resonates with our earlier contention that self-recognition is tied to recognition of the other. In other words, when we recognise our very being as human we simultaneously acknowledge that we have an internal relationship with any other human. To act with respect (*adab*) therefore means to act with humaneness. This is why scholars such as al-Attas (2005:23) maintain that merely acquiring knowledge – that is, knowing something for the sake of knowing it – is not the same as gaining an education. Unless education includes moral purpose, argues al-Attas (2005:23), it is not education. Moreover, to al-Attas (2005), *adab* does not only take into account notions of respect, it also refers to 'right action'. And education is the absorption of 'right action into the self, and hence shapes one's interactions with others' (al-Attas 2005:23).

Thus far we have argued that deliberative encounters with the unfamiliar and the yet-to-be-known create spaces for non-prescriptive and unconstrained practices of deliberation. It is through deliberative encounters that Islamic education, as premised on the Qur'anic text, continues to speak to multiple audiences in terms of time, history and diversity. We have also shown how these encounters must be practised on the basis of respect and regard for the other. To this end, encounters, as propagated through Islamic education, cannot be empty of respect or 'right action'. This brings us to the concluding section of this chapter, in which we pay attention to the foundational rationale of Islamic education.

Islamic education as an enhancement of justice and co-belonging

The notion of justice ('*adl*) in Islamic education is commonly associated with the concepts of equity (*qist*), judgement (*hukm*) and balance (*mīzān*), as reflected in the following verse:

> *O ye who believe! stand out firmly for justice, as witnesses to Allah, even as against yourselves, or your parents, or your kin, and whether it be (against) rich or poor: for Allah can best protect both. Follow not the lusts (of your hearts), lest ye swerve, and if ye distort (justice) or decline to do justice, verily Allah is well-acquainted with all that ye do.* (an-Nisā 4:135)

The Qur'an often and intensely emphasises justice and just human relations, comments Waghid (2011:7), which clarifies that the foundational rationale of Islamic education is in fact 'the achievement of *'adl* (justice) in relations among people'. This is because the attainment of justice is geared neither towards Muslims nor any other particular group. Rather, it is meant for all people of all time. Islamic education starkly contrasts with practices of exclusion, marginalisation and oppression inasmuch as it is opposed to notions of coercion, since none of these are commensurate with conceptions of *shūrā* (mutual consultation or engagement) or *ijtihād* (intellectual striving or independent critical judgement).

Al-Attas (1991:76) describes justice in Islam as referring to 'the relational situations of harmony and equilibrium existing between one person and another'. This means that if justice (*'adl*) is the foundational rationale for Islamic education, then the ultimate aim of a (Muslim's) life is to contribute towards cultivating harmonious and balanced relationships between him- or herself and others. And if the expectation upon each individual is to act justly, so that no harm is brought to him- or herself or others, then the type of community that will be constituted through such collective actions would be what the Qur'an refers to as a justly balanced community (*ummatan wasatan*): 'And thus have We willed you to be a community of the middle way, so that [with your lives] you might bear witness to the truth before all humankind [...]' (*al-Baqarah* 2:143).

To al-Qaradawi, Omer (2013) tells us, the first principle of moderate and justly balanced thought is a 'comprehensive understanding of Islam, which is characterized as being a creed and a way, knowledge and action, worship and interaction, culture and character, truth and strength, [as well as] an invitation and political engagement'. Islamic doctrine, explains al-Qaradawi (2010:9), appeals to Muslims to exercise moderation and to reject and oppose all kinds of extremism, including excessiveness, religiosity and austerity. Such a community (*ummah*), he continues, is a community of justice and moderation, and testifies against every deviation (al-Qaradawi 2010).

Such a community would thus be as committed to acting justly as it would be to acting against unjust acts, whether these be against kin or the self. For an individual, who is attached to a particular community (*ummah*), to act against individuals who have acted unjustly would require a measure of detachment from that community. In other words, detachment is necessary for the enactment of justice because if a person is too attached, then he or she might not want to act against a wrong. Although an individual may be attached to a particular community, he or she is unbounded by it – he or she belongs, and yet does not belong. Agamben (1993) explains that to be unbounded or detached from a community is in itself an acknowledgement that acting communally can engender unfavourable enactments. Inasmuch as an individual ought to be unbounded or detached, even while he or she is attached, the community is naturally unbounded. Inasmuch as any community is not monolithic or homogeneous – even when it is framed as Muslim, in this instance – such a community is persistently in flux, never constant. An unbounded community will always be in potentiality, because it is always shaped by the *ijtihād* (intellectual striving or independent critical judgement) of individuals, and hence by this or that action.

Islamic education recognises that communities are complex and collective constructions of individualities, described by Agamben (1993) as 'whatever singularity'. For Agamben, a conception of community does not presuppose commonality or identity as a condition of belonging (Mills 2008:129). Rather, in Agamben's (1993:86) view, a community is one in which '[whatever] singularities form a community without affirming an identity that humans co-belong, without any representable condition of belonging'. To the question of which kind of politics would accompany a community constituted by 'whatever singularities', Agamben (1993:87) responds: '[a] being whose community is mediated not by any condition of belonging (being red, being Italian, being Communist) [...] but by belonging itself'. These individuals seek nothing and lack nothing, continues Agamben (1993:87), and they are neither inside nor outside. They co-belong for the purposes of a shared purpose, and when that purpose is not shared they cease to co-belong. Such individuals 'co-belong without any representable condition of belonging' (Agamben 1993:87).

In sum, such a community would be constituted by the very act of doing justice to others, and by implication does not hesitate to detach itself from doing an injustice to them. Such a community remains in becoming, and is in perpetual restraint.

Conclusion and recommendations for future research

By adopting a post-structuralist analysis of Islamic education – and by specifically drawing on the Qur'anic text – we have offered arguments in support of why Islamic education, and hence Islam, is indeed aligned with criticality, diversity and openness to the new and the unexpected. We began by showing that a philosophy of Islamic education comprises concepts that exist on a continuum of socialisation (*tarbiyyah*), individualisation and reflective action (*ta'lim*) and social activism or just action (*ta'dib*). We then argued that as a pedagogical encounter the Qur'an offers two implications: learning is by nature an active and at times a disruptive encounter, and by inviting the believer or reader into the language of its text, the Qur'an confirms that its teaching and knowledge are unlimited. In this sense, new forms of knowledge may emerge in relation to particular contexts or experiences.

In conclusion, we argued that, by virtue of the emphasis placed by the Qur'an on *shūrā* (mutual consultation or engagement) and *ijtihād* (intellectual striving or independent critical judgement), Islamic education is underscored by a recognition of criticality, and agreement and disagreement. In drawing on the Qur'an's endorsement of the virtues of justice and just actions, we further argued that the foundational rationale of Islamic education is indeed that of justice. To act justly, we showed, is commensurate not only with treating others with dignity and honour, but also with what it means to co-belong to a particular community. The notion of co-belonging, we explained, implies both attachment and detachment, creating the necessary spaces to act against any injustices.

Our conception of a philosophy of Islamic education has a post-structuralist bias, primarily because our scholarship ventured into such a realm. But we are aware of other multiple understandings of Islamic education, of which absolutist (positivist), interpretivist and critical perspectives abound. Paradigmatically, we have situated our understanding of Islamic education within a post-structuralist theory of knowledge. We would be interested to know whether other notions of Islamic education could be framed and by implication would depart from our position as elaborated above.

References

Abu Zayd NH. 1998. Inquisition trial in Egypt. *Recht van de Islam*, 15:47–55.

Abu Zayd NH. 2004. *Rethinking the Qur'an: Towards a Humanistic Hermeneutics.* Amsterdam: SWP.

Abu Zayd NH. 2010. The Qur'an, Islam and Muhammad. *Philosophy & Social Criticism*, 36(3/4):281–294.

Agamben G. 1993. *The Coming Community: Theory out of Bounds Volume 1.* Translated by M Hardt. Minneapolis: University of Minnesota Press.

Alibasic A. 1999. The right of political opposition in Islam. *Al-Shajarah: Journal of the International Institute of Islamic Thought and Civilisation*, 4(2):231–296.

Arkoun M. 1991. Religion and society. In D Cohn-Sherbok. (ed). *Islam in a World of Diverse Faiths.* London: Macmillan. 134–177.

Arkoun M. 2002. *The Unthought in Contemporary Islamic Thought.* London: Saqi Books.

Al-Attas SMN. 1991. *The Concept of Education in Islam: A Framework for an Islamic Philosophy of Education.* Kuala Lumpur: The International Institute of Islamic Thought and Civilisation.

Al-Attas SMN. 2005. Islam and secularism. *Journal of Islamic Philosophy*, 1:11–43.

Al-Qaradawi Y. 2010. The 30 principles of moderate and balanced thought. Translated by YF Fahmy. Available: http://www.facebook.com/notes/...30-principles...balanced-thought/335048770632/. (Accessed 29 February 2016.)

Barlas A. 2002. *Believing Women in Islam: Unreading Patriarchal Interpretations of the Qur'an.* Austin: University of Texas Press.

Barthes R. 1988. The death of the author. In D Lodge. (ed). *Modern Criticism and Theory.* London: Longman. 166–195.

Cavell S. 1979. *The Claim of Reason: Wittgenstein, Skepticism, Morality and Tragedy.* Oxford: Oxford University Press.

Cavell S. 2004. *Cities of Words: Pedagogical Letters on the Register of the Moral Life.* Cambridge: Harvard University Press.

Hourani GF. 1985. *Reason and Tradition in Islamic Ethics.* Cambridge: Cambridge University Press.

Makdisi G. 1981. *Rise of Colleges: Institutions of Learning in Islam and the West.* Edinburgh: Edinburgh University Press.

Mills C. 2008. *The Philosophy of Agamben.* Stocksfield: Acumen.

Omer S. 2013. *Al-wasatiyyah* (moderation) as an agenda of the *ummah.* August 21. Available: https://medinanet.org/2013/08/al-wasatiyyah-moderation-as-an-agenda-of-the-ummah/. (Accessed 17 February 2017.)

Pohl F. 2009. *Islamic Education and the Public Sphere: Today's Pesantren in Indonesia.* Berlin: Waxmann.

Waghid Y. 2011. *Conceptions of Islamic Education: Pedagogical Framings.* New York: Peter Lang.

Wan Daud WMN. 2009. Dewesternization and Islamization: Their epistemic framework and final purpose. Paper presented at The International Conference on Islamic University Education in Russia and its Surrounding Areas, 27–30 September, Kazan, Russia. 1–18.

Chinese philosophy and education:

Philosophy of education in classical Confucianism

Kam-por Yu

Introduction

Chinese philosophy of education is characterised by competing schools of thought and differing stages of development. Making summaries or generalisations about these can result in misrepresentation or oversimplification, while focusing on the finer details may make the discussion more historical than philosophical. A more scholarly approach may be to focus on a particular philosopher or text. But for the purpose of this chapter, it may be advisable to do something in-between. We thus confine ourselves to classical Confucianism, using texts from a few writers, based on the assumption that within such a scope these texts are consistent and complementary.

Such an approach is intended to give readers, especially those from other cultural backgrounds, a rich and accessible account of Confucian philosophy of education. We intend the account to be educationally informative and philosophically interesting. And we seek to demonstrate that this ancient tradition still provides some valuable insights into and lessons for education today.

Texts in the Confucian tradition

This chapter relies mainly on four texts in the Confucian tradition, all Confucian classics: *The Book of Rites*, *The Book of Changes*, *The Analects* and *The Mencius*.

In *The Book of Rites* (or *Liji* 禮記), there is a piece of writing that includes a systematic and critical discussion of education. The piece, called *Xueji* (學記) or 'On Education' (Legge 2003:Vol 2:82–91; Lin 1966:241–251; Xu & McEwan 2016:9–18), is probably the world's first treatise on education, dated around 476–221 BCE. *Xueji* first talks about the importance of education, both for the formation of a good society and for the development of individual human beings. It then looks at the ancient or ideal system of education, which featured different levels of institutions, various stages of learning and the educational goals of these stages. It explores seven key principles of education, and the importance of the balance between curricular study and extra-curricular activities, as well as between serious learning and leisurely pursuits. This is followed by a critique of bad practices in education, and the listing of four causes of the success of education and six causes of its failure.

Xueji then discusses the pitfalls and good practices of learning and teaching, and ends with praise for the greatness of the role of the educator. This treatise brings out a number of important ideas about education, such as learner-based learning, motivation of the learner, the use of the enlightening approach instead of instillation, and the balance of formal and informal curricula. It also gives a perceptive account of good and bad educational practices. We intend to show that this account of education is still very much alive and relevant in the 21st century.

The Book of Changes (Minford 2014; Wilhelm 1989) is an unlikely text to which to refer about the topic of this chapter, as it has rarely, if ever, been used to shed light on the topic. *The Book of Changes* is usually taken as a book of oracle. But we understand the book as a work on the study of human affairs. Its 64 hexagrams represent 64 types of situation. For example, the *shi* (The Army 師) hexagram ䷆ represents the situation of commanding an army or going into battle, while the *meng* (The Uninitiated 蒙) hexagram ䷃ represents the situation of a child receiving education (Minford 2014:56–62; Wilhelm 1989:20–24). Each hexagram has six lines (either *yin* or *yang*), and each line represents a stage of development in the specific type of situation. For each stage, there are various opportunities and pitfalls, as well as right and wrong actions and responses.

The text about the *meng* hexagram comments specifically on each of the stages of education, which taken together constitute a coherent philosophy of education that emphasises the importance of learner motivation, respect for and trust of the educator, clear communication of the rules and expectations, encouragement and support, toleration and the appropriate use of punishment. Such a philosophy prioritises the successful learning of the learner, and guides the educator as to how to interact with learners. It sheds light on a number of key ideas in the philosophy of education, such as the use of hard methods and soft methods, the importance of understanding the learners, and the nature of the educator–learner relationship. In short, this text also systematically discusses education, though much more briefly than does *Xueji*.

A text that is commonly used in discussions of Confucian philosophy of education is *The Analects* (Lau 1992; Legge 1971). *The Analects* is a collection of the sayings of Confucius (551–479 BCE). This text covers many topics and contains only fragments, but it remains one of the major texts that we have for our use, based as it is on the ideas of the most authoritative figure in the Confucian tradition. Nevertheless, there are numerous significant points on education, the most well known of which is *youjiao wulei* (有教無類) (*The Analects* 15.39, Lau 1992:158), which literally means 'yes for education, no for classification'. This is usually taken to indicate that 'in education there is no classification', such as classification according to social class.

In Confucius's time, education was available only to the noble class. Confucius was the first person to make education available to anyone who sincerely wanted to learn. So the saying is usually translated as 'education for everyone'. However, the literal meaning of the saying is actually a much bolder and groundbreaking proclamation. It means that no classification of human beings is valid except that of education. People can only be distinguished as educated and uneducated, in the figurative sense of being cultivated or uncultivated (as opposed to the literal sense of attending school or receiving formal education). The Chinese word for education – *jiao* (教) – is closely related to the concept of cultivation or transformation. Other categories of human beings are invalid, such as Chinese and non-Chinese, noblemen and commoners, of superior origin and of inferior origin. This revolutionary idea puts education right at the centre of human civilisation.

Something that we can learn from *The Analects* (2.7, 2.8, 11.22; Lau 1992:13, 103) much more readily than from other Confucian texts is the principle of *yincai shijiao* (因材施教), or 'teach learners in accordance with their aptitude'. There are many examples of Confucius giving different answers, sometimes even opposing answers, to different learners who ask the same question. The answers are not supposed to be correct in general; each answer is appropriate to the learner concerned, and takes into consideration the learner's situation, thinking and attitudes, and strengths and weaknesses.

In sum, *The Analects* (Lau 1992) focuses on key ideas in education, such as universal education and teaching according to aptitude. Confucius was a pioneer in adopting an enlightening, learner-based approach that emphasised getting the best out of learners.

The next text that we use, *Mencius* (Lau 1984), is also indispensable for an adequate account of philosophy of education in classical Confucianism. Even the shortest list of philosophers in this context must include Mencius (372–289 BCE) in addition to Confucius, as Mencius is commonly regarded as the second greatest Confucian sage, following only Confucius himself. *Mencius* was written by Mencius himself, with the help of his disciples. In the text, he mainly talks about good governance, and the promotion of proper education is regarded as an important part of good governance. Mencius presents a conception of education that is highly typical in the Confucian tradition, but which may be quite alien to us today. His conception is not particularly related to the acquisition of knowledge; instead, it is about learning to be a human being. The goal of education is for a learner to become *chengren* (成人), a complete human being (*The Analects* 14.12; Lau 1992:135), or a *daren* (大人), a big human being (*Mencius* 4B12, 6A14; Lau 1984:163, 237), who understands human relationships and how to treat other human beings (Lau 1984:107).

This text sheds light on the purpose, the social function and the moral and personal developmental roles of education. Here, education is not about reading books or acquiring knowledge, but about self-understanding, self-strengthening, self-reflecting and self-correcting. These tasks embody the Chinese concept of self-cultivation (*xiushen* 修身), or the cultivation of virtue, which is extensively discussed in another classical work: *Daxue* (大學) or *The Great Learning* (Johnson & Wang 2012).

Viewed together, these four texts provide a clear and substantial picture of Confucian philosophy of education. After identifying the main emphasis and special features of these texts in relation to philosophy of education, we will assess Confucian philosophy of education on the basis of these texts.

The purpose of education

Education is conceived at both the individual and the collective levels in Confucian philosophy. On the one hand it is about the personal development of an individual. On the other hand it relates to the cultural enterprise of a society. As a matter of *personal development*, education begins and thrives with active learning, intrinsic motivation, reflection and self-realisation. Here, the educator is taken to be a watcher, facilitator, respondent, rectifier, forerunner or advisor. As a matter of *cultural enterprise*, education requires favourable social conditions, moral atmosphere and conscious effort. Here, the educator is seen as a planner, provider, expert or authority. In the Confucian view, these two aspects complement each other, and the success of the individual dimension of education is the foundation of the success of the social dimension of education.

Xueji (Lin 1966:241) makes a very strong statement on the superior status of education in public policy:

> *The desire to do right and to seek what is good would give a person a little reputation but would not enable him to influence the masses. To associate with the wise and able men and to welcome those who come from a distant country would enable a person to influence the masses, but would not enable him to civilize the people. The only way for the superior man to civilize the people and establish good social customs is through education. [...] Therefore the ancient kings regarded education as the first important factor in their efforts to establish order in a country.*

This idea of 'civilising the people' (*huamin* 化民) or 'transforming the people' is a recurrent theme in Confucian philosophy. For example, in the *Book of Documents*, it is said that the sage king Yao 'united and harmonized the myriad States of the Empire; and lo! The black-haired people were transformed' (Legge 1960:Vol 3:17). In the *Book of Filial Piety*, it is said a major goal in educating the people is 'to change the trends and customs of the people' (Yu 2015:158). At the root of such teaching, there is the idea that human beings are not born as fully human, but have to be cultivated and educated in order to become fully human, and good governance facilitates this kind of development.

Sometimes this theme of transforming the people is regarded as signifying the collective feature of Confucian education – the use of education to serve a social function. But this is at most a half-truth. Both Confucius and Mencius are indeed explicit in explaining the social dimension of education. Confucius holds that education should be the main enterprise of a society after issues of survival and livelihood have been addressed. See, for example, *The Analects* (13.9, Lau 1992:123), in which Confucius comments that once the population has grown, the people's livelihood needs to be improved, and after that the people should become educated. This implies that there are three stages in governance: survival, prosperity and education.

Mencius (*Mencius* 3A3, Lau 1984:107) further explains that the point of education is to teach people how to have human relationships, so that they can co-exist in peace:

> *This is the way of the common people: once they have a full belly and warm clothes on their back they degenerate to the level of animals if they are allowed to lead idle lives, without education and discipline. [...] to teach the people human relationships [renlun 人倫]: love between father and son, duty between ruler and subject, distinction between husband and wife, precedence of the old over the young, and faith between friends.*

Fundamentally, this idea of education entails learning to become human. In the Confucian conception, a person has to learn to become fully human or a complete human (*chengren* 成人). We are not born as humans, but only born with human nature, and we have to learn and develop our human nature in order to become truly human. In *Daxue*, this process is described as 'to illustrate illustrious virtue' (Legge 1971:356). 'Illustrious virtue' means that the root of such virtue is to be found in human nature; 'illustrating' the 'illustrious virtue' means that such a root has to be developed to become truly 'illustrious virtue'.

This account of human nature is described as 'human becoming', to be contrasted with a static account of 'human nature' (Ames 2001:81–92, 121–128). Everyone has the illustrious virtue inside themselves, but with a bright nature such virtue has to be cultivated in order for it to become truly bright. The process for achieving this, as explained in *Daxue*, is education or self-cultivation, which includes 'extension of knowledge', 'investigation of things', 'sincerity of the will' (getting rid of self-deception) and 'rectification of the mind' (Johnson & Wang 2012:135; Legge 1971:357–359). In this way, we can see how, from the Confucian perspective, education serves a social function and is associated with self-cultivation.

As noted by Ames (2016:22),

> *personal cultivation is certainly the root of the Confucian philosophy of education. [...] The close link between education and Confucian morality lie in the fact that they are both grounded in growth in our roles and relations.*

Education so conceived is not instrumental as a means to some desired end, but a transformative process that is an end in itself. We are educated to live intelligent lives, and become moral to act morally.

However, the social function of education must not be seen as being in conflict with educating the learner to become an independent, critical and self-initiating agent. As noted, in *Daxue*, the cultivation of virtue is said to have its foundation in 'extension of knowledge', 'investigation of things', 'sincerity of the will' and 'rectification of the mind'. In *Xueji*, the goals of education are the intellectual and moral accomplishments of the individual learner, where independent thinking, learner-based learning and self-motivation are emphasised, at least in the higher stages of education.

First-year students are observed to determine their ability to analyze classical texts, and how they might demonstrate their interests and aspirations in learning. Third-year students are evaluated on their commitment to learning and on their ability to get on well within the scholarly community. Fifth-year students are examined on the breadth of their learning and on their devotion to and respect for their teachers. Seventh-year students are judged on the quality of their scholarly debate and on their choice of friends. Students who had arrived at this level are recognized as having reached a basic level of achievement. By their ninth year of study, having mastered their subjects and applied their knowledge broadly and having established themselves and their goals firmly, then it can be said that students have become greatly accomplished. It is only then that they are able to cultivate and transform the people, and change old human habits and shape new enlightened ways of living. They will be able to bring those close by into harmonious accord and gain respect of those at a distance. This, then, is the exemplary way of teaching and learning. (Xu et al 2016:11, cf Lin 1966:243)

The lower goal of education is to ensure that the learner masters the basic skills of reading and writing, cultivates good learning habits and gets along well in social groups. Beyond such primary goals, there is the higher goal of cultivating the learner to become an independent thinker, able to make good judgements and stand on his or her own feet in his or her further pursuits. Therefore, education has two goals: social and individual. The *social goal* is 'to cultivate and transform the people, and change old human habits and shape new enlightened ways of living' (*huamin chengsu* 化民成俗) or 'to civilize the people and reform the morals of the country' (Lin 1966:243). This social goal is based on educating learners not as tools that can be used by others, but as having independent and enlightened minds, and being able to help other people to have the same: 'able to establish themselves and their goals firmly' (*qiangli er bufan* 強立而不反) or 'have a general understanding of life and to have laid a firm foundation for their character from which they could not go back' (Lin 1966:243). The fulfilment of this *individual goal* is a prerequisite of the fulfilment of the social goal.

As explained by the neo-Confucian, Zhu Xi (1130–1200),

> [i]n considering the purport of how the ancient sages and wise men instructed others in the pursuit of learning, I find that it was totally a matter of explaining and clarifying moral principle for the cultivation of one's person; after [such cultivation was accomplished] it was extended so that [this rectifying influence] might reach others. It was never merely a matter of concentrating on memorizing readings and devoting oneself to literary composition in order to fish for a fine reputation and get a profitable salary. (Kalton 1988:104)

To sum up, according to Confucian philosophy of education, education is both for the individual and the society. The overall goal is to make people better human beings. We start by making ourselves better human beings and then extend to others in order to help them (with their willing participation) to become better human beings as well. This is the process described as 'transforming the people'. It must not be confused with the collective ideal of education, which aims at shaping the people according to some socially desirable targets, as defined or understood by those in power. The individual and social dimensions of education, according to Confucianism, are not at odds and do not compete with each other, but rather complement and reinforce each other.

The method of education

Does education mean putting something into the learner or getting something out of the learner? Should education aim at maintaining some common standard, or fostering individuality? Is education more like manufacturing a utensil or growing a plant? For these questions, Confucian philosophy of education clearly prefers one answer to another, but it is also important to note that this is just a distinction between primary and secondary concerns, and the two opposing ends have their proper places in education.

As noted, the Confucian conception of education is not about the appropriation of external knowledge, but about the development of a person's humanity or the cultivation of a person's moral mind. So education is more like getting something out of the learner than putting something into him or her. The learner needs to find out the answer for him- or herself rather than obtaining it from the educator. As Mencius (*Mencius* 4B14, Lau 1984:163) points out, in learning the most important thing is to 'get it oneself' (*zi de zhi* 自得之): 'When he finds it in himself, he will be at ease in it; when he is at ease in it, he can draw deeply upon it; when he can draw deeply upon it, he finds its source wherever he turns'.

In *Xueji* (Lin 1966:247), it is said that a good educator has the following three characteristics:

1. He or she guides but does not lead (*dao er fu qian* 道而弗牽). He or she shows the way to the learner but does not take the learner's hand to walk each step.

2. He or she presses but does not suppress (*qiang er fu yi* 強而弗抑). He or she places some pressure on the learner, but does not suppress the thoughts of the learner.

3. He or she starts but does not deliver (*kai er fu da* 開而弗達). He or she makes sure that the process has started but will not bring the learner to the destination.

In the words of *Xueji* (Lin 1966:247):

> *The superior man guides his students but does not pull them along; he urges them to go forward but does not suppress them; he opens the way, but does not take them to the place. Guiding without pulling makes the process of learning gentle; urging without suppressing makes the process of learning easy; and opening the way without leading the students to the place makes them think for themselves. Now if the process of learning is made gentle and easy and the students are encouraged to think for themselves, we may call the man a good teacher.*

The learner is taken as an active explorer rather than a passive receiver, and what the educator does resembles inspiring more than instilling. It is important that the learner keeps motivated and inquisitive, and keeps thinking for him- or herself.

Confucius goes even further, suggesting that he does not provide guidance and response until the learner has encountered difficulty and tried hard to solve the problems by him- or herself. As he explains:

> *I never enlighten anyone who has not been driven to distraction by trying to understand a difficulty or who has not got into a frenzy trying to put his ideas into words. When I have pointed out one corner of a square to anyone and he does not come back with the other three, I will not point it out to him a second time. (The Analects 7.8, Lau 1992:57)*

In short, Confucius wishes his learners try by themselves first before he offers any help. For him, education is always a two-way process, never a one-way transmission. On the teaching of Confucius, Yan Yuan, Confucius's most outstanding learner, comments:

> *The more I look up at it the higher it appears. The more I bore into it the harder it becomes. I see it before me. Suddenly it is behind me. The Master is good at leading one on step by step. He broadens me with culture and brings me back to essentials by means of the rites. I cannot give up even*

> *if I wanted to, but, having done all I can, it seems to rise sheer above me and I have no way of going after it, however much I may want to. (The Analects 9.11, Lau 1992:79)*

These comments show as much about Yan Yuan's learning experience as about Confucius's style of teaching. The educator needs to know not just the contents well, but also the aptitude of the learner. The way the educator interacts with the learner is based on how much progress has been made. The teaching is learner-based, and varies according to the differences of the individual learners.

Confucius (*The Analects* 9.8, Lau 1992:79) even goes as far as saying that he teaches not by transmitting his own knowledge, but by inviting the learner to consider opposing views, to find out what is wrong with these views and then to develop his or her own thinking: 'Do I possess knowledge? No, I do not. A rustic put a question to me and my mind was a complete blank. I kept hammering at the two sides of the question until I got everything out of it'.

Evidently, Confucian philosophy of education does not focus on the educator transmitting knowledge to the learner or the learner imitating the educator. The methods of teaching are instead designed to help the learner to 'get it' him- or herself. Thus the educator 'guides but does not lead', 'presses but does not suppress' and 'starts but does not deliver'. The methods of questioning – presenting learners with options or possible answers, and leaving blanks in the educator's replies – all aim at encouraging learners to think for themselves and obtain the answers to the bewildering questions by themselves. Such methods are regarded as crucial for the learner to maintain an internal motivation to learn, and to have a sense of ownership of his or her learning.

Good and bad practices in education

In its discussion of good and bad practices in education, the Confucian text *Xueji* is particularly relevant. But we begin by looking at a much neglected discussion on education in *The Book of Changes*.

The *meng* hexagram of *The Book of Changes* (Minford 2014; Wilhelm 1989) is about educating the young one. A lot of advice about education can be found in this part of the book. The 'Judgment' of this hexagram says:

> *It is not I who seek the young fool;*
> *The young fool seeks me.*
> *At the first oracle I inform him.*
> *If he asks two or three times, it is importunity.*
> *If he importunes, I give him no information. (Wilhelm 1989:20)*

Two principles of education are illustrated in the above passage: 'The learner must first be motivated' and 'The learner must first have trust in the educator'. 'It is not

I who seek the young fool' but 'the young fool seeks me' means that the learner should voluntarily follow the educator, rather than the educator chasing after the learner. The learner must be self-motivated before genuine and meaningful learning can begin to take place. If the educator chases after the learner to make him or her learn, the learner will become even more reluctant to learn in the future. Education can be effective only if the learner has a desire to learn. If the educator were to beg or force the learner to learn, then the educator would have to make a lot of effort and the learner would learn very little.

The 'Judgment' also uses the oracle as an analogy to explain that asking the oracle the same questions more than once or twice means that there is no faith in the oracle, and hence the oracle has to stop. Similarly, if the learner has no trust in the educator, the misgiving in the learner will hinder him or her from learning. Even if the educator has repeated the information many times, the learner still will not benefit. It is therefore very important, according to Confucian tradition, for the learner to take the initiative and request the educator to teach, and for the learner to respect the educator. In short, two things are important at the initial stage of education: the curiosity of the learner and the reputation of the educator.

The *meng* hexagram distinguishes between six stages in education:

1. *Fa meng* (發蒙), or 'expose folly': Regulations and expectations should be clearly spelt out at the beginning, so that the learners know what they are supposed to do and will not be caught by surprise or angered when their mistakes are pointed out. This is also a way to prevent frustration and resentment.

2. *Bao meng* (包蒙), or 'tolerating folly': When the learner has done something below expectation, he or she should be tolerated as far as possible, and given support and encouragement. Confrontation, coercion and contestation should be avoided.

3. Watch out for temptation: Regular and engaged participation is the key to success, which is undermined by external temptation or frequent distraction. A learner succumbing to temptation is compared to a woman who gives up her manner upon seeing a rich man – such a woman must not be taken as a wife, it is said. If the learner is distracted by some 'bad' hobby, it is difficult to keep him or her focused on his or her studies.

4. *Kun meng* (困蒙), or 'entangled folly': The learner will inevitably encounter problems and challenges. This is normal. He or she must not become frustrated and must not give up.

5. *Tong meng* (童蒙), or 'childlike folly': This relates to approaching learning with an empty and eager mind. This is auspicious.

6. *Ji meng* (擊蒙), or 'punishing folly': This involves censure or punishment for the learner. The important thing is that its purpose is to rectify the situation. If, however, the punishment only makes the learner more rebellious, and the

learner escalates the confrontation, then the punishment does not suit the purpose and should not be used.

Thus, *The Book of Changes* (Wilhelm 1989:23) states:

> *In punishing folly*
> *It does not further one*
> *To commit transgressions.*
> *The only thing that furthers*
> *Is to prevent transgression.*

If the punishment makes the offender become a bigger criminal, then it is ineffective. If, however, the punishment causes the offender to stop making offences, then it is effective. The same applies to education. Punishing a learner is justified only when the punishment can help him or her to return to learning. If the punishment drives the learner further away from the learning, then it is not justified. In short, whether or not the punishment to be used is learner-based and care-based, both the avoidance of punishment and the administration of punishment rest on the same consideration.

A controversial issue in education concerns the use of hard methods (such as censure and punishment) and soft methods (such as care and encouragement). Significantly, in the Confucian view, while the soft methods are clearly preferred, the hard methods also have their proper place. The hard methods are made known to the learners at the beginning, but are used only as a last resort, and only to help them back onto the right track. The use of hard methods is thus supplementary in nature. Whether they are appropriate depends on the situation, the timing, the motive and their effectiveness.

This kind of complementary use of different methods can also be seen in *Xueji* (6, Lin 1966:244; Xu et al 2016:11–12), in which seven methods of teaching are mentioned, namely:

1. the use of ceremony to teach respect and piety
2. the use of songs to teach interpersonal communication
3. the use of drum and bell to teach discipline
4. the use of punishment to regulate behaviour
5. the sparing use of assessment, to allow self-development
6. the use of observation but not continual lecturing, to give learners time to think things out for themselves
7. the use of stage goals to help learners understand their place.

By contrast, some ways of teaching are regarded as anti-educational. *Xueji* (Lin 1966:246) makes a lively critique of such bad practices:

> *The teachers of today just go on repeating things in a rigmarole fashion,*
> *annoy the students with constant questions, and repeat the same things*

over and over again. They do not try to find out what the students' natural inclinations are, so that the students are forced to pretend to like their studies, nor do they try to bring out the best in their talents. What they give to the students is wrong in the first place and what they expect of the students is just as wrong. As a result, the students hide their favorite readings and hate the teachers, are exasperated at the difficulty of their studies and do not know what good it does them. Although they go through the regular course of instruction, they are quick to leave it when they are through. This is the reason for the failure of education today.

In the above passage, the educator is criticised for having the following two main faults:

1. Failing to let people show their sincerity (*shiren buyou qicheng* 使人不由其誠): The educator just teaches what he or she has to teach, and fails to understand the learners. As a result, the educator does not know the true thinking and feelings of the learners, and fails to help them move forward from where they currently stand.
2. Failing to make the best of people's talent (*jiaoren bujin qicai* 教人不盡其材): This is also related to failing to understand the learners, as well as not knowing their potential, strengths and weaknesses. As a result, the learners may have potential of which they are unaware, and which thus remains underdeveloped, while the learners themselves feel frustrated and lacking in self-confidence.

Xueji (Lin 1966:246–247; Xu et al 2016:13) highlights four *good practices* that lead to success, namely:

1. prevention (*yu* 豫): preventing bad habits before they arise
2. timeliness (*shi* 時): giving the learners things when they are ready for them
3. order (*xun* 孫): teaching subjects in the proper sequence
4. mutual stimulation (*mo* 摩, literally 'friction'): letting learners admire the excellence of other learners or letting them learn from their peers.

Xueji (Lin 1966:247; Xu et al 2016:13) also lists six common *bad practices* in education, which lead to failure, namely:

1. to forbid after habits are formed
2. to teach after the opportunity has passed
3. to teach without the proper sequence
4. to study alone, without friends
5. bad company that would encourage the learners to go against the educators
6. bad pastimes, which would cause the learners to neglect their studies.

The basic idea is that the educator does not just give to the learner what he or she regards as good for the learner. He or she has to understand the learner's psychology, motivation, difficulties, talents, levels, interests and so on in order to seize the best teaching moment, teach in the right order and capitalise the resources around the learner that are helpful to him or her, such as learning from his or her peers.

Implications for educational theory and practice

Confucian philosophy of education has a number of remarkable implications for educational theory and practice. The following are some better-known examples.

Whole-person education

As pointed out, the purpose of education according to the Confucian ideal is to become a better human being, rather than to become a tool that is useful to other people and that can be sold at a good price. For Confucius, this is also the education to become a gentleman, or gentlewoman. Confucius (*The Analects* 2.12, Lau 1992:13) distinguishes between the two: '[T]he gentleman is no vessel'. A vessel has value in being useful to other people, but Confucian education does not aim at training people to become useful in this way. There is nothing wrong with being useful to others, but the kind of education that trains people to become useful is regarded as a lower form of education, which can go hand in hand with whole-person education but is neither necessary nor sufficient for such education. A human being can be more than a mere vessel, as the following dialogue shows:

> *Tzu-kung asked, "What do you think of me?"*
> *The Master said, "You are a vessel."*
> *"What kind of vessel?"*
> *"A sacrificial vessel"* (*The Analects* 5.4, Lau 1992:37)

Tzu-kung was not happy to hear Confucius call him a vessel, as Confucius's saying – that 'the gentleman is no vessel' – must be well known to him. This is a way to criticise him as not yet attaining the level of a gentleman. But it is not a very serious criticism, as it is not wrong to be a vessel, and there are also different kinds of vessels that are of different kinds of value to society. A sacrificial vessel, for example, is made of jade, and thus has cultural as well as commercial value. However, clearly, according to this Confucian conception, education is for the mind and character of the learner: 'Men of antiquity studied to improve themselves; men today study to impress others' (*The Analects* 14.24, Lau 1992:141). 'Men of antiquity' is used as an honorific term, and 'men today' is used in a derogatory way. Therefore learning to improve ourselves or learning to become better human beings is regarded as the superior form of learning, and learning to make ourselves useful or impressive in the eyes of other people is regarded as an inferior form of learning.

The Confucian classics distinguish between 'small learning' (*xiao xue* 小學) and 'great learning' (*da xue* 大學). Small learning aims at educating the learner to become a useful member of society, whereas great learning aims at developing the mind and cultivating virtue. Great learning is open to everyone, the only prerequisite being that the learner must seek to develop his or her humanity and become a full human. As Mencius (*Mencius* 7A33, Lau 1984:279) comments, 'the business of a Gentleman' is 'to set his mind on high principles', which is 'to be moral'.

Teaching according to aptitude

Since education is not about making the learners into some sort of product, but rather getting the best from them, the educator must understand the learners first before it can be determined which ways of teaching can serve their development better, suit their needs more closely and get the most and best out of them. Confucius is well known for his idea of *yincai shijiao* (因材施教), or 'teaching according to aptitude'. He is particularly perceptive in recognising the strengths and weaknesses of his learners, in relation to which he gives discerning individual comments: 'Shih is radical', 'Shang is conservative', 'Chai is stupid', 'Tsan is slow', 'Shih is one-sided', 'Yu is rash', 'Shih is perceptive', 'Yu is resolute', 'Chiu is talented' (*The Analects* 6.8, 11.16, 11.18, Lau 1992:49, 101).

Interestingly, the so-called strengths and weaknesses are relative and contextual. A feature regarded as a strength can become a weakness in another context. So the above comments are not so much positive or negative comments as they are observations that highlight the salient feature of a learner which implies both strength and weakness that has to be magnified or rectified.

Here is an example of Confucius's (*The Analects* 11.22, Lau 1992:103) principle of teaching according to aptitude:

Tzu-lu asked, "Should one immediately put into practice what one has heard?" The Master said, "As your father and elder brother are still alive, you are hardly in a position immediately to put into practice what you have heard."

Jan Yu asked, "Should one immediately put into practice what one has heard?" The Master said, "Yes, one should."

Kung-His Hua said, "When Tzu-lu asked whether one should immediately put into practice what one had heard, you pointed out that his father and elder brothers were alive. Yet when Jan Yu asked whether one should immediately put into practice what one had heard, you answered that one should. I am puzzled. May I be enlightened?"

The Master said, "Jan Yu holds himself back. It is for this reason that I tried to urge him on. Tzu-lu has the drive of two men. It is for this reason that I tried to hold him back."

The principle of teaching according to aptitude implies that the educator must learn about his or her learners before he or she can teach them, and there is no single, best teaching method that suits the needs of all the learners.

The dual emphasis on reflective thinking and knowledge acquisition

The Confucian perspective on education emphasises personal development, and so a person's reflective thinking is essential. But there must be a solid knowledge base for his or her reflective thinking to be effective. For this reason, knowledge acquisition is also regarded as fundamental in education. That is to say, the importance of knowledge acquisition is derivative, but in practice it is a prerequisite for serious learning. As a result, there is a dual emphasis on reflective thinking and knowledge acquisition in Confucianism. As Confucius states, 'If one learns from others but does not think, one will be bewildered. If, on the other hand, one thinks but does not learn from others, one will be imperiled' (*The Analects* 2.15, Lau 1992:15). And also: 'Once I went without food all day and without sleep all night thinking, but I found that this did me no good at all. It would have been better for me to have spent the time in learning' (*The Analects* 15.31, Lau 1992:157).

The emphasis on the complementarity of opposites is a salient feature of Confucian philosophy. The opposites are *yin* and *yang*, which complement each other, rather than good and bad, which eliminate each other. Readers interested in a further discussion of this aspect of Confucian philosophy are invited to read Yu (2014:70–76). There is a similar emphasis in education. Reflective thinking and knowledge acquisition compete for the attention of the educator and the learners, and it is easy to focus on one at the expense of the other. It would be misleading to say that one is important and the other is not. They should instead be seen as complementary, and a healthy measure of both is needed in order for a balance to be struck.

Conclusion and recommendations for future research

Chinese philosophy of education is frequently (mis)understood through stereotypes about traditional China, or practices in contemporary China, rather than careful study of the relevant Chinese classics. Closer study reveals that these relevant texts present many liberating and critical ideas, which are as fresh today as they were 2 500 years ago. This philosophy also has a number of practical implications, coming directly from the theory, which are still perceptive and valuable nowadays. Examples include 'mind the beginning', 'watch a lot and intervene a little', 'seize the learning moment', 'guide but do not lead', 'make prompt remedy', 'know your learner' and 'make progress in stages'.

However, Confucian philosophy of education makes some controversial contentions, such as the purpose of education is to 'become a fully human being' for ourselves or to 'transform the people' for the good of human society. This seems to be at odds with the modern ideal, which emphasises individual choice and social need. Confucian philosophy of education suggests that both the individual and the society should be reformed, and that individual choice and social needs cannot be taken at face value. Some people may see this as an outdated kind of perfectionism, while others may see it as an antidote to modern consumerism.

We have looked at just the Confucian stance in this chapter, without critically examining it or comparing and contrasting it with rival theories. Such critical study may initiate meaningful work for further research.

Many of the ideas outlined in this chapter, such as 'inspiring not instilling', 'knowing the strengths and weaknesses of the learners', 'making the best of the learner's talent' and 'helping the learners to get the answers by themselves' may seem to be timeless ideas, or at least aligned with modern educational theory. By contrast, some ideas in Confucian philosophy of education may be challenged by modern educators, such as the use of censure and punishment (hard methods) in addition to care and encouragement (soft methods), the emphasis on the authority of the educator and the importance of respecting the educator, and the refusal to apply one unified standard for all learners (as exemplified in the principle of teaching according to aptitude). Critical discussion of such ideas in Confucian philosophy of education, in contrast with the prevailing or influential contemporary theories, would also be interesting for further research.

Thus, in spite of its alternative or controversial ideas, Confucian philosophy of education can still be regarded as very much alive and vibrant today, worthy of the attention and close scrutiny of modern education theorists.

References

Ames RT. 2001. *Confucian Role Ethics: A Vocabulary*. Hong Kong: Chinese University Press.

Ames RT. 2016. On teaching and learning (*Xueji* 學記): Setting the root in Confucian education. In D Xu & H McEwan. (eds). *Chinese Philosophy on Teaching and Learning: Xueji (學記) in the Twenty-First Century*. Albany: State University of New York Press. 21–38.

Johnson I & Wang P. (trs). 2012. *Daxue and Zhongyong*. Hong Kong: The Chinese University Press.

Kalton MC. (tr). 1988. *To Become a Sage: The Ten Diagrams on Sage Learning*. New York: Columbia University Press.

Lau DC. (tr). 1984. *The Mencius*. Hong Kong: Chinese University Press.

Lau DC. (tr). 1992. *The Analects*. Hong Kong: Chinese University Press.

Legge J. (tr). 1960. *The Chinese Classics*. Vols 1 to 5. Hong Kong: Hong Kong University Press.

Legge J. (tr). 1971. *Confucian Analects, The Great Learning, and the Doctrine of the Mean*.

New York: Dover.

Legge J. (tr). 2003. *Li Chi: The Book of Rites* [1885]. Vols 1 and 2. Oxford: Oxford University Press.

Lin Y. (ed & tr). 1966. *The Wisdom of Confucius*. New York: The Modern Library.

Minford J. (tr). 2014. *I Ching*. New York: Penguin.

Wilhelm R. (tr). 1989. *I Ching or Book of Changes*. London: Arkana.

Xu D & McEwan H. (eds). 2016. *Chinese Philosophy on Teaching and Learning: Xueji (學記) in the Twenty-First Century*. Albany: State University of New York Press.

Xu D, Yang L, McEwan H & Ames RT. (trs). 2016. On teaching and learning (*Xueji* 學記). In D Xu & H McEwan. (eds). *Chinese Philosophy on Teaching and Learning: Xueji (學記) in the Twenty-First Century*. Albany: State University of New York Press. 9–18.

Yu K. 2014. The Confucian vision of peace. In T Shogimen & V Spencer. (eds). *Visions of Peace: The West and Asia*. London: Ashgate. 67–84.

Yu K. 2015. The Chinese tradition of filial piety and the Confucian philosophical reconstructions. *Bochumer Jahrbuch zur Ostasienforschung (BJOAF)*, 38:145–160.

Buddhism and education:
Right speech for freedom from suffering

Pradeep Dhillon

*Friend, there are two conditions for the arising of right view: the voice of another and wise attention (*parato ca ghoso, yoniso ca manaskaro*). These are the two conditions for the arising of right view.* – Mahāvedadallasutta (Nance 2013:366)

Introduction

It is difficult to state precisely what a Buddhist conception of education *is*. It is easier to say what it is *for* – freedom from suffering, or *moksha* – although the full meaning of the phrase 'freedom from suffering' may not be clear. In this chapter we offer some of the reasons for these difficulties as well as clarification, in order for us to gain a deeper understanding of what Buddhism can offer education. We focus on the Buddhist philosophy of language developed by the philosopher Nagarjuna (150–250 CE) and the importance of educating for right speech. Nagarjuna (Garfield 1995) argues that attention to language is central to the understanding and practice of Buddhist thought.

Buddhist foundational texts are difficult to identify, because much of the early philosophy in the tradition was developed and transmitted orally. As many scholars have pointed out, the historical figure we take to be 'the Buddha' – a philosopher/educator named Siddhartha Gautama, born in Eastern Nepal in 563 BCE and christened Buddha Shakyamuni after attaining 'enlightenment' – was only one among many in a tradition of philosophical and spiritual educators. Gautama taught throughout the Indian sub-continent in the sixth century BCE, but there were buddhas before him, and there have continued to be buddhas after him (Prebish 2008).

Following the Buddha's death around 483 BCE, his followers divided his teachings into three collections: *Vinaya Pitaka*, which were the rules governing the monastic life; *Sutta Pitaka*, the collected discourses of the Buddha and some of his disciples; and *Abhidhamma Pitaka*, or 'higher teachings', a collection of commentaries that developed over time and contain detailed analyses and philosophical presentations of the *Sutta Pitaka* discourses. Because Siddhartha Gautama and his early interpreters delivered all of his philosophical and educational treatises orally, there is no single written record that we can take to be the foundational text of Buddhism.

After Gautama's death, the Buddhist teachings travelled from northeast India down to Sri Lanka, and then out to Tibet, China and Japan and eventually the West. Along the way, they absorbed local cultural and philosophical traditions. Even the earliest of these cultures often had sophisticated systems of writing and philosophical thought. As a result, Buddhist scholarship offers a staggering array of debates, theoretical positions and practices. Presenting a simple introduction to the philosophical system would 'take several volumes' (Emmanuel 2013:8). Over the centuries, Buddhism has developed many varied traditions and sects, emerging through both written and oral Buddhist interpretive scholarship (Klein 1994). This proliferation of viewpoints and the acceptance of such plurality make it difficult to speak of Buddhism in a singular overarching manner in order to draw out its significance for education.

The debates around this philosophical tradition are sophisticated and plentiful, as is to be expected in any philosophical system that emphasises the use of reason and critical thinking. Consider, for example, the debates between realism and idealism, empiricism and rationalism, and non-self and personhood (Humble 1999; McCagney 1997; Phunstsho 2005). This robust body of interpretive scholarship illustrates Buddhism's long tradition of valuing individual reasoning, on the grounds that the world is known and knowable to us through both perception and inference. The Buddhist tradition is sceptical of hearsay evidence and guesswork. As Buddha says to his learners, the Kalamas, as recounted in the *Kalama Sutta*, or *The Buddha's Charter of Free Inquiry* (Thera nd):

> *Come, Kalamas. Do not go upon what has been acquired by repeated hearing; nor upon tradition; nor upon rumor; nor upon what is in a scripture; nor upon surmise; nor upon an axiom; nor upon specious reasoning; nor upon a bias towards a notion that has been pondered over; nor upon another's seeming ability; nor upon the consideration, "The monk is our teacher." Kalamas, when you yourselves know: "These things are good; these things are not blamable; these things are praised by the wise; undertaken and observed, these things lead to benefit and happiness," enter on and abide in them.*

Woven into the fabric of Buddhism, then, and arising from its reliance on individual reason, is a plurality of theoretical approaches. But while it may be tempting to liken the Buddha's insistence on reason to that of Kant – and the parallels with Kant's (1996) essay 'What Is Enlightenment?' are no doubt striking – it is important to keep in mind that for the Buddha, reason alone was not sufficient for bringing about sound and appropriate moral outcomes, nor were such outcomes the chief purpose of the cultivation and exercise of reason.

Buddha's view of reason was pragmatic: He recognised the intrinsic value of reason, but saw its ultimate value in its potential to liberate human beings from suffering. Siderits (2015) recounts Buddha's famous metaphor, in which he 'compares someone who insists that the Buddha answer these questions [about the nature of reason] to someone who has been wounded by an arrow but will not have the wound treated until they are told who shot the arrow, what sort of wood the arrow is made of, and the like'. The metaphor expresses Buddha's sense that reason should be applied in a targeted way to treat our wounds, and not used merely to indulge our curiosity about syllogistic inessentials. This pragmatic conception of reason lends cohesion to a diverse array of Buddhist texts.

Although the origins and formation of the Buddhist scriptural canon remains mostly obscure to modern scholarship, one of the earliest to be written down was the Pali canon of the Theravada school. According to the Theravada school, this writing occurred in Sri Lanka in the latter half of the first century BCE. Other early schools produced canons in various Middle Indian dialects. Important elements of these canons have been preserved in Sanskrit and in Chinese translation (Emmanuel 2013:2). As Buddhist thought spread to Tibet and China, translations of the Pali canon no doubt existed, and increasingly different interpretations emerged as quite distinct strands of Buddhist thought and practice.

From here came the three distinct living Buddhist traditions as we know them today: *Hinayana*, *Mahayana* and *Vajrayana*. These are often loosely translated as the 'Little Vehicle', the 'Great Vehicle' and the 'Diamond, or Hard, Vehicle' respectively. Roughly, *Hinayana* focuses on individual efforts at obtaining nirvana, *Mahayana* concentrates on the importance of assisting others in attaining peace after we have achieved *bodhisattva* (expert) status, and *Vajrayana* suggests that this could be accomplished in one lifetime, as opposed to the many lifetimes assumed by the first two traditions. Each has distinctive conceptual patterns and practices, and has generated a large literature of scholarly debate, interpretation and disputation.

Even though Buddhism has varied traditions and sects, contemporary Buddhist scholars increasingly agree that all iterations of Buddhist thought share core concepts, and that these are laid out in the early Pali texts (*Sutta Pitaka*) and their Chinese counterparts, the *Agamas*. This fact puts into perspective the contributions of philosophers such as Nagarjuna, who is considered to be the greatest of Buddhist philosophers, perhaps second only to the Buddha himself: 'The great Indian fathers of east Asian and Tibetan Buddhism were completely familiar with this material and treated it as the authoritative word of the Buddha' (Gethin 1998:44). Nagarjuna is remembered for his subtle contributions to Buddhist thought.

In this chapter we take Gautama Buddha's discourses to be foundational to the system of thought that we refer to as 'Buddhism', and we see Nagarjuna's (Garfield 1995) philosophy of language as stemming from these early discourses. Even though the Buddhist tradition has many strands, we follow Buddhist scholars such as Harvey (2012) in holding that all of these strands are based in the tradition that we know as Buddhism, regardless of the continuing debates among and between them, and the varying interpretations of gross and arcane points in this philosophical tradition. Further, although we take no stance on the relationship between philosophy and religion in the Buddhist tradition, we maintain that philosophy was important to the Buddha and the Buddhist scholars who followed him. The Buddha himself did not develop various branches of philosophical thought, but subsequent followers did, and highly sophisticated treatments of branches of philosophy – such as epistemology, philosophy of mind, philosophy of language, and logic – are to be found. Philosophical study was not pursued for intellectual reasons alone but was entered into pragmatically, to improve the human condition.

The Buddhist emphasis on the pragmatic view of reason is significant. On this basis we argue that Buddhism has a rightful place within the field of philosophy of education, particularly moral education. In the Buddhist view, humans as moral agents generally have two responsibilities, namely:

1. to refine their moral selves, as emphasised by the *Hinayana* tradition
2. to do that and help others pursue their own moral development, as stressed in the *Mahayana* tradition.

Both forms of moral development have a pragmatic end: The *Dhamma*, or the Path, is valuable only insofar as it enables us to develop understanding and practices that in turn release us from the suffering which is the mark of the human condition. The Buddha cautions that once we have achieved an end to suffering, we must not cling to our educators or their teachings, but rather let them go. 'In this respect,' Emmanuel (2013:5) explains, 'the Buddha likened his Dhamma to a raft: the usefulness of the teaching lies in helping us to reach the other shore. But once there, we must let it go.' In this view, then, particularly as articulated by Nagarjuna (Garfield 1995), right knowledge that is the foundation of right action arises from affectivity and rationality working together. Furthermore, once we have achieved right knowledge, we must let go of our attachments to, and reliance on, the 'raft' provided by educators and their teachings.

To draw out the relationship between the Buddhist tradition and the philosophy of education would require many volumes. We therefore limit our remarks to first laying out the philosophical underpinnings common to all strands of Buddhist thought, specifically the Buddhist conceptions of suffering, emptiness and impermanence that inform ideas of how and why education takes place. We then examine Nagarjuna's (Garfield 1995) theory of the non-self and interdependence to argue for the place of language in moral education within the Buddhist tradition.

The philosophical underpinnings of Buddhism: From suffering to salvation

In Buddhism, the primary characteristic of the human condition is suffering, and the main source of our suffering is ignorance: We do not recognise that all phenomena are transitory and interdependent, including ourselves. This existential impermanence leads logically to what the Buddha refers to as 'emptiness': No phenomenon has any essence or 'self' that remains stable and unchanged over time. No objects, real or abstract, have intrinsic substance (*svabhava*). All phenomena arise within a mutually determining network of causes and effects, and nothing exists independently of the contexts and conditions within which it is embedded.

In this view, personhood is taken to be a combination of the physical, the psychological, the cognitive and the perceptual, and personal identity is a 'perpetual procession of thought, ideas, and emotions' (Emmanuel 2013:6). We desire, and desperately try to cling to, objects, people and conditions, thinking we can hold on to them once we possess them, unaware that they can be neither possessed nor held since they are momentary and changing. It is tempting to see a parallel with Hume's (1978:78) notion of the human mind as a theatre where 'perceptions successively make their appearance; pass, repass, glide way, and mingle in an infinite variety of postures and situations'. However, for the Buddha, as Emmanuel (2013) reminds us, the insight – and, more importantly, the appropriate use of reason and philosophical reflection – is the key to working towards the cessation of suffering. Thus, philosophical understanding is placed at the heart of educational practice in this tradition.

Crucially, Buddhism's emphasis on ignorance of the actual conditions of 'emptiness' relies on a distinction between two kinds of reality: 'conventional' and 'ultimate'. If suffering is caused by ignorance of the co-dependent nature of the self and by existential impermanence, then the way out of this suffering is through being educated into and following the *Dhamma*. Through philosophical reflection, we can gain knowledge of the causal conditions under which the objects of desire appear, change and disappear. In this way, we can cut through this ignorance, freeing ourselves from the birth-and-rebirth cycle of *samsara*, to attain *nibbana* (nirvana in the Indian tradition).

For the Buddha, this takes two mutually dependent forms: the *philosophical reflection* of the practitioner-learner (*arhat*), as supplemented with *meditative practice* in the company of and support from fellow travellers, the community (*sangha*). In other words, suffering adheres to life even when we are in relatively stable and satisfying states of mind and circumstances. Not only are positive and negative experiences transitory, but our desire to hold on to what we perceive as good experiences and to find strategies to escape the unfortunate ones are futile and serve only to produce even more suffering.

In sum, Buddhism in all its varieties takes suffering to be constitutive of life. To exist, in this view, is to suffer.

The Buddha's teachings, as drawn from the *Sutta Pitaka*, are distilled in the *Dhamma*. This text is divided into two components: philosophical understanding and practice. The *philosophical* component is found in the text the 'Four Noble

Truths', which sets forth the truths that are known to the noble ones who have found peace. These truths provide the theoretical foundation to the Buddhist's search for the cessation of suffering. The *practical* component of the *Dhamma*, entitled the 'Eightfold Path', instructs readers on how to build practices based on the truths and thereby be freed from suffering. These two texts were originally intended to be a unified education in theory and practice. But especially in the West, the philosophical Four Noble Truths have generated the increasingly sophisticated academic field of Buddhist studies, while the more practical Eightfold Path is usually followed by lay people and led by an educator.

Buddha's philosophical guidelines to freedom from suffering

The Four Noble Truths seek to provoke the cognitive response of understanding. The truths are as follows:

1. The truth of suffering (*dukkha*) – demanding awareness that to be human is to suffer. This is true not only when we undergo unfortunate experiences, but also when we pass through pleasant or even joyful experiences, as we know that they will not last.
2. The truth of the origin of suffering (*samudaya*) – requiring us to know the source of human suffering. It offers us the theory of the emptiness of people, which depends on the assumption that all phenomena are transitional and arise from a complex network of conditional causes.
3. The truth of the cessation of suffering (*nirodha*) – declaring that we are not doomed to suffering; that is, suffering is not inevitable.
4. The truth of the path to the cessation of suffering (*magga*) – telling us that there is a path out of the condition of suffering.

Buddha's practical guidelines to freedom

The practice of *Dhamma* as encapsulated in the Eightfold Path is tied to the fourth noble truth, namely the path that the *arhat* needs to undertake in order for peace to be attained. This practical component of Buddhism is generally stressed in Western popular culture and embraced by the laity, even in the case of eminent Buddhist educators such as Hanh (1998). One of the few attempts at a practical philosophical analysis of *Dhamma* is that of Nnanavamsa and Krishnasamy (2014). They point out that the Eightfold Path, an expansion of the fourth of the truths, is itself divided into three sections: wisdom, morality and concentration (Nnanavamsa & Krishnasamy 2014:3):

1. The first section of the Eightfold Path, focusing on wisdom (*Paññā*), 'includes the first two factors of *Sammā-Ditthi* (Right View or Understanding) and *Sammā-Sankappa* (Right Thought)' (Nnanavamsa & Krishnasamy 2014:1). The

first factor serves a purely epistemological purpose. Through philosophical reflection, we come to understand the truth and origin of suffering. Given this understanding, we realise that our desires are futile in the face of continual change. The second factor thus requires us to let go of misplaced emotions such as lust, hatred and cruelty (Nnanavamsa & Krishnasamy 2014:2).

2. The second section of the Eightfold Path focuses on morality (*Sila*), which 'includes *Sammā-Vacca* (Right Speech), *Sammā-Kammanta* (Right Action), and *Sammā-Ajiva* (Right Livelihood)' (Nnanavamsa & Krishnasamy 2014:1). This section is meant to direct individuals to use language that is not harmful or misleading; to act in a way that avoids killing, stealing and sexual misconduct; and to earn a living in a manner that supports the discipline of the Path and does not cause direct or indirect harm (Nnanavamsa & Krishnasamy 2014:2).

3. Finally, the third section of the text is devoted to concentration (*Samadhi*), which directs epistemological practice. It focuses on the last three elements of the Path: '*Sammā-Vāyama* (Right Effort), *Sammā-Sati* (Right Mindfulness) and *Sammā-Samādhi* (Right Concentration)' (Nnanavamsa & Krishnasamy 2014:1). In this section we are encouraged to try to replace any bad thoughts that we may have with good, positive thoughts; to pay close attention to our bodies, our feelings, and our thoughts, ideas and state of mind through the activity of meditation; and to carefully follow the correct steps of meditation (Nnanavamsa & Krishnasamy 2014:3).

At every stage on the Path, we are called on to use reasoned contemplation to gain right understanding from which right action, speech and appropriate material action flow. This is different from the first part of the Eightfold Path, which lays out the precepts that focus on the path to *nirvana*, because in the second section we are required to *develop* our capacity in obtaining right understanding and right action. In other words, while the two sections are integrated, the first promotes right understanding and the second builds, through practice, the capacity necessary for Buddhist belief and action. This practice, which is considered to lead to epistemological and moral sophistication, is meditation. And contemplative reflection must also be guided by morality. The accuracy of philosophical analysis that we develop through reflection should be in the service of right understanding that would lead to right action. This injunction forbids the use of meditative practice that could lead to knowledge which could be used to harm others. In other words, when properly pursuing *Dhamma*, all the stages of the Eightfold Path are involved in the pursuit of freedom from suffering.

Nagarjuna on emptiness, language and education

Having explored the basic Buddhist philosophical concepts of suffering, emptiness and impermanence, and the guidelines for achieving freedom, we now turn to the question of how this freedom and salvation might be achieved, through a focus on Nagarjuna (Garfield 1995). We consider how the *arhat*, or Buddhist practitioner, can fulfil the original soteriological-educational intention set by the Buddha himself – pursuing salvation through education – by highlighting the importance of right and contextually appropriate speech. Education brings salvation by fostering the development of language and speech that contributes to moving us away from suffering towards freedom. The early Buddhists recognised the significant function of language and speech and the subtleties involved in appropriate usage, as is clearly seen in the words of the poet Mātṛceṭa (born 105 CE). Mātṛceṭa addresses the Buddha with these words:

> *Sometimes you, a knower of times and hearts, did not speak even though questioned;*
> *Sometimes you approached others and fashioned a discourse,*
> *Elsewhere, having excited interest, you spoke [...]*
> *There is no method or power by which you did not try*
> *To rescue the miserable world*
> *From the terrible hell of samsara.* (Shackleton Bailey 1951:175)

This interest in contextually appropriate language use is different from, but complementary to, the use of language in logical reasoning, which is the other crucial soteriological-educational use for language in both Indian and Buddhist philosophy.

To explore the complexities of Buddhist thinking about language, we now turn to the work of Nagarjuna, who as mentioned is sometimes called the second Buddha. Nagarjuna's critical philosophy is said to have founded the *Madhyamaka*, or School of the Middle Way, within the *Mahayana* Buddhist philosophical tradition. In this section we examine how Nagarjuna's functional account of language is based on his ideas about language's emptiness (conventionalist usage). We see language as playing an important, though little explored, role in Nagarjuna's thought. Looking closely at how language functions in his work, we see that he values diversity of thought and language, and emphasises the ethical importance of adapting language to context. Finally, we draw out the implication of Nagarjuna's thought to the question of Buddhist education, unpacking what it tells us about praxis/skilful means in the use of language to relieve suffering. This section is based on Garfield (1995).

Emptiness and interdependence: The conventionalist use of language

Nagarjuna was trained in Indian logic and dialectical reasoning, but did not ascribe to the Hindu ontology that a statement must refer to something – even if just an abstract entity – in order to have meaning. Rather, Nagarjuna shared with the Buddhists who came before him the view that all phenomena dependently co-arise and so are without a stable nature, substance or essence. Following this reasoning, language does not refer to anything, although it still has practical uses established through convention (Gudmunsen 2014). In Nagarjuna's conception of emptiness, he goes a step further than earlier Buddhists by arguing that the concept of 'emptiness' is itself 'empty': It does not exist by itself, independently, nor does it refer to a transcendental reality beyond or above phenomenal reality. In other words, Nagarjuna makes a radical move within the Buddhist tradition by dissolving the distinction between the two realities, ultimate and conventional, on which the tradition had rested thus far. For Nagarjuna, nothing has any *svabhava*, or intrinsic nature; everything is thoroughly *prabhava*, or interdependent.

Nagarjuna goes on to propose that if nothing has *svabhava*, then the things on which we take a certain object to be dependent are also 'empty'. He offers the metaphor of a chariot (the two-wheeled horse-drawn vehicle used in ancient racing and warfare). While we can break down the chariot into its component parts, he points out, such as the carriage, the wheels, the spokes and the axles, these parts do not in themselves indicate the stable entity that is a chariot. In other words, they do not contain within themselves any attribute of 'chariotness'. Moreover, they can be broken down further into the components that gave them their existence, and so on. All we can do is work with the use to which a chariot, and by extension its parts, can be put.

It is not surprising that Nagarjuna's contemporaries called him a nihilist, or at the very least an anti-essentialist. This debate over the emptiness or functionality of language continues among Buddhist philosophers to this day. As Eckel (1978:333–334) reminds us:

> *Theories of language play an important part in the Maadhyamika philosophy of the early period, [...] because the disputes between Maadhyamika and rival Indian schools were often, at bottom, cast in terms of disagreements over the use of language. This is perhaps a natural consequence of the Maadhyamika critical method. Maadhyamika philosophers were more interested in devising a critical scheme for removing their opponents' misconceptions than they were in building their own positive theory.*

This thoroughgoing conventionalism is a key distinguishing feature of Nagarjuna's theory of language. His other, and more subtle, point is that even saying that all is 'empty' is itself empty, since saying this cannot refer to anything that *is not*, and hence cannot be asserted. However, relying on conventional usage, he argues that at least language is useful in letting him point to the 'emptiness' of all things. In this way, Nagarjuna provides a functional account of language.

Language and context: Diversity and adaptation

As noted by Schroeder (2000), scholarship on Nagarjuna has long focused on his metaphysics and epistemology, and has done so in a way that assumes, without explicitly discussing, the important role that language plays in his thought. In recent years, Buddhist scholars trained in the Western philosophical tradition have been preoccupied with whether Nagarjuna's philosophy exemplifies nihilism, anti-essentialism and anti-realism (Siderits & Katsura 2013). Spackman (2014) suggests that nihilistic interpretations of Nagarjuna in contemporary Buddhist philosophy are waning but not extinct. He argues (Spackman 2014:151),

> *The nihilist reading is the radical view that the central claim in Nāgārjuna's writings is that nothing whatsoever exists in any sense, either at the level of the ultimate truth* (paramārthasatya) *or at the level of the conventional truth* (saṃvṛtisatya). *Such a view is to be contrasted with what is arguably the prevailing contemporary account – or better, family of accounts – of Nāgārjuna, which I will call the anti-essentialist interpretation, some form of which is maintained, for instance, by Jay Garfield, David Seyfort Ruegg, David Kalupahana, and Frederick Streng.*

Spackman (2014) goes on to explain the view of these philosophers in general terms: Nagarjuna, they propose, denies that things have intrinsically existent properties, but does not deny the existence of things altogether. The nihilists and the anti-essentialists agree that for Nagarjuna, things do not exist intrinsically and independently. By contrast, the anti-essentialists see him as allowing a different way of existing, one that is dependent on other things and human knowers.

For Spackman (2014), neither of these positions provides an adequate account of Nagarjuna's standpoint. He argues, instead, for what he calls the 'conventionalist interpretation' (Spackman 2014), which we have been pursuing. Drawing on interpretations of certain key verses, Spackman (2014) demonstrates that both the nihilistic accounts and the anti-essentialist accounts fall short of what Nagarjuna seeks to accomplish. Roughly, for the nihilists, Nagarjuna's position of radical and absolute 'emptiness' is incoherent, since nothing can ever be asserted. The anti-essentialists, through what Spackman (2014) takes to be arbitrary interpretations of key texts, wish to preserve the 'emptiness' thesis by maintaining the idea of conventional truth.

Spackman (2014:160), however, argues that the conceptualist proposes a way of thinking about Nagarjuna's notion of emptiness not by 'equating conventional existence with interdependent existence, as the anti-essentialist does, but by viewing conventional existence statements as applying the standard concept of existence without endorsing its svabhāva-related content'. Spackman thus draws attention to a relation, albeit a tenuous one, between language and thought that both the nihilists and the anti-essentialists miss. He concludes by asserting, significantly, that 'from the conceptualist perspective, if everything is empty of independent existence, it is not possible to understand conceptually how things can appear as they do to our conventionalist minds at all' (Spackman 2014:170).

We enter this debate with Spackman not so much to settle the dispute between nihilistic and anti-essentialist readings of Nagarjuna as to show the important role that language plays in Nagarjuna's thought. Some scholars have suggested that Nagarjuna wrote several texts – some for lay people, some esoteric, some philosophical to the point of seeming arcane even to the most sophisticated of scholars – using varieties of language in order to be comprehensible to audiences with varying degrees of philosophical education (Lindtner 1986). That is, he uses right speech – speech that is appropriate to context and in right relationship with the speaker, and thus ethical – to communicate his thoughts to a diverse audience.

From thought to action: The praxis of skilful means

Despite the centrality of language in Nagarjuna's thought, and the importance of *upaya-kausalya* (skilful means) in Buddhist philosophy more generally, Schroeder (2000) notes that the philosophical scholarship on Nagarjuna from early to present times has focused almost entirely on his metaphysics and epistemology. Scholars have made little effort to consider the *upaya* (praxis) inherent in Nagarjuna's thought, even though the development of *upaya-kausalya* is stressed throughout Buddhist philosophy, including *Mahayana* philosophy (Schroeder 2000). For Schroeder (2000:559), Pye's *Skilful Means* is among the few scholarly works to explore this relationship between thought and action, including linguistic action. As Pye (2003:1) comments:

> *"Nirvana", "bodhisattva," "emptiness" [...] and so on have all been considered in this way and that, but apart from occasional references and brief definitions [the concept of] "skilful means" has scarcely been attended to at all. A concept which has been used to explain the very existence of Buddhism as a functioning religious system demands closer attention.*

Schroeder (2000) especially disapproves of Western philosophers who concentrate on Nagarjuna's metaphysics. This approach is motivated by the assumption that, for Nagarjuna, in keeping with the second noble truth, and the first section or stage in the Eightfold Path, liberation from suffering depends on undertaking metaphysical analysis. As mentioned, the debates among Buddhist scholars rest primarily on trying to determine whether Nagarjuna was a nihilist, a conventionalist, an anti-essentialist or an absolutist: 'Whether or not his dialectic of "emptiness" (sunyata) undermines all positive philosophical positions, it is commonly assumed that Nagarjuna is dealing with important metaphysical problems and that he thinks Buddhist praxis is somehow incomplete without it' (Schroeder 2000:559).

Schroeder (2000) wishes instead to read Nagarjuna through the lens of *upaya*. Not to do so, in his view, is like suggesting that the *Dhamma* can be separated from its role in providing guidance for action, and even religious context, and can be taught without any particular audience in mind. This is the mistaken, unskilful approach that he claims most Western philosophers take when they study Buddhist thought (Schroeder 2000). Unlike traditional Western metaphysics, he argues, Buddhist thought in general, including that of Nagarjuna, 'is not concerned with the nature of space and time, causality, personal identity, or consciousness, and [instead] it resists the tendency to conceptualize [itself] apart from Buddhist praxis' (Schroeder 2000:559).

For example, rather than analysing Nagarjuna's notion of emptiness, Schroeder (2000) seeks to show how the notion is related to Buddhist practice. He rebukes those who might think that this focus on practice is un-philosophical (Schroeder 2000). For him, 'skill-in-means', the Eightfold Path, is philosophy, even though it is differently conceived (see, for example, Schroeder 2000:568). He points out that the entire Buddhist tradition consists of following the example of the Buddha, who refused to undertake philosophical analysis and discourse without its soteriological (salvation-related) aspects (Schroeder 2000).

A central point for Schroeder (2000), then, is that scholars are mistaken when they take the various schools of Buddhist philosophy engaged primarily in metaphysical examination to mean that they could establish the right view that would, in turn, place them on the path to liberation. Rather, he suggests (with reference to Kasulis's text 'Philosophy as metapraxis'), it would be more appropriate to call their philosophical investigations a 'metapraxis' (Schroeder 2000). These philosophers undertake theoretical investigations in order to determine the best meditative practice. In Schroeder's (2000) view, Nagarjuna's critiques of the metaphysics proposed by the various schools are not motivated solely by the purpose of pointing to the inconsistencies that he perceives in existing schools of thought. Rather, his philosophical work is motivated by laying bare their attachment to the more concrete and less abstract meditative practices they have developed.

These positions are jealously defended through philosophical debate and argument. For Schroeder (2000:569), Nagarjuna takes the conflict that arises between theories and schools of thought as stemming not so much from differences in views – these differences being innocuous in themselves – as from the 'blind grasping' of their proponents. The Buddha himself, Schroeder (2000:569) argues, 'initially refused to "Turn the Wheel" because people were so "cloaked" in "habitual tendencies," and he attacked the "sixty-two" prevailing philosophical systems in India not because they were metaphysically incorrect but because the people who espoused them were "caught in the net" of attachments'.

In other words, skilful means comprise the ability to cut through philosophical reflection in order to combine it with effective meditative practice. No doubt, he contends, philosophical reflection provides insight into how the mind and world work, but these outcomes are merely stepping stones to the real purpose of attaining liberation from suffering (Schroeder 2000). In an often-quoted section from the *Majjhima-nikaya*, part of the pre-*Mahayana* canon, the Buddha cautions us against taking teachings and philosophical reflection as more than helpful devices: 'If you cling to it, if you fondle it, if you treasure it, if you are attached to it, then you do not understand that the teaching is similar to a raft, which is for crossing over, and not for getting hold of' (Conze 1954:87).

Schroeder (2000) goes so far as to point out that in order to understand fully the role of *upaya* in Nagarjuna's thought, we need to keep in mind that within the *Mahayana* tradition, which he founded, *upaya* was created to oppose meditative practices that had become orthodox. Nagarjuna welcomed the pluralism found in the various positions held by different schools of thought, and in adjusting the teaching – both the mode of presentation and the content – in recognition of the diversity of the audience.

Nagarjuna argues that we could not have the same teachings for everyone, in the same way that the same medicine cannot be prescribed for all illnesses. Schroeder (2000:562) reminds us that in the early *Mahayana* texts, such as the *Prajnaparamita*, the *Lotus Sutra* and *Vimalakirtinirdesa*, the Buddha is an exemplary 'physician' 'because he knows the different illnesses of sentient beings, and he knows how to administer the appropriate "medicine." He knows what to say, when to remain silent, and when to prescribe the best "cure." To preach Buddhism without such sensitivity, we are told, is "bad medicine."'

What Schroeder (2000) is really objecting to is the universalisation of forms of human suffering, and the fact that Nagarjuna is too often depicted by Buddhist scholars, both ancient and contemporary, as presenting 'emptiness' as a general cure for that suffering. This tendency to universalise implicitly invokes stable dispositions, a stable set of teachings and stable modes of teaching. This runs counter to Nagarjuna's philosophy. That is, in so doing, they run afoul of the idea of *upaya* itself and unravel the very philosophical system they are trying to explain.

Nagarjuna's emphasis on conventional usage of language, diversity of thought and varieties of practice and teaching tie in with the Eightfold Path's insistence on 'rightness'. The 'rightness', according to Nagarjuna, does not have to do with some absolute correctness, but rather with being appropriate to the context. This leads us to examine in more detail context and *upaya* as pertaining to language use in educating for freedom from suffering.

Context and right speech in education

Based on our foregoing discussion of Nagarjuna (Garfield 1995), we now consider more fully how the Buddhist tradition conceptualises education for freedom from suffering: specifically, the proposal that education entails the acquisition of the right (contextually appropriate) use of language. Like Schroeder, Nance (2013) foregrounds the role of context in creating meaning. However, Nance (2013) works with a more robust theory of language, which is not surprising since his focus is right speech rather than *upaya* in general. He explains that Buddhist education requires the cultivation of right view, right speech and so on, as part of a many-stranded, mutually reinforcing complex of ideals that depend on practice in order to be achieved (Nance 2013). As the *arhats* practise living out these ideals, their views grow clearer and more accurate. The buddhas are those who have perfected these attributes and are pre-eminent educators. That said, within Buddhism, others who are far enough along the way are also permitted to teach those learners less advanced than themselves. The goal of all teaching is to free others from their suffering.

Through meditation and philosophical reflection, buddhas gain deep general insights into the human condition, which are expressed as general teachings. In the process, they also develop skilful means for successful teaching. Acknowledging that teaching occurs in both verbal and non-verbal modes, with the focus on language, Nance (2013) reminds us that the buddhas are also excellent and effective users of rhetoric. That is, they can adapt their message to the needs of their learners. Indeed, it is their moral duty to do so, because they are responsible not just for being proficient philosophers but also, ultimately, educators. As Nance (2013:367) explains, scholars agree that 'buddhas see things as they are not merely *presently* and *locally*, but *tenselessly* and *universally*'. In other words, buddhas not only express teachings that apply to all people, everywhere, they also adjust their speech to suit the needs and interests of particular persons and specific audiences. In order for their speech to be widely applicable, their language needs to flexible. We need an account of this flexibility if we are to teach it to others.

Indian Buddhists distinguish between a teaching's *vyanjana* (formal structure) and its *artha* (meaning). A single meaning can be expressed in many ways, and a single expression allows for many meanings. This flexibility of language opens possibilities for expressing the same thought in several ways, and using many expressions to communicate the same thought. Like Schroeder, Nance (2013) notes that much of the philosophical work done within the Buddhist tradition focuses on the general truths that form the core of the belief system. However, just as knowledge of grammar is not enough to make a person an effective speaker of a language, knowledge of Buddhist general truths is not enough to make a person moral.

Rather, Nance (2013) pays attention to *upaya* in speech – that is, the skilful means of using language or rhetoric. In particular, he wishes to focus on what he calls responsiveness when examining language used appropriately within specific contexts involving specific speakers. This notion of responsiveness, he says, 'mark[s] a variety of actions of body, speech, and mind that range from complex formulations of judgment involving a fine-grained appraisal of unfolding events to swift reactions that may seem to those who engage in them to involve no judgments at all' (Nance 2013:367).

Furthermore, Nance (2013:367) takes responsiveness to be a 'contingent feature of action', and therefore a given action may or may not bear this quality. This contingency and possibility of choice makes context central to our understanding of our ability to respond appropriately to actions in general, and to speech in particular. Drawing on the *Mahāvedadallasutta*, Nance (2013:366) reminds us that 'the voice of another and wise attention [...]: these are the two conditions for the arising of right view'. Both of these conditions point to the importance of context in developing skilful means in the use of language.

Conclusion and recommendations for future research

In this chapter we have sought to lay out the central concepts of Buddhist thought, with a focus on Nagarjuna's philosophy of language. For Nagarjuna (Garfield 1995), all speech, even soliloquies, occur within a context and with a speaker. We need to pay attention to that context as we formulate what we are going to say and how we say it. This attention is not malicious – it does not seek to find weaknesses in order to inflict harm. Rather, it is suffused with the educator's concern for the well-being, and ultimate liberation, of the learner. Furthermore, as educators and learners talk and listen to each other, the educator, too, becomes a learner. Within the conversational context, they both struggle to cultivate 'right view', to end their own suffering and that of others.

The Buddhist tradition offers a rich resource for conceptualising how the right use of language is cultivated through a process of education. That process centres on both solitary reflection and communal practice to culminate in freedom from suffering. To understand the nature and purpose of this educational process, we can draw on the work of Nagarjuna, the 'second Buddha', who gives us a coherent basis for making generalisations about a Buddhist conception of education, even though this body of knowledge is notoriously difficult to disentangle due to its multiplicity of texts and diverging traditions.

With reference to the concept of 'emptiness', Nagarjuna (Garfield 1995) claims that there is no enduring, foundational self. Instead the self, or non-self, as he calls it, arises interdependently from the world around us. For this reason, language is taken to constitute our thinking of ourselves as we relate to each other and the material world more generally. We can thus use Nagarjuna to argue for the place of language in moral education in the Buddhist tradition. This approach deepens the Buddhist understanding of 'emptiness', 'non-self' and 'interdependence' as these concepts play out in moral education. This educational intention lies at the heart of freedom from suffering, originally articulated by the Buddha himself.

The focus of this chapter – that is, on one aspect (language) of the system of thought of a particular philosopher (Nagarjuna) – draws out the relevance of language to philosophy of education more generally. It was important, as far as possible, to present the philosophy in its own terms. This is but a beginning of the contribution to a more robustly cosmopolitan philosophy of education. The tradition is rich and varied and there is much work to be done as the field seeks to become truly international.

References

Conze E. 1954. *Buddhist Texts through the Ages*. New York: Philosophical Library.

Eckel MD. 1978. Bhaaviveka and the early Maadhyamika theories of language. *Philosophy East and West*, 28(3):323–337.

Emmanuel SM. 2013. Introduction. In SM Emmanuel. (ed). *A Companion to Buddhist Philosophy*. Oxford: Wiley. 1–10.

Garfield JL. (tr). 1995. *The Fundamental Wisdom of the Middle Way: Nāgārjuna's Mūlamadhyamakakārikā*. New York and Oxford: Oxford University Press.

Gethin R. 1998. *The Foundations of Buddhism*. Oxford: Oxford University Press.

Gudmunsen C. 2014. *Wittgenstein and Buddhism* [1977]. London: Palgrave Macmillan.

Hanh TN. 1998. *The Heart of the Buddha's Teaching: Transforming Suffering into Peace, Joy, and Liberation: The Four Noble Truths, the Noble Eightfold Path, and other Basic Buddhist Teachings*. New York: Broadway Books.

Harvey P. 2012. *Introduction to Buddhism: Teachings, History and Practices*. 2nd ed. Cambridge: Cambridge University Press.

Humble M. 1999. The realist-idealist debate in Buddhist philosophy. Unpublished thesis, University of Oxford, Oxford.

Hume D. 1978. *A Treatise of Human Nature* [1738–1740]. Oxford: Clarendon.

Kant I. 1996. An answer to the question: What is enlightenment? [1784]. In MJ Gregor. (ed). *Practical Philosophy*. Cambridge: Cambridge University Press. 11–22.

Klein AC. 1994. *Path to the Middle: Oral Madhyamika Scholarship of Kensur Yeshey Tupden*. Albany: State University of New York Press.

Lindtner C. 1986. *Master of Wisdom: Writings of the Buddhist Master Nāgārjuna*. Berkeley: Dharma.

McCagney N. 1997. *Nagarjuna and the Philosophy of Openness*. Lanham: Rowman & Littlefield.

Nance R. 2013. The voice of another: Speech, responsiveness, and Buddhist philosophy. In SM Emmanuel. (ed). *A Companion to Buddhist Philosophy*. Oxford: Wiley. 366–376.

Nnanavamsa & Krishnasamy P. 2014. Buddha's philosophical interpretation of the Eightfold Path. *Indian Streams Research Journal*, 4(8):1–6.

Phunstsho K. 2005. *Mipham's Dialectics and the Debates on Emptiness: To Be, Not to Be or Neither*. London: Routledge.

Prebish C. 2008. Cooking the Buddhist books: The implications for the new dating of the Buddha for the history of early Indian Buddhism. *Journal of Buddhist Ethics*, 15:1–21.

Pye M. 2003. *Skilful Means: A Concept in Mahayana Buddhism*. 2nd ed. London and New York: Routledge.

Schroeder J. 2000. Nagarjuna and the doctrine of 'skillful means'. *Philosophy East and West*, 50(4):559–583.

Shackleton Bailey DR. 1951. *The Śatapañcāśatka of Mātṛceṭa*. Cambridge: Cambridge University Press.

Siderits M. 2015. Buddha. In the Stanford Encyclopedia of Philosophy Archive, Spring. Available: http://plato.stanford.edu/archives/spr2015/entries/buddha/. (Accessed 19 February 2017.)

Siderits M & Katsura S. 2013. *Nāgārjuna's Middle Way: Mulamadhyamakakārikā.* Sommerville: Wisdom.

Spackman J. 2014. Between nihilism and anti-essentialism: A conceptualist interpretation of Nāgārjuna. *Philosophy East and West,* 64(1):151–173.

Thera Ven. S. (tr). nd. *Kalama Sutta: The Buddha's Charter of Free Inquiry.* Available: http://www.buddhanet.net/e-learning/kalama1.htm. (Accessed 19 February 2017.)

Post-structuralism and education:

Anti-foundationalism and the critique of the philosophy of the subject

Michael Peters and Tina Besley

Introduction

This chapter charts some of the most significant post-structuralist developments and their impact on education – not only on education philosophy but also on policy, feminist thought and postcolonial studies. We begin with the assumption that post-structuralism represents both a theoretical response and a form of criticism of its immediate predecessor paradigm – structuralism – with which it shares certain similarities as well as differences. Both movements have had a strong impact and continue to affect educational philosophy and theory, especially in relation to questions of the text, criticism, 'reading', writing and subjectivity. The twin movements have thus had great influence in most fields of education.

This chapter starts by reviewing the decade of French structuralism, before engaging with the conceptual underpinnings, key issues and debates. We end the chapter with applications and implications for educational theory and practice.

A decade of French structuralism

The term 'structuralism' was coined by the Russian linguist Roman Jakobson (1896–1982) in 1939, and was developed simultaneously by Ferdinand de Saussure (1857–1913) in Geneva and Louis Hjelmslev (1899–1965) in Copenhagen. The movement pointed the way to understanding a sign (a word) as that which links the signifier (the sound or image) to the signified (the concept or meaning). It presented the ideas that underlying every system is a structure comprised of binary oppositions, and that human behaviour is governed by 'deep structure' of which we are often unaware. The origins of structuralism can be found in the movement of European formalism beginning with Jakobson's establishment of the Society for the Study of Poetic Language (OPOJAZ) in St Petersburg and the Moscow Linguistic Circle around 1914 or 1915. Russian formalism, which began somewhat earlier and included such luminaries as Viktor Shklovsky (1893–1984), Vladimir Propp (1895–1970) and Boris Eichenbaum (1886–1959), developed a scientific approach as opposed to the then current psychological or historical approach to poetic language and literature. Formalists insisted on the autonomy of language.

In conversation with Trombadori in the early 1980s, Michel Foucault (1926–1984) (1991:86–87) distinguishes structuralism from existentialism and phenomenology in the French context, and attributes its origins to the older, larger movement of Russian formalism:

> *[Structuralism's] real origin is found in an entire series of investigations developed in the U.S.S.R. and Central Europe around the 1920s. This great cultural expansion, in the fields of linguistics, mythology, folklore, etc., which had preceded and in a certain sense coincided with the Russian Revolution of 1917, had afterwards been swept away and almost crushed by the Stalinist steamroller. Structuralist culture had then ended up circulating in France through more or less underground channels that were little known at any rate: think of the phonology of Troubetzkoy, or of the influence of Propp on Dumézil and Lévi-Strauss, etc.*

Foucault (1991:87) further comments that 'structuralism had been the great cultural victim of Stalinism', but at the moment of de-Stalinisation intellectuals freed from official ideologies tried to recover the political innovation of formalism associated with the October Revolution. 'A left culture that was not Marxist was about to emerge', he argues, and goes on to suggest that 'a certain way of putting theoretical problems, without centering any longer on the "subject"; then, of forms of analysis that, though rigorously rational, were not of the Marxist variety' (Foucault 1991:90, 93). For Foucault (1991), this early structuralist movement meant that the tradition of the subject and subject-centred reason was exhausted. Structuralism and semiotics made individual subjectivity a relational attribute of the system, and thereby decentred the Cartesian–Kantian autonomous subject that was the centrepiece of so much liberal thinking in law, philosophy and education.

The structuralist movement in France began with *Anthropologie Structurale* by Claude Lévi-Strauss (1908–2009), first published in 1958, and ended a decade later with Jean Piaget's (1896–1980) *Le Structuralisme*. In that period the structuralist circle included Jacques Lacan (1901–1981), Louis Althusser (1918–1990), Roland Barthes (1915–1980) and the earlier works of Foucault, all of whom employed structuralism as a method to provide readings of Freud, Marx, popular culture and epistemology. Structuralism became the basis of an intellectual movement that was applied across the humanities and social sciences.

In education, Piaget's (1970a) stages of cognition, and Althusser's Marxist readings in political economy, dominated educational sociology. Piaget's thought was seen as 'a general theory of the structure of natural and [...] logico-mathematical systems', and was later 'conceived as dynamic, "constructive" (genetic [...]) processes' (Turner 1973:351). He explains: 'A critical account of structuralism must begin with a consideration of mathematical structures, not only for logical but even for historical reasons', and he informs us that 'the structural models of Lévi-Strauss [...] are a direct adaptation of general algebra' (Piaget 1970a:17). For Piaget

(1970b) the critical concept is the 'group' understood mathematically, a system consisting of a set of elements together with an operation or rule of combination that form the foundation of algebra. Groups are the prototype of structures, and the formal abstractions of logico-mathematical rules for transformation have applications in mathematics, logic, physics, biology and language. Piaget's (1970a) innovation has been to apply this model to the human mind, and to children's thinking in particular.

By contrast, Althusser developed a form of structuralist Marxism in opposition to the humanist Marxism that was current in the heyday of existentialism and phenomenology, emphasising that Marxism was a science which studied objective structures. Althusser and Balibar (1970) argue that with *The German Ideology* Marx departed from the humanism that characterised his early works, thereby creating an epistemological break that developed a new problematic of the science of history. Althusser's (1970) essay 'Ideology and Ideological State Apparatuses', which discusses the reproduction of the conditions of production, has been particularly influential in educational sociology because it names education as one of the principal ideological state apparatuses (ISAs), along with religion, the family, communications and culture. His work strongly influenced structuralist accounts such as Bowles and Gintis's (1976) classic text *Schooling in Capitalist America*, which argues for a structural correspondence between school organisation and that of the workplace.

Lacan's (2002) structuralist reading of Freud constitutes a departure from the humanism of ego psychology under the motif that 'the unconscious is structured like a language', and leads to the hypothesis of the 'mirror stage' as a means of explaining the formation of the Ego. Lacan's (2002) metapsychology is an account of the development of the human psyche and a curative psychoanalytic practice. It has had enormous influence on a generation of thinkers, including those we call 'post-structuralists'; his influence on education has become more evident in recent decades (see, for example, Britzman 1992; Roseboro 2008).

Anglo-American philosophy of education in the 1960s and 70s was largely uninterested in these developments, if not unaware of them altogether, being more strongly influenced by the revolution in analytic philosophy. Philosophy of education in the English-speaking world tended to be oblivious of developments in French structuralism or European formalism even though they were similar products of the broader 'linguistic turn', albeit based on different conceptions of language.

There was little disciplinary crossover between analytic philosophy of education and structuralist theory, partly because of methodological differences. Analytic philosophers proceeded by reducing philosophical problems to their constituent parts, as exemplified in Russell's (2010) 'Logical Atomism' of 1924 and Wittgenstein's *Tractatus Logico-Philosophicus* of 1922, whereas structuralist philosophers developed an approach that considered particulars to be parts of an integrative and synthetic whole – that is, the system or structure. Where the former is seen as a scientific 'problem-solving' approach, the latter, tied more to literature, art and the humanistic tradition, tends to be both historically and politically orientated. Some would argue that the split is emblematic of the wider division between analytic and Continental philosophy, and essentially of the difference between Kant and Hegel, although the place of both Wittgenstein and Heidegger complicate this picture and the differences today seem less a question of metaphysics than of style (Peters 2002; Peters & Marshall 1999).

The conceptual underpinnings

As pointed out by Peters and Wain (2003:60),

> *post-structuralism is a difficult term to define. It has often been confused with its kinship term, postmodernism [...] We can distinguish between the two terms by recognizing the difference between their theoretical objects of study. Poststructuralism takes as its theoretical object "structuralism," whereas postmodernism takes as its theoretical object "modernism." Post-structuralism can be characterized as [an intellectual movement], a style of philosophizing, and a kind of writing, yet the term should not be used to convey a sense of homogeneity, singularity, and unity.*

Generally, the conceptual issues underpinning post-structuralism emerged as a series of critiques of structuralism, including its ahistoricism, aculturalism and pseudo-scientific status, revealing alleged 'universal' structures of culture, cognition and language. The most important source of inspiration for post-structuralism was the French reception of Nietzsche. 'Where Marx was seen to play out the theme of power in his work, and Freud gave a conceptual priority to the notion of desire, Nietzsche was read as a philosopher who did not prioritize or subordinate the one concept over the other. [His] philosophy offered a way forward that *combined both power and desire*' (Peters 2001:3) – themes that were absent from analytic approaches to education at the time.

In the 1960s, a group of scholars under the influence of Nietzsche, including Derrida, Deleuze, Foucault, Lyotard, Kristeva and Irigaray, began to question the operating assumptions of the European movement of structuralism that understood human culture, cognition and activity on the model of structural linguistics. The first Nietzsche conferences in France were held at the Royaumont Abbey in 1964, and were organised by Deleuze (Schrift 2010), who in his closing address mentioned five major themes, namely:

1. the necessity of interpretation
2. the will to power
3. relations of affirmation and negation
4. the Dionysian affirmation in the eternal return
5. his relation to other philosophers, including Marx and Freud.

The German publication *Nietzsche* by Heidegger in 1961 was a powerful stimulus to French thought. The second Nietzsche conference, held in 1972, led to a renewal of contemporary French philosophy. This philosophy shifted away from the strictures and scientism of structuralism towards a reversal of Platonic metaphysics, a suspicion of the values of 'truth', a greater sensitivity to philology and rhetoric, a concern for meaning and Being, and a radicalisation of the concepts of interpretation, perspective and difference. With Nietzsche's assistance, French philosophers understood how to respond to the structuralist lament of 'the death of the subject', by raising questions about the constitutive individual and situated agency that emphasised history and the manufacture of subjectivity without privileging a consciousness isolated from history or culture. This Nietzschean philosophy played out methodologically in educational theory in terms of the culturally and historically embedded and enacted subject, paying greater attention to questions of intersubjectivity and considering learning as a relational and collective phenomenon.

Post-structuralism, which began as a critique of structuralism, soon achieved paradigmatic status, and was received beyond France in the English-speaking world in the 1980s, perhaps dating from the paper 'Structure, Sign, and Play in the Discourse of the Human Sciences', which Derrida presented in the USA in 1966. As Peters (2009:158) elaborates,

> the *"decentering"* of structure, of the transcendental signified, and of the sovereign *subject, Derrida suggests – naming his sources of inspiration – can be found in the Nietzschean critique of metaphysics and, especially, of the concepts of Being and truth, and in the Freudian critique of self-presence, as he says, "the critique of consciousness, of the subject, of self-identity and of self-proximity or self-possession" (ibid. 280), and, more radically, in the Heideggerean destruction of metaphysics, "of the determination of Being as presence" (ibid).*

Key issues and debates

Themes from Nietzsche and Heidegger that influenced post-structuralism and educational theory began with a critique of the realist tradition going back to Plato, and advanced an anti- or post-epistemological standpoint that is sometimes referred to as 'anti-foundationalism' or 'post-foundationalism'. This position denies the existence of a fundamental principle that serves as the foundation for knowledge and enquiry, or that such a foundation is necessary for knowledge, ethics and politics. Post-foundationalism tries to go beyond foundationalism. For post-structuralists there are no foundational certainties that guarantee knowledge, politics or ethics. This anti-foundationalism is often associated with anti-realism about meaning and reference, or with what Rorty (1979) calls 'anti-representationalism', which involves the rejection of the picture of knowledge as accurate representation and of truth as correspondence to reality.

Sometimes the attacks on foundationalism are an outcome of the concept of analyticity – after rejecting the Kantian distinction between scheme and content, it is no longer clear what this concept or the concept of analysis in philosophy actually means. Anti-foundationalism at times draws on arguments from science and mathematics, utilising Gödel's (1965) incompleteness theorems to demonstrate the inherent limitations of any formal axiomatic system involving arithmetic. Heisenberg's (1958) uncertainty principle concerns mathematical inequalities asserting a fundamental limit to the precision with which certain pairs of physical properties of a particle can be known simultaneously, and Einstein's (1921) theory of relativity as a theory of space – time holds, among other things, that the laws of physics are the same for all observers in uniform motion relative to one another. The naturalism of post-structuralism and pragmatism recognises no real difference between philosophy and science, and many of the philosophical theories of post-structuralists are based on empiricism. Post-foundationalism acknowledges that reflection and thought, while both rational and critical, are generally conditioned by the historical and cultural context, yet it is still possible to achieve knowledge, albeit as provisional, infinitely revisable and fallible.

With the attack on the realism of Plato comes an attack on Platonic essentialism. Post-structuralist philosophy is anti-essentialist in the sense that properties are not considered universal and unchanging, but rather radically contingent on the historical context. Post-structuralism entertains a suspicion of transcendental arguments and viewpoints, and rejects canonical descriptions and final vocabularies. Alongside Lyotard's (1984) talk of the 'suspicion of metanarratives', we might add the turn to narrative and narratology, more generally – *petite récits* pitted against metanarratives. We might also add an emphasis on linguistic use and the *therapeutic view of philosophy* – that is, an ethos, above all, concerning philosophy as a critique of language summed up best in Wittgenstein's (1953:47) famous comment, in *Philosophical Investigations*, that 'philosophy is a battle against the bewitchment of our intelligence by means of language'.

This is a view that underlies the development of the social sciences and cultural studies in the latter half of the 20th century. It is perhaps sloganised in the twin methodological imperatives of the linguistic turn, the significance of representation and the turn to social practices on the one hand, and the attempt to overcome the dualistic thought, the search for certainty and essences, and the subjectivism that are the legacies of Cartesian thought on the other. Encouraged by Wittgenstein's (1953) expert disassembly of the Cartesian worldview and model of subjectivity, we might entertain a model of education as openness, engagement and *copoiesis* (co-creation), one that is more suited to the global, networked and digital environment in which we live.

Many of the critiques – anti-foundationalist and seeking to decentre the humanist subject – served to revisit and develop new theories of meaning, forms of textual criticism and analysis, and differing notions of 'author' and 'reader'. Their combined effect was to expose the underlying metaphysics of the structuralist model of the text and culture as logocentric, based on an optional and hierarchical set of binary oppositions and power relations embodying the dualisms of self/other, speech/writing, rational/emotional, signifier/signified, symbolic/imaginary, male/female and so on. These post-structuralist investigations revealed the objectivist and universalist constructions of 'scientific objectivity' and 'universality' that accompanied the rise of the West.

In addition to doing work that engages directly with specific philosophers, post-structuralist thinkers have developed distinctive forms of analysis (grammatology, deconstruction, archaeology, genealogy, semanalysis and governmentality). Often they developed these forms as critiques of specific institutions (the family, state, prison, clinic, school, university, factory, armed forces, and even philosophy itself) and theorisations of a range of media ('reading', 'writing', teaching, television, the visual arts, the plastic arts and film, and forms of electronic communication).

Much of what is currently known as discourse theory, or critical discourse analysis (CDA), used extensively in educational and social science research, emerged directly from Foucault's (1981:52) inaugural lecture 'The order of Discourse', given in France in December 1970, in which he famously claimed that 'in every society the production of discourse is at once controlled, selected, organised and redistributed by a certain number of procedures whose role is to ward off its powers and dangers, to gain mastery over its chance events, to evade its ponderous, formidable materiality'.

This text provides a strong contrast to the approach of analytic philosophy (of education) to language through the analysis and clarification of concepts one step removed from reality. Foucault (1981) highlights the differences between an analytic approach based on logocentrism and 'logophobia' and his genealogy, which focuses on the relationship between discourse and power. Thus, this strategic text emphasises the differences between an analytic philosophy of education which seeks the clarification of concepts underlying educational practices and a Foucauldian or post-structuralist philosophy of education that adopts an approach to language through a theory of discourse which acknowledges the effects of power and desire.

Foucault (1981) discusses 'procedures of exclusion' (prohibitions, divisions and the true/false opposition), various procedures internal to discourse and conditions of access to discourse (with reference to the speaking subject). He also explores philosophical themes such as the notion of *ideal truth* as the law of discourse, and of *immanent rationality* as a principle of unfolding for discourse, by way of the themes of the founding subject, of originating experience and of universal mediation (Foucault 1981). 'We must call into question our will to truth, restore to discourse its character as an event, and finally throw off the sovereignty of the signifier,' he argues (Foucault 1981:66).

Foucault (1981) proposes two kinds of analyses for the future: a critical analysis and a genealogical analysis. In opposition to four notions that have dominated the traditional history of ideas – signification, originality, unity and creation – Foucault (1981) advances the notions event, series, regularity and the possible conditions of existence. On this basis, history does not privilege the position of the individual event, but rather relates it to the series which defines it, thereby revealing it as an event within a more enduring social, economic or political structure. No longer consciousness and continuity, or sign and structure, but rather events and series.

Foucault (1981) moves away from the formal linguistic analysis of language to focus on power–knowledge relations within disciplines linked to the institutional production of knowledge through the historical formation of discourses, where it is used in the social construction and governance of groups and individuals. This shift indicates a radical departure from more traditional forms of discourse theory that followed from the model of European formalism to emphasise power diffused and embodied in discourse, knowledge and 'regimes of truth'. Foucault's 'power–knowledge' signifies that power is constituted through accepted forms of knowledge, scientific understanding and 'truth'. This is a very different account from analytic philosophy, which tends to ignore questions of historical context to settle on logical structure and a correspondence theory of truth where fact-stating sentences picture the world. As Bowman (2014) suggests:

> *Despite its many internal differences, a first tenet of poststructuralism is arguably this:* institutions form subjects. *Michel Foucault picked up the baton of his colleague Louis Althusser, who argued in "Ideology and Ideological State Apparatuses" (Althusser 1977) that social institutions mould individuals and make them into "subjects". Foucault deepened and developed this argument in a series of book-long studies of the way institutions produce "knowledge" (about "subjects") and then accrue a kind of "power" over them.*

Significant links are also made between post-structuralism and postcolonialism through Foucault's (1981) notion of discourse. Postcolonialism is above all a discourse that examines Western representations and depictions of the East. Said's *Orientalism*, a founding text of postcolonialism first published in 1978, is a study of the power relations involved in the construction of a discourse by Western scholars about the 'Orient' on the basis of stereotypes. As Said (1979:2) argues: 'Orientalism is a style of thought based upon ontological and epistemological distinction made between "the Orient" and (most of the time) "the Occident".'

According to Said (1979:3), the Western representation of Other as exotic, deviant and different is inextricably connected to 'dominating, restructuring, and having authority over the Orient'.

Postcolonial theory in education exemplifies the influence of a critical tradition, including theorists such as Fanon, Said, Bhabha and Spivak, that reflects cultural theory buttressed by arguments and methods of post-structuralism (Andreotti 2011; Hickling-Hudson, Matthews & Woods 2004). 'Postcolonial studies,' Tarc (2009:195) notes, 'are slow to come to education, in part because postcolonial studies threaten to undo education, to unravel the passionately held-onto thought and knowledge of the modern Western-educated student and scholar.'

Implications for educational theory and practice

Post-structuralism represents a special relationship with education and the humanities responsible for generating new models of reading, writing and criticism, especially with the so-called 'cultural turn'. Its insights and theoretical innovations began to be adopted in the field of education in the 1990s and have grown into a sustained research programme dedicated to their refinement in the application of individual post-structuralist philosophers. A substantial body of work now examines post-structuralism and education on the basis of studies of Foucault, Derrida, Lyotard and others in philosophy of education, and in other areas such as learning theory, curriculum theory and history, adult education, music education, physical education and so on. As well as presenting work on individual philosophers, educational philosophers have begun to revisit and unpack the founding influences on post-structuralist philosophy, writing texts, for example, on Nietzsche, Heidegger and Levinas. In addition, educational philosophers have adopted approaches from post-structuralism to examine the subjectivity of learners and educators under neoliberalism and in the digital world.

The first texts in philosophy of education appeared in the late 1980s, to flourish in the 1990s and become more specialised based on individual philosophers and in a range of educational fields and sub-fields thereafter. Among the first contributions to this emerging literature were Cherryholmes's (1988) *Power and Criticism: Poststructural Investigations in Education*, Ball's (1990) *Foucault and Education*, Aronowitz and Giroux's (1991) *Postmodern Education*, Lather's (1991) *Getting Smart: Feminist Research and Pedagogy with/in the Post-Modern* and Sarup's (1993) *An Introductory Guide to Post-Structuralism and Postmodernism*.

These texts are strikingly different from the texts that had come to characterise analytic philosophy of education. They are more engaged with the world through policy, criticism or political movements. They take the question of power (and desire, though less so) to be central, and tend to apply the insights of various post-structualist thinkers to educational issues. Aronowitz and Giroux (1991:15) argue for the significance of popular culture in the curriculum: 'Postmodern educators believe the curriculum can best inspire learning only when school knowledge builds upon tacit knowledge derived from cultural resources that students already possess. For example, electronically mediated popular culture [...] is treated by postmodern education as a legitimate object of knowledge'.

Aronowitz and Giroux (1991:93) go on to articulate a power–knowledge concept in terms of sites of cultural production: 'Knowledge has to be viewed in the context of power, and consequently the relationships between writers, readers, and texts have to be understood as sites at which different readings, meanings, and forms of cultural production take place'. These authors use the term 'border pedagogy' to indicate that education and the curriculum no longer have firm foundations, and that educators need to focus on knowledge and experience through which 'students can author their own voices and construct their own identities' (Aronowitz & Giroux 1991:128). Subjectivities, identities and critical approaches to popular culture are themes reiterated as a feature of the postmodern world.

Peters (1995) was the first to present Lyotard's ideas on education, focusing on Lyotard's (1984) *The Postmodern Condition*, a book that sparked a debate about the legitimation of knowledge and the end of metanarrative, which dominated for at least a decade and led to an unhelpful polarisation with German critical theory. Lyotard's work, first published in Paris in 1979, was important in that it developed a particularly original interpretation of the state of knowledge in the most highly developed societies, reviewing and synthesising a wide range of material on contemporary science, the sociology of post-industrial society and studies of postmodern culture. Lyotard (1984) brought together diverse threads and separate literatures in a prophetic analysis that signalled an epochal break with the so-called 'modern era'.

Peters (1995) features a short Foreword by Lyotard, and includes essays by Readings and Marshall, among others. In this connection Dhillon and Standish (2000) focus on the recurrent theme of education in Lyotard's work. Blake et al (1998, 2002), indicating a radical shift in style and thinking, bring themes of post-structuralism directly to the heart of philosophy of education in the United Kingdom and beyond, investigating moral standards and education in the age of nihilism. Together and individually, their work constitutes a turning point for British philosophy of education, opening it up to Continental influences in ways not seen previously.

Usher and Edwards (1994) approach postmodernism (and use it as a synonym for post-structuralism) as a set of challenges to education that is, they maintain, founded on the discourse of modernity as one of the 'grand narratives' supported by the Enlightenment ideals of individual freedom, critical reason and progress. Walkerdine (1988, 2002) adopts the perspective of critical psychology based on non-foundational and psychoanalytic concepts to investigate the production of rationality and, in later work, questions of gender, girlhood and subjectivity.

Davies (1989, 2014), also a scholar of subjectivity, and strongly influenced by Judith Butler, pursues a range of topics centred around pedagogy, children, gender, ethics and collaborative writing. Morss (1990, 2013) uses post-structuralist thought to develop alternatives to developmental psychology and cognition after Piaget, leading him to talk of 'postmodern psychologies'.

Pinar (2004), Pinar and Reynolds (1992) and Pinar et al (2008) apply post-structuralism to understanding the curriculum, unsettling it as something stable, assumed and official. Stronach and MacLure (1997) employ post-structuralism and deconstruction in the research of methodology and policy critique, investigating alternative ways of reading and writing educational research. Ball (1994) develops an approach to understanding education reform that draws on both critical theory and post-structuralism. Peters (1996) focuses on the critique of subject-centred reason to criticise neoliberal constructions of the subject in education that rest heavily on the assumption of economic man.

These texts make up a selection of the work of the early leaders in the English-speaking world. Ranging across the sub-fields of education, they began to destabilise the official consensus concerning the aims, methods and teaching practices of the modernist education project. These texts emulated the diversity of the main movements in philosophy, history, psychology, child development, curriculum, feminist and gender studies, research methodology and policy studies. Rooted in linguistics and aspects of structuralism, post-structuralism in education was not solely a philosophical development or movement – it instead incorporated elements of structuralism and, thus, also linguistics and a range of aligned disciplines.

Post-structuralism in education then began to spread its influence to other sub-fields, such as mathematics, music education, environmental education and adult education (Bell et al 2000; Brown 2001; Gough & Whitehouse 2003; McKenzie 2004; Richerme 2015; Roth 2012; Usher, Bryant & Johnston 1997). It also started engaging in the deeper studies of individual thinkers of the 1970s in Paris, including Foucault, Derrida, Deleuze, Guattari, Lyotard, Kristeva, Irigaray and Barthes (Besley & Peters 2009; Biesta & Egéa-Kuehne 2001; Peters & Besley 2007; Peters & Biesta 2009; Peters et al 2009) and the structuralist predecessors such as Lacan and Althusser, as well as those who inspired the Paris generation: Nietzsche, Heidegger, Spinoza and Bergson.

Conclusion and recommendations for future research

The complexities of every intellectual movement defeat a neat summary, especially as they fall into place in histories or anthologies. Rarely do movements arrange themselves in decades or in easy-to-follow charts of who influenced whom. Certainly this is the case in education, where post-structuralism was picked up by the second generation of thinkers outside Paris, outside France and increasingly in non-Western countries, where new formations, theories and concepts have taken root, especially in extended discourses of postcolonialism, gender, youth and what we might call 'subjectivity studies' of learners and educators. In this regard the work of Waghid, Higgs and Le Grange, among others, in South Africa warrants special mention. Waghid's (2011, 2014a) work on democracy and Islamic education, and the work of all these authors on African philosophy of education and ubuntu (Higgs 2003, 2009; Le Grange 2015; Waghid 2014b), represents a move away from Western ethnocentrism and indicates greater respect for indigenous philosophy.

Any history of post-structuralism in the vast terrain of education needs to take account of methodological innovations – especially the prevalence of critical discourse analysis, but also genealogy, grammatology and a host of other approaches – alongside the theories and concepts. It must also recognise the resistances to post-structuralism of some inflexible, determined analytic philosophers, from liberals and from Marxists. One group of self-styled cultural heroes, mostly aging white ('grumpy') men, have wanted to 'clear the decks of such junk theory and debilitating "political" posturing because of the urgent tasks ahead for socialists' (Hill et al 2002:3). Peters (2001) seeks explicitly to disabuse people of the notion that post-structuralists and Marxists belonged to opposing camps, by examining the relations of Foucault, Deleuze, Guattari, Derrida and Lyotard to French Marxism. Attempts to propose new thinking do not take kindly to the 'literalists' who base themselves on one interpretation of a text, who maintain an authority in relation to the word and police its 'authentic version'. Investigating the relations between education, post-structuralism and politics is exactly what is needed in understanding, critiquing, reflecting upon and organising resistance against the forces and orthodoxy of neoliberal capitalism.

The future of post-structuralist philosophy of education depends not only on the deepening of scholarship through a return to readings of Nietzsche, Heidegger and other early progenitors, but also a widening of the circle of academic philosophers across cultural traditions and gender divisions. Post-humanism, postcolonialism and indigenous philosophy are often seen as successors to post-structuralism, yet these might also be lines of future investigation.

References

Althusser L. 1970. Ideology and ideological state apparatuses: Notes towards an investigation. In L Althusser. (ed). *Lenin and Philosophy and Other Essays*. New York: Monthly Review Press. 127–186.

Althusser L & Balibar E. 1970. *Reading Capital* [1968]. Translated by B Brewster. London: New Left Books. Available: https://www.marxists.org/reference/archive/althusser/1968/reading-capital/. (Accessed 14 March 2017.)

Andreotti V. 2011. *Actionable Postcolonial Theory in Education*. New York: Palgrave Macmillan.

Aronowitz S & Giroux H. 1991. *Postmodern Education: Politics, Culture, and Social Criticism*. Minneapolis: University of Minnesota Press.

Ball SJ. 1990. *Foucault and Education*. London: Routledge.

Ball SJ. 1994. *Education Reform: A Critical and Post-Structural Approach*. Buckingham: Open University Press.

Bell A & Russell C. 2000. Beyond human, beyond words: Anthropocentrism, critical pedagogy, and the poststructuralist turn. *Canadian Journal of Education*, 25(3):188–203.

Besley T & Peters MA. 2009. *Subjectivity and Truth: Foucault, Education, and the Culture of Self*. New York: Peter Lang.

Biesta G & Egéa-Kuehne D. 2001. *Derrida and Education*. London: Routledge.

Blake N, Smeyers P, Smith R & Standish P. 1998. *Thinking Again: Education after Postmodernism*. New York: Praeger.

Blake N, Smeyers P, Smith R & Standish P. (eds). 2002. *The Blackwell Guide to the Philosophy of Education*. Oxford: Blackwell.

Bowles S & Gintis H. 1976. *Schooling in Capitalist America: Educational Reform and the Contradictions of Economic Life*. New York: Basic Books.

Bowman P. 2014. Poststructuralism, postcolonialism, postmodernism. 23 January. Available: http://ranciere.blogspot.hr/2014/01/poststructuralism-postcolonialism.html. (Accessed 21 February 2017.)

Britzman D. 1992. The terrible problem of knowing thyself: Toward a poststructural account of teacher identity. *Journal of Curriculum Theory*, 9(3):23–46.

Brown T. 2001. *Mathematics Education and Language: Interpreting Hermeneutics and Post-Structuralism*. Dordrecht: Kluwer Academic.

Cherryholmes CH. 1988. *Power and Criticism: Poststructural Investigations in Education*. New York: Teachers College Press, Columbia University.

Davies B. 1989. *Frogs and Snails and Feminist Tales: Preschool Children and Gender*. Sydney: Allen & Unwin.

Davies B. 2014. *Listening to Children: Being and Becoming*. London: Routledge.

Dillon P & Standish P. (eds). 2000. Lyotard: *Just Education*. London: Routledge.

Einstein A. 1921. The meaning of relativity. Four lectures delivered at Princeton University, May, Princeton, New Jersey. Available: http://www.gutenberg.org/files/36276/36276-pdf.pdf. (Accessed 21 February 2017.)

Foucault M. 1981. The order of discourse [1970]. Translated by I McLeod. In R Young (ed). *Untying the Text: A Poststructuralist Reader*. Boston: Routledge & Kegan Paul. 48–78.

Foucault M. 1991. But structuralism was not a French invention. In M Foucault. *Remarks on Marx: Conversations with Duccio Trombadori*. Translated by RJ Goldstein & J Cascaito. New York: Semiotext(e). 83–113.

Gödel K. 1965. On undecidable propositions of formal mathematical systems [1934]. In M Davis. (ed). *The Undecidable: Basic Papers on Undecidable Propositions, Unsolvable Problems and Computable Functions*. New York: Raven Press Books. 39–74.

Gough A & Whitehouse H. 2003. The 'nature' of environmental education research from a feminist poststructuralist viewpoint. *Canadian Journal of Environmental Education*, 8:31–43.

Heisenberg W. 1958. *Physics and Philosophy*. New York: Harper.

Hickling-Hudson A, Matthews J & Woods A. (eds). 2004. *Disrupting Preconceptions: Postcolonialism and Education*. Brisbane: Post Pressed.

Higgs P. 2003. African philosophy and the transformation of educational discourse in South Africa. *Journal of Education*, 30(1):5–22.

Higgs P. 2009. Towards an indigenous African educational discourse: A philosophical reflection. In S Majhanovich, C Fox & AP Kreso. (eds). *Living Together: Education and Intercultural Dialogue*. Dordrecht: Springer Science+Business Media. 159–172.

Hill D, McLaren P, Cole M & Rikowski G. (eds). 2002. *Marxism against Postmodernism in Educational Theory*. Maryland: Lexington Books.

Lacan J. 2002. The instance of the letter in the unconscious, or reason since Freud [1966]. In J Lacan. *Écrits: A Selection*. Translated by B Fink. New York and London: WW Norton. 412–441.

Lather P. 1991. *Getting Smart: Feminist Research and Pedagogy with/in the Post-Modern*. Oxford: Routledge.

Le Grange L. 2015. Ubuntu/Botho as ecophilosophy and ecosophy. *Journal of Human Ecology*, 493:301–308.

Lyotard J-F. 1984. *The Postmodern Condition: A Report on Knowledge* [1979]. Minneapolis: University of Minnesota Press.

McKenzie M. 2004. The 'willful contradiction' of poststructural socio-ecological education. *Canadian Journal of Environmental Education*, 9:177–190.

Morss J. 1990. *The Biologising of Childhood: Developmental Psychology and the Darwinian Myth*. London: Lawrence Erlbaum.

Morss J. 2013. *Growing Critical: Alternatives to Developmental Psychology*. London: Routledge.

Peters MA. (ed). 1995. *Education and the Postmodern Condition*. Westport and London: Bergin & Garvey.

Peters MA. 1996. *Poststructuralism, Politics and Education*. Westport and London: Bergin & Garvey.

Peters MA. 2001a. *Poststructuralism, Marxism and Neoliberalism: Between Theory and Politics*. Lanham: Rowman & Littlefield.

Peters MA. (ed). 2002. *Heidegger, Education and Modernity*. Boulder: Roman & Littlefield.

Peters MA. 2009. Derrida, Nietzsche and the Return to the Subject. In MA Peters & G Biesta. 2009. *Derrida, Deconstruction and the Politics of Pedagogy*. New York: Peter Lang.

Peters MA & Besley T. 2007. *Why Foucault? New Directions in Educational Research*. New York: Peter Lang.

Peters MA & Biesta G. 2009. *Derrida, Deconstruction, and the Politics of Pedagogy.* New York: Peter Lang.

Peters MA & Marshall JD. 1999. *Wittgenstein: Philosophy, Postmodernism, Pedagogy.* New York and London: Bergin & Garvey.

Peters MA & Wain K. 2003. Postmodernism/Post-structuralism. In N Blake, P Smeyers, RD Smith & P Standish. (eds). *The Blackwell Guide to the Philosophy of Education.* Oxford: Blackwell. 57–72.

Peters MA, Besley T, Olssen M, Maurer S & Weber S. (eds). 2009. *Governmentality Studies in Education.* Rotterdam: Sense.

Piaget J. 1970a. *Genetic Epistemology.* Translated by E Duckworth. New York: Columbia University Press.

Piaget J. 1970b. *Structuralism* [1968]. Translated by C Maschler. New York: Harper & Row.

Pinar W. 2004. *What Is Curriculum Theory?* New York and London: Routledge.

Pinar W & Reynolds W. 1992. *Understanding Curriculum as Phenomenological and Deconstructed Text.* New York: Teachers College Press, Columbia University.

Pinar WF, Reynolds WM, Slattery P & Taubman P. (eds). 2008. *Understanding Curriculum: An Introduction to the Study of Historical and Contemporary Curriculum Discourses.* New York: Peter Lang.

Richerme LK. 2015. Philosophy in the music classroom: Poststructuralist lessons from *The Lego Movie. Music Educators Journal,* 102(1):62–68.

Rorty R. 1979. *Philosophy and the Mirror of Nature.* Princeton: Princeton University Press.

Roseboro D. 2008. *Jacques Lacan and Education: A Critical Introduction.* Rotterdam: Sense.

Roth W-M. 2012. Re/writing the subject: A contribution to post-structuralist theory in mathematics education. *Educational Studies in Mathematics,* 80:451–473.

Russell B. 2010. Logical atomism [1924]. In B Russell. *The Philosophy of Logical Atomism.* London and New York: Routledge. 126–150.

Said E. 1979. *Orientalism.* New York: Vintage.

Sarup M. 1993. *An Introductory Guide to Post-Structuralism and Postmodernism.* 2nd ed. Athens: University of Georgia Press.

Schrift AD. (ed). 2010. Poststructuralism and critical theory's second generation. Volume 6. In AD Schrift. (ed). *The History of Continental Philosophy.* London and New York: Routledge.

Stronach I & MacLure M. 1997. *Educational Research Undone: The Postmodern Embrace.* Philadelphia: Open University Press.

Tarc AM. 2009. Postcolonial studies as re-education: Learning from JM Coetzee's *Disgrace.* In RS Coloma. (ed). *Postcolonial Challenges in Education.* New York: Peter Lang. 195–214.

Turner T. 1973. *Genetic Epistemology* by Jean Piaget. Review. *American Anthropologist,* 752:351–373.

Usher R & Edwards R. 1994. *Postmodernism and Education.* London: Routledge.

Usher R, Bryant I & Johnston R. 1997. *Adult Education and the Postmodern Challenge: Learning Beyond the Limits.* London: Routledge.

Waghid Y. 2011. *Conceptions of Islamic Education: Pedagogical Framings.* New York: Peter Lang.

Waghid Y. 2014a. *Pedagogy out of Bounds: Untamed Variations of Democratic Education.* Rotterdam: Sense.

Waghid Y. 2014b. *African Philosophy of Education Reconsidered: On Being Human.* New York and London: Routledge.

Walkerdine V. 1988. *The Mastery of Reason.* London: Routledge.

Walkerdine V. 2002. *Critical Theory, Critical Practice.* London: Lawrence & Wishart.

Wittgenstein L. 1922. *Tractatus Logico-Philosophicus.* Translated by CK Ogden. London: Kegan Paul.

Wittgenstein L. 1953. *Philosophical Investigations.* Translated by GEM Anscombe. Oxford: Basil Blackwell.

Index

C

chaos theory
    education with an ethos of
        empowerment 85–86
    equity and renewal 80–81
    fear perpetuated in education
        systems 79–80
    key issues 76
    knowledge and power, balance
        of 81–82
    moral foundations for education
        systems 80–81
    principled non-conformance
        75, 76
    recommendations for future
        research 85–86
    repetitive strain and human
        indignity 82–83
    traditional and popular cultures
        81–82
    truth, freedom and human dignity
        83–84
circular structure of educational
    experience 58–59
classical Confucianism and education
    characteristics of good educators
        159–160
    civilising role of education
        155–156
    complementarity of opposites 166
    good and bad practices in
        education 160–164
    humanising role of education 156
    implications for educational theory
        and practice 164–166
    method 158–160
    purpose of education 155–158
    recommendations for future
        research 166–167
    reflective thinking and knowledge
        acquisition 166
    six stages in education 161–162
    small and great learning 164–165
    teaching according to aptitude
        165–166
    teaching methods 162
    texts 152–155
    whole-person education 164–165
co-belonging and justice, in Islamic
    education 147–149
community in Islamic education
    148–149
complexity theory
    key issues 77–79
    protection of human rights and
        responsibilities 77–79
conditioning by social structuring 41
consequentialism as related to
    morality 21–22
context and right speech 181–183
cosmopolitanism 10–11
counter-science 42–43, 44
criticality
    anthropomorphism 123
    three ontological domains
        123, 124
critical theory
    critique 109
    in education 111–113
    emancipation 109
    goals in society 108–111
    hegemonic ideologies 110
    historical beginnings 107–108
    social transformation 110
    see also decolonisation
critical thinking 34
critical vs scientific methodologies
    41–42
critique 109
culture and the struggle for scientific
    meaning 4

curriculum
aesthetic literacy 43–45
and phenomenology 45–46
Curriculum and Assessment Policy
Statements (CAPS) 47, 51–52
curriculum, reconceptualisation of
47–48

D

decolonisation
as African critical theory work
113–115
as binary of dominators and
subordinates 117–118
higher education systems,
centrality 115–116
and particularisation of knowledge
118
recommendations for future
research 116–118
and violence 116–117
see also critical theory
deep structures in universities
126–127
dehumanising effect of systems theory
where ethos is absent 73–74
deliberative encounters 9–10
and respect 145–147
dialectical hermeneutics *see*
hermeneutics, dialectical
dominators and subordinates binary
117–118

E

education
with an ethos of empowerment
85–86
context and right speech 181–183
critical theory in 111–113
emptiness and language 175–181

educational research, hermeneutics
and education 60–61
Eightfold Path 174–175
emancipation 109
emptiness, language and education
175–181
ethos of empowerment 85–86
experience as touchstone 14–15

F

facts, values and pragmatism 16–18
feminism
African 93
black 93
conceptual underpinnings 90–93
liberal 92
Marxist 93
misconceptions of 94–95
postmodern/post-structuralist 94
radical 93
recommendations for future
research 103–104
social 93
feminism on the African continent
95–97
African feminism, common
features in 100–101
implications for education in
Africa 101–103
neo-feminism 99–100
state feminism 98
stiwanism 99
womanism and motherism 98–99
Four Noble Truths 173–174
freedom, truth and human dignity
83–84

G

guerrilla realism 128–129

www.ingramcontent.com/pod-product-compliance
Lightning Source LLC
Chambersburg PA
CBHW050745100426
42739CB00016BA/3441